THE CAMBRIDGE COMPANION TO
POSTHUMAN

The Cambridge Companion to Literature and
its kind to gather diverse critical treatments of the posthuman ~~
ism together in a single volume. Seventeen scholars from six different countries
address the historical and esthetic dimensions of posthuman figures alongside
posthumanism as a new paradigm in the critical humanities. The three parts and
their chapters trace the history of the posthuman in literature and other media,
including film and video games, and identify major political, philosophical, and
techno-scientific issues raised in the literary and cinematic narratives of the
posthuman and posthumanist discourses. The volume surveys the key works,
primary modes, and critical theories engaged by depictions of the posthuman
and discussions about posthumanism.

BRUCE CLARKE is Chair of the Department of English and the Paul Whitfield
Horn Professor of Literature and Science at Texas Tech University, USA. His
widely published research areas focus on nineteenth- and twentieth-century
literature and science, with special interests in systems theory, narrative theory,
and ecology. Since 2011 he has been the Advisor for the European Society for .
Literature, Science, and the Arts (SLSA-EU).

MANUELA ROSSINI works in the Vice Rectorate for Research at the University
of Basel, Switzerland, where she is also an associated researcher in the
Department of English. She is the current President and Executive Director of
SLSA-EU. Her research focuses on critical posthumanism, animal studies, feminist materialism, cultural studies of science, and inter- and transdisciplinary
methodology.

A complete list of books in the series is at the back of this book

THE CAMBRIDGE
COMPANION TO

LITERATURE AND THE POSTHUMAN

EDITED BY
BRUCE CLARKE
MANUELA ROSSINI

CAMBRIDGE
UNIVERSITY PRESS

CAMBRIDGE
UNIVERSITY PRESS

University Printing House, Cambridge CB2 8BS, United Kingdom

One Liberty Plaza, 20th Floor, New York, NY 10006, USA

477 Williamstown Road, Port Melbourne, VIC 3207, Australia

4843/24, 2nd Floor, Ansari Road, Daryaganj, Delhi – 110002, India

79 Anson Road, #06–04/06, Singapore 079906

Cambridge University Press is part of the University of Cambridge.

It furthers the University's mission by disseminating knowledge in the pursuit of education, learning, and research at the highest international levels of excellence.

www.cambridge.org
Information on this title: www.cambridge.org/9781107086203
DOI: 10.1017/9781316091227

© Cambridge University Press 2017

First published 2017

Printed in the United States of America by Sheridan Books, Inc.

A catalogue record for this publication is available from the British Library.

Library of Congress Cataloging-in-Publication Data
NAMES: Clarke, Bruce, 1950– editor. | Rossini, Manuela, editor.
TITLE: The Cambridge companion to literature and the posthuman / edited by Bruce Clarke and Manuela Rossini.
DESCRIPTION: New York, NY : Cambridge University Press, 2016. | Series: Cambridge companions to literature
IDENTIFIERS: LCCN 2016026619 | ISBN 9781107086203 (hardback)
SUBJECTS: LCSH: Literature and technology. | Humanism in literature. | Mass media and technology. | Human beings in literature. | BISAC: LITERARY CRITICISM / Semiotics & Theory.
CLASSIFICATION: LCC PN56.T37 C36 2016 | DDC 809/.93356–dc23
LC record available at https://lccn.loc.gov/2016026619

ISBN 978-1-107-08620-3 Hardback
ISBN 978-1-107-45061-5 Paperback

CONTENTS

Contents

FIGURES

CONTRIBUTORS

Mario Aquilina, University of Malta

Ridvan Askin, University of Basel

Ron Broglio, Arizona State University

Ivan Callus, University of Malta

Bruce Clarke, Texas Tech University

Claire Colebrook, Pennsylvania State University

Lisa Diedrich, Stony Brook University

Jason W. Ellis, New York City College of Technology, CUNY

Stefan Herbrechter, University of Coventry

Kevin LaGrandeur, New York Institute of Technology

Manuela Rossini, University of Basel

R. L. Rutsky, San Francisco State University

Anneke Smelik, Radboud University Nijmegen

Karl Steel, Brooklyn College and the Graduate Center, CUNY

Jeff Wallace, Cardiff Metropolitan University

Kari Weil, Wesleyan University

Lisa Yaszek, Georgia Institute of Technology

Literature, Posthumanism, and the Posthuman

The Literary Posthuman

In 1977, literary scholar Ihab Hassan published a scholarly article in the form of a performance script, "Prometheus as Performer: Toward a Posthumanist Culture? A University Masque in Five Scenes."[1] This piece is often cited as the original announcement within the critical humanities of the advent of a "posthumanist culture." Describing the ways that the sciences and technologies of that moment were breaking up the engrained image of "man" while prompting renewed flights of Promethean questing, Hassan's remarks are worth recalling from the vantage of 40 years' hindsight: "At present, posthumanism may appear variously as a dubious neologism, the latest slogan, or simply another image of man's recurrent self-hate. Yet posthumanism may also hint at a potential in our culture, hint at a tendency struggling to become more than a trend ... We need to understand that five hundred years of humanism may be coming to an end, as humanism transforms itself into something that we must helplessly call posthumanism" (843). Moreover, engaging with supercomputer HAL from Stanley Kubrick's movie *2001 – A Space Odyssey* (1968), he adds that "the human brain itself does not really know whether it will become obsolete – or simply need to revise its self-conception. ... Will artificial intelligences supersede the human brain, rectify it, or simply extend its powers? We do not know. But this we do know: artificial intelligences, from the humblest calculator to the most transcendent computer, help to transform the image of man, the concept of the human. They are agents of a new posthumanism" (846). Registering the critique of the humanist subject already extant in structuralism as well as the appearance of the cyborg as a cultural figure, Hassan's early survey of the posthumanist landscape remains entirely serviceable today.

Yet the passages I have cited come forward not in any ponderous manner but as dramatized in a comedic vein of "postmodern performance" (831), to wit, a "University Masque" whose characters are Pretext, Mythotext, Text, Heterotext, Context, Metatext, Postext, and Paratext. In the decades that have elapsed since then, in overall fulfillment of Hassan's predictions, the interrogation of humanism's long reign has indeed become a new paradigm within the humanities – a discourse we must still "helplessly call posthumanism" as an umbrella term covering diverse approaches and viewpoints.

Nonetheless, we do well to remember the humorous tonality – indeed, the audacious literary styling – of Hassan's seminal cultural meditation. Even while critical attention and philosophical treatment have been extracting the more sober lineaments of an ever-enlarging set of posthumanist discourses, literary treatments cannot help but turn the image of the posthuman into narrative play, into performance pieces of one sort or another.

The risible side of the literary posthuman is nicely captured in Mark McGurl's 2012 essay "The Posthuman Comedy."[2] McGurl notes that the posthuman image is cultivated most vigorously in literary forms that high humanist taste once derided, for which one uses "the term genre fiction (its science fiction and horror variants in particular) … those literary forms willing to risk artistic ludicrousness in their representation of the inhumanly large and long" (538). In our own cultural era, when the claims of posthumanism are being taken increasingly seriously, the posthuman comedy arises as "scientific knowledge of the spatiotemporal vastness and numerousness of the nonhuman world becomes visible as a formal, representational, and finally existential problem" (537). Ironically enough, it is we humans who are turning the tables, one after the other, on our own cherished pretensions, for instance, to personal autonomy, to impersonal objectivity, to collective significance in the cosmos. Ethically speaking, to practice posthumanism means to relinquish claims of spiritual absolution from natural contingencies. The comic tonality of the posthuman image results when such ontological decentering of the human is depicted in a bathetic light, as a sort of pratfall deflating human affectations or ostentations, especially by foregrounding abiding human affinities with the inorganic machine or the nonhuman animal.

McGurl's distinction between the posthuman comedy's first and second acts helpfully maps the modern and contemporary fields of discussion traversed by this *Cambridge Companion to Literature and the Posthuman*. Spanning the modernist sensibility – references are to Henri Bergson's 1901 treatise on comedy and Charlie Chaplin's 1936 *Modern Times* – and connecting it to the post-World War II era of the cyborg, the posthuman comedy's first act is the one "in which we realize that we cannot be understood apart from our technological prostheses" (549). The second act then follows the strong recent turn in posthumanist discourse from the machinic posthuman to the planetary nonhuman:

> While mechanism in the modern technological sense is one key to comedy, even more basic are the mechanisms of nature, the entire realm of natural processes that enclose, infiltrate, and humiliate human designs. The second act of the posthuman comedy is in this sense a turn (and continual return) to naturalism, one in which nature, far from being dominated by technology, *reclaims*

technology as a human *secretion*, something human beings under
the right conditions naturally produce and use.   (550)

McGurl's cosmic comedy unveils the profound naturalistic currents driving
posthumanist discourse at the moment, coming in on waves of natural
science channeled through quantum theory, symbiotic theory, complexity
theory, and systems theory.[3] These currents have converged to describe life
altogether as a "secretion" of the material-energetic cosmos as that has
coalesced in the Earth system. In their term of evolutionary emergence and
transformation, *all* living beings "secrete technology" as a matter of course –
from laterally transferred genetic packets distributing metabolic capacities
among microbes to metazoan acquisitions of bones, beaks, eyes, wings, and
fingers.[4] The pervasive preoccupation with hybridity in both the profuse
productions of the posthuman imaginary and the diverse discourses of posthumanism are repercussions of these recognitions. Nature at all scales is
penetrating the prior boundaries we thought to place around the human
essence.

The Posthumanist Academy

The past decade has witnessed growing numbers of seminars and conferences
dedicated to topics such as "The Nonhuman," "Radical Methodologies for
the Posthumanities," and "Approaching Posthumanism and the
Posthuman." Special issues on posthumanist topics have appeared in jour-
nals such as *Biography, Cultural Critique*, the *European Journal of English
Studies, Postmedieval, Subjectivity*, and *Subject Matters*. Moreover, curri-
cula in academic departments across the world testify to the development of
posthumanism into a substantial and vibrant topic crossing many fields.
Literary critics and historians have brought a range of theoretical and meth-
odological paradigms to their examination of the posthuman, contributing
to the development of the humanities into the posthumanities.

Posthumanism comprises responses by writers, artists, and scholars to the
general intellectual ecology of contemporary modernity, reactions and
engagements symptomatic of a growing awareness that the human (as
"we" have known and conceptualized it for at least 500 years) is an incoherent concept. However, the various doctrines of posthumanism may be
distinguished in principle from the many notions of the posthuman. We have
employed the term "posthuman," poised ambiguously between noun and
adjective, for expressions such as the cybernetic posthuman, the posthuman
subject, posthuman bodies, the posthuman condition, posthuman culture, or
posthuman society. Here the term refers to images and figurations in literary
and cultural productions, in various genres and periods, of states that lie

before, beyond, or after the human, or into which the human blurs when viewed in its essential hybridity.

Instances of the posthuman present an image, extant or speculative, coupling the human to some nonhuman order of being. This formula is epitomized by the figure of the cyborg, in which a cybernetic or computational technology is spliced to an organic body. The phenomenal fecundity of the cyborg imaginary has been vigorously developed in narrative fictions, in particular, in science fiction and cyberpunk literature. The cybernetic posthuman is sometimes portrayed as an inevitable future, or in a manner continuous with transhumanist visions. The apotheosis of prosthetics would be the downloading of the human mind into a computer – a posthuman scenario developed in earnest 30 years ago in the roboticist Hans Moravec's *Mind Children* and brought to the screen in movies like *Transcendence*. However, these and other related fantasies are better termed instances of retro-humanism. Transhumanist prostheses are skeuomorphs of humanism, vestiges of heroic aspirations that preserve rather than challenge the Cartesian mind–body split so definitive of Western modernity and the Eurocentric myth of progress as technoscientific development.

Alongside such historical and esthetic dimensions of the posthuman imaginary one can also track the reflective and critical discourses of posthumanist philosophies. For instance, drawing on the French philosopher Jacques Derrida's notion of supplementarity – based in the first instance on the way that writing can be considered a *technical supplement* to the capacity for spoken language – one can expand the range of phenomena by which posthumanism observes the inhuman or nonhuman other inhabiting the ostensibly human and so deconstructing the humanist concept of the human. The digital prosthesis is only one among the many forms of the nonhuman supplement. In contrast to images of the cybernetic posthuman as trans- or super-human, posthumanist discourses promote neither the transcendence of the human nor the negation of humanism. Rather, critical posthumanisms engage with the humanist legacy to critique anthropocentric values and worldviews. Posthumanist scholars have brought attention to the potential as well as the fault lines of humanist knowledge production while also problematizing the narrative of the progressive trajectory of the posthuman.[5]

Posthumanism questions how relations between humans and nonhumans operate within the environments where they are assembled. What forms of political agency, what codes of ethics, but also what aesthetic principles would be needed to arrive at a posthumanist world? It is certainly no coincidence that such questions are being discussed today, that the figurations of the posthuman mentioned above proliferate in our time, or that the venerable traditions of humanism are now under challenge. In the face of global threats (ecocides, climate change, human and nonhuman extinctions) unfolding in real time, posthumanism is a historically specific response to our present moment and currently possible forms of futurity. However, neither the current situation nor this line of critical thinking nor its esthetic reworkings have suddenly emerged *ex nihilo*. The humanist era itself has never been a homogenous and fully consensual affair. If the limits of the human have always exercised both our thinking and our esthetic practices, then some aspects of what is now termed "posthumanism" and "the posthuman" go as far back as the beginning of the human itself.

The Cambridge Companion to Literature and the Posthuman

Because figures of the posthuman have a long prehistory, the *Cambridge Companion to Literature and the Posthuman* begins with chapters on premodern literary periods. At issue is the extent of modern technology's role in or responsibility for humanity's becoming posthuman or posthumanist. This volume's authors are skeptical of simple one-way links between the rapidly accelerating potential for radical technological modifications and the proliferation of posthuman figurations in literature, film, and philosophy. Rather, a current challenge for posthumanist thinking is to confront the specters of those premodern animals, gods, angels, monsters, and other real and conceptual entities that, in order to keep the human "proper," humanist modernity had to expel. In doing so, we find that the prehistory of the posthuman underscores our evolutionary situation from its very beginning as inextricably bound up with the nonhuman, technical and otherwise. In the context of posthumanism and the posthuman, then, literature and fiction have always been privileged speculative discourses haunted by the ghosts of humans, nonhumans, and posthumans.

Part I: Literary Periods

The first section of the *Cambridge Companion to Literature and the Posthuman* presents a selected genealogy of the posthuman in literature from the Middle Ages to the present. Karl Steel's chapter "Medieval" opens this volume with a meticulous posthumanist critique of premodern literature. Determining the medieval period's dominant rules for being human clarifies these rules' potential sites of failure. In Steel's analysis, the dominant form of medieval humanism defined the human as "not animal," as possessing a body destined for immortality, and as receiving supposedly unique endowments of language and free will. Steel interrogates each of these points of differentiation of the human in a set of texts – among them the life of Christina the Astonishing, Marie de France's werewolf tale, "Bisclavret," and *Barlam and Iosaphat*, the medieval Christian adaptation of the life of the Buddha – from which one conclusion is that "a great deal of medieval art and literature is indifferent or even hostile to any systematic effort to cordon humans off from other life." Steel brings to light other literary instances that counter enterprise par excellence has to be revised. Part II offers a glimpse at what is happening to literature under posthumanist conditions.

Chapter 6 turns immediately to the genre most commonly associated with the literary posthuman, science fiction (SF). Lisa Yaszek and Jason W. Ellis catalog a wide range of science-fictional literary productions, characterizing the works of authors from Mary Shelley, Nathaniel Hawthorne, Edgar Allan Poe, H. G. Wells, and Olaf Stapledon, to A. E. Van Vogt, Arthur C. Clarke, Theodore Sturgeon, Philip K. Dick, William Gibson, Joanna Russ, and Octavia Butler. Yaszek and Ellis's historical narrative observes that while proto SF authors of the nineteenth century responded to the emergence of modern scientific principles with stories about the dubious results of scientific experiments designed to alter human bodies and life processes, early and mid-twentieth-century SF writers responded to the ascendancy of engineering, eugenics, and cybernetics with stories about beings that were hybrids of organic and technological components. Since then, newer technologies of simulation and replication have engendered a wide range of stories about the meaning and value of posthumanity, especially when conceived, particularly by feminist authors, as a way to envision the overcoming of past and present prejudices and social injustices.

In Chapter 7, Kari Weil writes that while autobiography might be regarded as the most humanist of genres, one whose authors sought to depict the autonomy and agency of the self in relation to its world, the most important examples of the genre have always questioned what it means to be human. Just as the genre arose, with St. Augustine's *Confessions*, from a concern for self-divisions between soul and body, for connections to God and to sin, so do many contemporary life writings put in question where our humanness is located and to what extent we are able to discover it. Weil traces recent posthumanist contestations of autobiography's humanist subject, seeking to locate and describe a posthuman subject in recent autobiographical works in various narrative mediums by autistic author Temple Grandin, video artist Bill Viola, and writer-philosopher Hélène Cixous. "We might then come to think," she notes, "of a posthumanist autobiography as one that attempts to know or at least account for that in- or non-human out of and through which one comes to recognize and be recognized as a 'human' self."

In "Comics and Graphic Narratives," Lisa Diedrich explores how notions of posthuman subjectivity may be constituted by formal innovations in mingling verbal and visual expressions. These hybrid literary forms have become important resources for communicating about a range of ethical and esthetic issues in modes that purely textual literary genres cannot duplicate. Chapter 8 focuses on the hybrid subjects constituted by "graphic medicine," the comics and graphic narratives that have followed developments in medicine and the life sciences. Diedrich's examples of such graphic memoirs and narratives range from *Epileptic* by French cartoonist David B. and *Marbles: Mania, Depression, Michelangelo, and Me* by Ellen Forney to *Mom's Cancer* by Brian Fies and "Becoming Bone Sheep" by Martina Schlünder, Pit Arens, and Axel Gerhardt. For medical practitioners, patients, and families and caregivers dealing with suffering, illness and disability, such narratives help to rethink the boundaries of health, life and death, and not least of all, the status of the human in its entanglement with nonhuman, equally precarious and liminal lives.

In Chapter 9, Anneke Smelik examines popular images of the cyborg in science-fiction film. Unlike earlier figures of the mad scientist producing evil machines, the cinematic cyborg is no longer a figure that instills fear or anxiety. Instead, it points to profound desires for "posthumanization" through fusion with machines and their technologies. The scientific imaginary in cinema has stimulated the self-fashioning of posthuman bodies: in the digitized cinema of the last decade, the posthuman predicament takes the form of spectacular images expressing memories, emotions, and experiences in loops of time and space where present, past, and future are all connected. Smelik pays particular attention to recurrent cinematic tropes and techniques to register the psychic and somatic interiority of the cyborg body: subjective point-of-view (POV) shots, scenes of self-reparation before a mirror, emphasizing a machine agent's capacity for self-reflection, and various technological mediations of memory, suggesting continuity between organic and machinic capacities to remember experiences, to forget, or to refashion self-recollections. The popularity of the cyborg body in science-fiction films has translated into cultural practices of enhancing and altering the human body by entering into intimate relationships with the machines themselves. These cinematic narratives have thus become a significant agency of "posting" the human.

It may be that literature and literary culture are not where the main action is today. Perhaps the world of letters is not straightforwardly reconcilable with the digital cultures that dominate the posthuman age. It might thus seem that there is no longer any place for discussions of "literariness" or the "singularity of literature" that once dominated literary theory. More fundamentally still, literature itself – as discourse, tradition, institution, practice, field of study and focus for diverse investments and passions, even now in this moment of its announced precariousness – is claimed to be losing much of its recognizable form, resonance, and valence. In other words, there is a congruence between the posthuman and the "post-literary." In Chapter 10, "E-Literature," Ivan Callus and Mario Aquilina explore such ideas. What does literature become within a posthuman imaginary, and what exactly would the "post-literary" be? Their chapter considers how the practice and theory of electronic literature appear to be more intuitively complementary with posthumanism than is the case with literature's and criticism's more orthodox guises, though it also cautions against overinterpretation of the seeming affinities between the post-human and the post-literary.

Part III: Posthuman Themes

The *Cambridge Companion to Literature and the Posthuman* concludes by identifying major philosophical, political, esthetic, and existential perspectives raised in fictional and other discourses about the posthuman. Following our literary genealogy of the posthuman and its main motifs, modes, and narrative mediums, Part III moves the discussion to primary issues of posthumanism, as these appear in literature and related discourses, themes constituting the major theoretical fields on which discussions about the posthuman are currently playing out. As a rethinking of the human, the nonhuman, and their shared environments, posthumanism is a key component of current trends in ecological theory, animal studies, social systems theory, gender and sexuality studies, object-oriented ontology and speculative realism, as well as in the ongoing debates on the nature of the "Anthropocene" and on the prospect of climate change radically transforming conditions for all life on Earth. Thus, we present chapters on the nonhuman, on posthumanist relationships with various forms of bodies, objects, and technologies, and on the shapes we can conceive of "post-anthropocentric" futures.

In Chapter 11, Bruce Clarke examines the category of the nonhuman in relation to the discourses of the posthuman and of posthumanism. Whereas the post- of the posthuman carries along the connotation of temporal relations, the non- of the nonhuman posits an atemporal relation between the human and its others. Nonetheless, the nonhuman also has a conceptual history that runs parallel to the emergence of the notion of the posthuman. Attention to the nonhuman is a factor in Bruno Latour's distinction of the nonmodern from the postmodern, in Romanticism and the sublime in William Wordsworth's *Prelude*, in natural selection in Darwin's *Origin of Species* and the extraterrestrial alien in H. G. Wells's *The War of the Worlds*, in the modernist misanthropy in D. H. Lawrence's *Women in Love*, and in Ronald Wright's satirical near-future apocalyptic fantasy in *A Scientific Romance*. The present theoretical moment has crafted a positive concept of the nonhuman, a mobile signifier under which to place the multifarious ontological positivities currently imputed to the other-than-human.

Manuela Rossini argues in "Bodies" that within posthumanist discourse since the 1970s, the "nonhuman turn" is to a large extent accompanied by, if not the result of, a heightened critical attention to "corpo-reality," the material being of the body. In the wake of feminist interventions and Michel Foucault's work, the body acquired a history. It has since been analyzed as socially and culturally constructed in terms of gender, race, class, sexuality, ability, and other categories of corporeal difference. More recently, however, such discursive constructionism has also been challenged, notably by feminist new materialism and other approaches that deprioritize language as what makes human beings special and superior. Within these new analytical frameworks, and influenced by quantum theory and the new biology, the (human) body is understood as a porous ecosystem, dependent on other organic as well as nonorganic and nonhuman matter and beings for its survival. The *Cambridge Companion to Literature and the Posthuman* altogether testifies to nature–culture entanglements and evolutionary "transcorporeality" across the species divide. Chapter 12 examines such material-semiotic figurations of posthuman bodies and embodiment in late twentieth- and early twenty-first-century writings. It focuses in particular on French philosopher Jean-Luc Nancy's post-transplant essay "L'Intrus" ("The Intruder") and Shelley Jackson's widely discussed hypertext *Patchwork Girl* (a rewriting of *Frankenstein*). These discussions are intersected by brief references to Jackson's *my body – a Wunderkammer*, her tattoo project "Skin," her stories in *The Melancholy of Anatomy*, and her print novel *Half Life*, all paradigmatic examples of the posthuman *corpus* as always already intertextual and *in*-formed by its contingent "outsides."

In Chapter 13, Ridvan Askin reviews how traditional humanist approaches to literature tend to overlook the status of the literary text as an object in its own right, and thus, how literature operates not by virtue of what it is *about* but by virtue of what it *is*. One route to a posthumanist theory of literature, he proposes, is via explorations of its ontological constitution, that is, its status as an *esthetic object* that acts upon us in cognitive and bodily ways. Drawing on the Russian formalist Viktor Shklovsky's "Art as Device," Gilles Deleuze's philosophy of becoming, and the recent resurgence of speculative thought and metaphysics in continental philosophy, Askin lays a groundwork for treating literary texts as lures for affective encounters, displacing attention from humanist subjectivities to nonhuman objectivities. With readings of Margaret Fuller's *Summer on the Lakes, in 1843* and Charles Olson's "The Ring of" as test cases, Askin traces how literary texts qua esthetic objects constitute veritable speculative experiments in metaphysics.

R. L. Rutsky reminds us in "Technologies" that heightened literary engagement with the promises and threats of mechanical technologies go back at least to the eighteenth century if not to the Renaissance. More recently, from Fritz Lang's *Metropolis* to Richard Power's *Galatea 2.2*, figurations of the posthuman have been depicting technological systems as living systems, oscillating between technologies that mimic human life and those that portray a mechanized inversion of human life. However, changing conceptions of the posthuman have emerged precisely in concert with corresponding changes in the conception of technology. New concepts of the posthuman have emerged as technologies have increasingly come to be seen more broadly as complex and interactive environments, populations, systems, networks, and processes, which need neither serve nor imitate human life. Alongside treatments of pertinent theoretical authors, including Bernard Stiegler, Herbert Marcuse, Guy Debord, and Donna Haraway, Rutsky assembles a wealth of literary and filmic examples in which conceptual changes toward technology are mirrored in posthuman images of altered human relations to the planetary environment. Technological developments presage a nonhumanist post-humanity in which human beings come to be superseded by complex bundles of interactions, processes, and networked systems.

The *Cambridge Companion to Literature and the Posthuman* comes to an apt conclusion with Claire Colebrook's chapter on "Futures." How we conceive of the posthuman has direct implications for our imagined and possible futures, both in utopian and dystopian dimensions. Colebrook searches through a range of speculative futures, giving special attention to the statements of leading philosophers, including Jacques Derrida, Richard Rorty, Bernard Stiegler, Gilles Deleuze, Félix Guattari, Manuel De Landa, and Bruno Latour. She also contemplates their posthuman futures under the shadow of Friedrich Nietzsche's concept of eternal return. The image that arises from her survey is complex, one of "multiple worlds, multiple futures, and multiple lines of time," and this is precisely what one finds in the literature and cinema of the last century and the current moment. Twenty-first-century film and fiction in particular have both challenged and intensi-fied the modern awareness of humans as exceptional, not just in moral terms, but as a geological force. We just may be too exceptional for our own good. Many of our imagined futures are now posthuman only insofar as humans begin to witness the end of their own being. Literary texts depict such images of the future in literal rather than theoretical terms.

NOTES

1. Ihab Hassan, "Prometheus as Performer: Toward a Posthumanist Culture?" *The Georgia Review* 31.4 (Winter 1977): 830–50.
2. Mark McGurl, "The Posthuman Comedy," *Critical Inquiry* 38 (Spring 2012): 533–53.
3. See, for instance, Karen Barad, *Meeting the Universe Halfway: Quantum Physics and the Entanglement of Matter and Meaning* (Durham: Duke University Press, 2007); Jane Bennett, *Vibrant Matter: A Political Ecology of Things* (Durham: Duke University Press, 2010); Bruce Clarke, "Evolutionary Equality: Neocybernetic Posthumanism and Margulis and Sagan's Writing Practice," in *Writing Posthumanism, Posthuman Writing*, ed. Sidney I. Dobrin (Anderson, SC: Parlor Press), 275–97; Manuel De Landa, *A Thousand Years of Nonlinear History* (New York: Zone Books, 1997); Niklas Luhmann, "The Autopoiesis of Social Systems," in *Essays on Self-Reference* (New York: Columbia University Press, 1991), 1–20; Lynn Margulis, *Symbiotic Planet: A New Look at Evolution* (New York: Basic Books, 1998); Humberto Maturana and Francisco J. Varela, *Autopoiesis and Cognition: The Realization of the Living* (Boston: Riedel, 1980); and Cary Wolfe, *What is Posthumanism?* (Minneapolis: University of Minnesota Press, 2010).
4. See Bruce Clarke, ed., *Earth, Life, and System: Evolution and Ecology on a Gaian Planet* (New York: Fordham University Press, 2015).
5. For a detailed survey of these issues, see Stefan Herbrechter, *Posthumanism: A Critical Analysis* (London: Bloomsbury, 2013).

ACKNOWLEDGMENTS

We would like to thank Ivan Callus and Stefan Herbrechter, co-directors of the Critical Posthumanism Network, for sharing their thoughts on all matters posthuman/ist; Cary Wolfe for his example and encouragement; all the contributors to this volume for their patience and diligence; and other friends and colleagues too numerous to mention but certainly including Stacy Alaimo, Rosi Braidotti, John Bruni, Oron Catts, Richard Grusin, Vicki Kirby, Lynn Margulis, Colin Milburn, and Dorion Sagan.

CHRONOLOGY 1: THE POSTHUMAN

1920	D. H. Lawrence, *Women in Love*
1920	Kurt Schwitters, "Merz"
1922	Virginia Woolf, *Jacob's Room*
1923	Gertrude Stein, "If I Told Him"
1924	*L'Inhumaine*, dir. L'Herbier Marcel
1927	J. B. S. Haldane, "The Last Judgment"
1927	*Metropolis*, dir. Fritz Lang
1928	Wyndham Lewis, *Tarr* (2nd, revised version)
1929	Clare Winger Harris, "The Evolutionary Monstrosity"
1929	Leslie F. Stone, "Out of the Void"
1930	Lilith Lorraine, "Into the 28th Century"
1930	Olaf Stapledon, *Last and First Men*
1931	Edmond Hamilton, "The Man Who Evolved"
1932	Aldous Huxley, *Brave New World*
1933	Laurence Manning, "The Man Who Awoke"
1934	C. L. Moore, "No Woman Born"
1934	E. E. "Doc" Smith, *Triplanetary*
1935	Harry Bates, "Alas, All Thinking!"
1936	H. P. Lovecraft, *The Shadow Out of Time*
1937	Dorothy Quick, "Strange Orchids"
1938	Samuel Beckett, *Murphy*
1938	George S. Schuyler, *Black Empire*
1938	E. E. "Doc" Smith, *Galactic Patrol*
1940	E. E. "Doc" Smith, *Gray Lensman*
1940	A. E. Van Vogt, *Slan*
1942	Isaac Asimov, "Runaround"
1942	E. E. "Doc" Smith, *Second Stage Lensmen*
1948	E. E. "Doc" Smith, *Children of the Lens*
1948	Judith Merril, "That Only a Mother"
1949	George Orwell, *Nineteen Eighty-Four*
1950	E. E. "Doc" Smith, *First Lensman*
1953	Arthur C. Clarke, *Childhood's End*
1953	Charles Olson, "The Ring of"
1953	Lewis Padgett, *Mutant*
1953	Theodore Sturgeon, *More Human Than Human*
1954	Philip K. Dick, "The Golden Man"
1958	Samuel Beckett, *Krapp's Last Tape*
1959	Carol Emshwiller, "Day at the Beach"
1960	Mary Armock, "First Born"
1964	Daniel F. Galouye, *Simulacron-3*
1964	Phyllis Gottlieb, *Sunburst*

CHRONOLOGY 2: POSTHUMANISM

1976	Jacques Derrida, *Of Grammatology* (English translation)
1976	Thomas Weiskel, *The Romantic Sublime*
1980	Humberto Maturana and Francisco Varela, *Autopoiesis and Cognition*
1981	Jean Baudrillard, *Simulation and Simulacra*
1981	Heinz von Foerster, *Observing Systems*
1984	Jean-François Lyotard, *The Postmodern Condition* (English translation)
1984	Patricia Waugh, *Metafiction*
1985	Donna Haraway, "A Cyborg Manifesto"
1986	Temple Grandin, *Emergence: Labeled Autistic*
1987	Gilles Deleuze and Félix Guattari, *A Thousand Plateaus* (English translation)
1987	William Irwin Thompson, ed., *Gaia: A Way of Knowing*
1987	Brian McHale, *Postmodernist Fiction*
1988	Linda Hutcheon, *A Poetics of Postmodernism*
1988	Hans Moravec, *Mind Children*
1989	Slavoj Žižek, *The Sublime Object of Ideology*
1991	Fredric Jameson, *Postmodernism*
1991	Jean-François Lyotard, *The Inhuman* (English translation)
1992	Jacques Derrida, *Acts of Literature*
1992	Brian McHale, *Constructing Postmodernism*
1993	Scott Bukatman, *Terminal Identity*
1993	Bruno Latour, *We Have Never Been Modern* (English translation)
1994	Gilles Deleuze, *Difference and Repetition* (English translation)
1994	Gilles Deleuze and Félix Guattari, *What Is Philosophy?* (English translation)
1994	Bernard Stiegler, *Technics and Time, 1: The Fault of Epimetheus*
1995	Judith Halberstam and Ira Livingston, eds., *Posthuman Bodies*
1995	Niklas Luhmann, *Social Systems* (English translation)
1996	Anne Balsamo, *Technologies of the Gendered Body*
1996	Margrit Shildrick, "Posthumanism and the Monstrous Body"
1996	Joseph Tabbi, *The Postmodern Sublime*
1999	Giorgio Agamben, *The Man without Content*
1999	Erica Fudge, Ruth Gilbert, and Susan Wiseman, eds., *At the Borders of the Human*
1999	N. Katherine Hayles, *How We Became Posthuman*
1999	R. L. Rutsky, *High Techne*
2000	Neil Badmington, *Posthumanism*

2000	Pamela Caughie, ed., *Virginia Woolf in the Age of Mechanical Reproduction*
2000	Michael Hardt and Antonio Negri, *Empire*
2002	Elaine Graham, *Representations of the Post/Human*
2002	Annemarie Mol, *The Body Multiple*
2002	Margrit Schildrick, *Embodying the Monster*
2003	Giorgio Agamben, *The Open: Man and Animal*
2003	Jeffrey Jerome Cohen, *Medieval Identity Machines*
2003	Donna Haraway, *The Companion Species Manifesto*
2003	Lynn Margulis and Dorion Sagan, *Acquiring Genomes*
2003	Cary Wolfe, *Animal Rites*
2004	Neil Badmington, *Alien Chic: Posthumanism and the Other Within*
2004	Andy Clark, *Natural Born Cyborgs*
2004	Susan Squier, *Liminal Lives*
2007	Karen Barad, *Meeting the Universe Halfway*
2008	Bruce Clarke, *Posthuman Metamorphosis*
2008	Jacques Derrida, *The Animal that Therefore I Am* (English translation)
2008	Donna Haraway, *When Species Meet*
2008	Quentin Meillassoux, *After Finitude* (English translation)
2008	Colin Milburn, *Nanovision: Engineering the Future*
2009	Bruce Clarke and Mark B. N. Hansen, eds., *Emergence and Embodiment*
2010	Stacy Alaimo, *Bodily Natures*
2010	Jane Bennett, *Vibrant Matter*
2010	Graham Harman, *The Quadruple Object*
2010	Bruno Latour, "An Attempt at a 'Compositionist Manifesto'"
2010	Cary Wolfe, *What is Posthumanism?*
2011	Levi R. Bryant, *The Democracy of Objects*
2012	Stefan Herbrechter and Ivan Callus, eds., *Posthumanist Shakespeares*
2012	Patricia MacCormack, *Posthuman Ethics*
2012	Kari Weil, *Thinking Animals*
2013	Rosi Braidotti, *The Posthuman*
2013	Mary Bryden, ed., *Beckett and Animals*
2013	Stefan Herbrechter, *Posthumanism*
2013	Kevin LaGrandeur, *Androids and Intelligent Networks in Early Modern Literature and Culture*
2014	Ridvan Askin, Andreas Hägler, and Philipp Schweighauser, "Introduction: Aesthetics after the Speculative Turn"

PART I

Literary Periods

I

KARL STEEL

Medieval

Treating medieval posthumanism may seem a ludicrous task, since, at least in common wisdom, the Middle Ages lacked the technology, philosophical habits, or looming ecological collapse that would enable or encourage a dissolution of a settled belief in human supremacy; or, it simply lacked a recognizable humanism altogether. Some of these contradictory, albeit aligned, caricatures of the period leave premodernity mired in a jealously guarded anthropocentrism, masked under a theocentrism, without the suspicion, let alone the comparative anatomy or genetics, that would allow humanism to get over itself. Or they imagine the medieval as essentially instinctual, because of its presumptive submission to some universal religion; its hostility to science and to this world as a whole; its adherence to millennia-old textual traditions, transmitted mechanically and uncomprehendingly; and, finally, its squalor and savagery, in which an ovine populace cowered before a "feudal" lord in a non-politics in which sovereign and law were one and the same. In either case, in the long development of posthumanism, the Middle Ages is presumably what must be sloughed off. Modernity needed to await what the medieval lacked, namely the invention of the individual, a systematic atheism, and other such discursive developments that might finally save us from, or deliver us entirely to, the technoindustrial catastrophes and mass extinctions of our present.[1]

This chapter aims to shake up these prejudices, by examining a set of "hot spots" in medieval thinking, primarily concerning the human body, human language, and, finally, the problems inherent to the belief in human free choice. My survey should be understood not as attempting to identify a kind of "proto posthumanism" in the Middle Ages but as suspicious about the very temporal boundaries of "proto" and "post," and, especially, as arguing that any systematized humanism will always fissure under the pressure of its own efforts at coherence. Posthumanism does not follow humanism; rather, it is inherent in its own claims.

Humans and/as Animals

The Middle Age's most systematic attempts to define the human were chiefly devoted to distinguishing humans from all other worldly, mortal life. The first obvious difficulty was one of vocabulary. No medieval word in French, English, or Latin functioned exactly like the modern English or French words "animal."[2] The medieval genre of the bestiary – natural histories, often lavishly illustrated, loaded with moral commentary – invariably treated lions, dogs, wolves, eagles, sometimes stones; but they sometimes considered humans as well, understanding them to be, at least for the purposes of the genre, an animal like any other.[3] In Old French, "animality" is simply the set of faculties any given living thing possesses, while the closest etymological derivative of "animal," "almaille" or "aumaille," means only "livestock" or even just "horned livestock" rather than all nonhuman life.[4] A Middle English encyclopedia explains that "all that combines flesh and the spirit of life," that is, the *anima*, "is called an animal, whether it is an airy beast like a bird, a watery beast like a fish, or those that go on the ground, like humans or wild or tame beasts."[5] Another text speaks of humans and "other beasts."[6]

For its part, medieval Latin tended to divide nonhuman fauna into either domesticated animals, termed *pecores* or *jumentes*, or wild or dangerous animals, termed *bestiae* or *ferae*. *Bruti*, another common word, when appended as an adjective to "animal," meant most irrational fauna, but it tended to leave out snakes, insects, toads, and other creeping things, which were instead collected under the name of *reptiles*. Conversely, the Latin word "animal" could include a number of possible groups. For example, the entry on "animal" in the Alan of Lille's twelfth-century dictionary of theological terms neatly assembles several quite distinct meanings: like the Middle English above, as describing humans or any creature whatsoever having a soul capable of sensation (that is, nonvegetal living things); or only "brute" animals, used in the Bible, as when Noah and his sons go into the ark with all animals; and sometimes, surprisingly, *only* rational animals, as when Psalms 144:16 says, "Thou openest thy hand, and fillest with blessing every living creature [in the Latin Vulgate, 'animal']," which was, as Alan explains, a category that could include only humans, since none but rational creatures could receive this blessing.[7] Furthermore, a great deal of medieval art and literature is indifferent or even hostile to any systematic effort to cordon humans off from other life. This sentiment operates most obviously in material that developed independent of academia, monastic textuality, or other professionalized, closely supervised Christian literacies. A work like the fourteenth-century Icelandic *Saga of Hrolf Kraki*, set in sixth-century

Denmark, perhaps derived from much older sources, features, among other characters, a prince transformed into a bear by a wicked queen, killed by his father, and fed to his beloved, who bears three sons: one merely a great leader, another with dog's feet, and the other an elk from the navel down. *Hrolf Kraki* considers these brothers more wonderful than horrifying.[8] Another Old Norse work, the thirteenth-century *Konungs skuggsjá* (King's Mirror), draws on Irish writing and storytelling to imagine the fate of men driven mad by battle: they flee into the woods, where they grow feathers, and "run along the trees almost as swiftly as monkeys or squirrels."[9] Marie de France's twelfth-century "Bisclavret," like her other lais, professes to be based on the native stories of Brittany. This werewolf story does nothing to condemn the monster, neither does it imagine him to be cursed or diseased, but instead portrays him as being simply what he is: his wife is the story's villain, because she betrays him as soon as she learns of his dubious humanity.[10]

Another set of stories sought to free nobles from a mundanely human ancestry by associating their lines with animal or otherwise nonhuman progenitors. The mythical King Avidus of Crete, begotten upon the king's wife by a necromancer, thrived as a child, despite being repeatedly thrown to hungry beasts. Nurtured by deer's milk and thereby taking on the deer's own fleetness, he finally becomes king, where his nonhuman kinship allows him to invent the paradigmatically human technologies of domestication of oxen, plowing, and the planting of wheat.[11] Finally, the Lusignans, one of the noblest houses of Europe, promoted the myth of their descent from Melusine, who, once a week, secretly took on the form of a dragon, and whose children tended to be as monstrous as she was. Melusine abandons her family when her husband and brother-in-law refuse to be satisfied until they know her true nature.[12] In these and many other similar medieval tales, the category of the human is simply insufficient either for illustrating intense emotional states or for distinguishing nobility from more quotidian people. And in "Bisclavret" and *Melusine*, the human functions as little more than a pathetic prejudice and a temptation to normalize.

Nonetheless, even absent a clear linguistic division, and against this mass of storytelling, mainstream medieval thought, like mainstream thought now, remained committed to arguing that humans were a uniquely special form of life. When Marx says that "man can be distinguished from animals by consciousness, by religion, or anything else you like,"[13] almost no medieval thinker would disagree with him. His "anything else you like" sounds like nothing so much as a slight adaptation of Saint Augustine of Hippo's assertion that humans surpass "brute beasts" by "his reason or mind or intelligence, or whatever we wish to call it."[14] For the strain of medieval thought that Marx inherited and, we might say, automatically repeated, humans alone among mortal creation had reason, language, free choice, an immortal soul, the capacity to laugh, the upright posture that was itself the physical manifestation of their unique capacity to analyze things "as such," and so on.

A few examples will suffice to give a sense of what will likely strike moderns or supposed postmoderns as all too familiar. Here, again standing for Christian doctrine as a whole, Augustine affirmed that "the human mind, when judging visible things, can recognize that it itself is better than all visible things."[15] Here representing secular thought, the thirteenth-century political theorist Marsilius of Padua affirms, without any reference to ethology, that "man alone among the animals is said to have ownership or control of his acts," that is, we alone have free will.[16] From these jealously guarded unique possessions followed a set of rights and obligations: chiefly the right to be treated as an object of direct care (while, as in Kant, nonhuman animals could only be indirect objects of care) and the concomitant right not to be treated as merely a thing.[17]

Within this reasoning, humans could demonstrate their rational particularity more directly, not through displays of rational behavior – writing poetry, building churches, generating philosophy, and the like – but rather by dominating animals, for, according to this reasoning, no rational creature would allow itself to be so debased. The abbot Ratramnus of Corbie's ninth-century "Letter on the Cynocephali" finally determines that these dog-headed monsters are human and therefore deserve a missionary outreach, not on the basis of their political organization, nor from their use of clothing, itself evidence of their shame or modesty, but rather because they domesticate other animals: no animals but humans, reasons Ratramnus, keep livestock.[18] Similarly, if more cartoonishly, several medieval biographers found evidence of Charlemagne's sovereignty and warrior virility in his outsized appetite for animal flesh. Not only could he split a man into two with a single blow of his sword, or lift a fully armored man above his head; he also "ate but little bread, but at once he would eat a quarter of a ram, or two hens, or a goose, or a swine's shoulder, or a peacock, or a crane, or a whole hare."[19]

Certainly, some beasts could be treated well: like the moderns, medieval people kept pets, favoring lapdogs and other small animals, like squirrels, dormice, or even the occasional badger.[20] Elites admired and even mourned their horses, dogs, and hawks; the latter, for example, were sent to the shrines of saints to be healed, and those who mocked this saintly solicitude for mere beasts tended to find themselves blinded or paralyzed.[21] And being compared to a beast, even behaving like a beast, was not necessarily a moral or political catastrophe. Chivalric literature and heraldry frequently and favorably likened knights to lions, boars, bears, or eagles.[22] The avidity of the hungry Charlemagne looks like nothing so much as the bestial appetites of the giants and monstrous boars of medieval romance, or the barbaric carnivorousness of the Scots or Mongols in medieval polemic ethnography. Yet this diet, even in a document written by and for an ideally ascetic clergy, aims only to praise a masculinity whose outsized force disdains merely human rules. In all this material, we see yet another example of how human elites sought to naturalize their own supremacy, even amid a general practice of scorning most bestial life. Then as now, the intersection of class and humanity benefits some animals and harms most humans.

We can clearly discern this scorn in poems like a short French satire poem, "Contempt for Peasants," which pretends to be astonished that peasants should eat fish, beef, or wheat, when they should be pasturing on all fours on thorns and roots, like other livestock.[23] We can even more clearly discern it in medieval texts that imagined certain kinds of bodies as properly edible. A fifteenth-century Middle English monastic poem, "Disputation Between the Body and Worms," delights in its horrific representation of a beautiful woman now thronged with hungry vermin in the grave, thus joining itself to other medieval misogynist works that imagined women as particularly fleshly and putrid.[24] Meanwhile, the crusading fantasy sometimes splits Christian from Muslim bodies by imagining the latter as, essentially, meat. During a war against Iberian Muslims, the Norman knight Rotgerio fed his captives to each other, "dividing them up for food as if they were pigs."[25] A Middle English romance of Richard the Lionheart admires its hero for his enthusiasm for eating Saracens, whose bodies he found more restorative and delicious than the finest pork.[26]

One of the most elaborate of such stories is a popular fourteenth-century legend that during the Holy Family's exile from the threat of Herod, Jesus played with children from among the Jewish community, occasionally striking his playmates dead or resurrecting them. Understandably growing nervous, the Jewish families hid their children, in, of all places, an oven, placed under guard. When the guard tells Jesus that the oven contains only pigs, Jesus responds by transforming the Jewish children into just that.[27] According to some versions of the story, this is why Jews refuse to eat pork. The story may have been promulgated as a response to still other anti-Semitic stories that imagined Jews kidnapping Christian children and basting and roasting them like meat,[28] thus answering one anthropophagic legend with another: pigs are, after all, the one large domestic animal raised only to be eaten. These and other such tales remind us that the question of human recognition, and the accompanying question of who or what will be treated "as animals," will always be answered in ways that fall unequally and cruelly on the most vulnerable, and that any promise of technobiological or philosophical "escape" from humanism must always remember those humans deemed insufficient: too bodily, too emotional, too sick.[29] The category of the human has always endangered certain humans.

Even amid this unrelenting humanism, a posthumanism still remained possible, at least implicitly articulated by medieval textuality's own unrelenting attempts to set humans apart from the rest of creation. I might hesitate to call this critique – or, more precisely, this failure – of humanism a *post*humanism, since it did not follow a clearly articulated humanism so much as it surrounded it, ran alongside it, or even inevitably followed efforts to define human supremacy, which, as they do so often, devoured the very humanity this humanism was meant to defend. The remainder of this chapter will examine logical problems inherent to claims for the ultimate immortality of the human body and the aligned claims for the uniquely human possession of language and of free will, both evidence of the immortal, rational soul that humans, alone among animals, were thought to possess.

Mobile and Everlasting Bodies

First, immortality. Only a few scattered medieval thinkers allowed that nonhuman animals might have immortal souls like humans: all living things had souls, but only rational souls lived forever. The opposite position, that all souls were mortal, entirely immanent to this material world, was typically reserved in medieval writings for pagans or "natural philosophers," invented only as strawmen awaiting defeat by right belief. One medieval thinker, however, did develop this point on his own: this was Blaise of Parma, a late medieval Italian called by his contemporaries the "Doctor Diabolicus." Until his forced recantation in 1396, Blaise argued that the soul was entirely immanent to matter. He maintained no boundary that would reserve spontaneous generation only to the "imperfect" animals like gnats, bees, mice, eels, and toads, arguing instead that humans, along with their rational soul, could emerge spontaneously, so that life was itself nothing more than one more material effect of the action of celestial bodies upon this planet.[30]

Against this position, mainstream medieval humanism held that not only the rational soul but also the human body would enter into immortality. While all nonhuman worldly life was destined for death, humans, by contrast, would be reunited with their own reconstituted bodies upon the Day of Judgment. For this belief, based on a pre-Cartesian notion of the "psychosomatic unity" of the human subject, the human body was both mortal and, like the soul, promised to immortality, either to the eternal stasis of paradise or to the eternal flux and degradation of hell.[31] This "posthuman" body frees

8

the body of the mortal and even corporeal limitations of being a body, both for good and for ill, by realizing the inherent perfection and inescapable perpetuity of the human self that was lost when God expelled Adam and Eve from Eden.

The full terror of this posthuman condition may be discerned in the Thomas of Cantimpré's thirteenth-century life of Christina Mirabilis ("the Astonishing"), who was from what is now Sint-Truiden in modern-day Belgium. After dying briefly, and then being restored to life, she now has the benefits of the resurrection body, but in this world. She first eats a meal, as if to demonstrate that her body is indeed a real body. Later, however, she feeds only on her own milk and throws herself into a series of purgatorial punishments, leaping into fires or boiling pots, standing for hours on end in the frigid Meuse, stretching herself out on professional instruments of torture, lying in new graves, and whirling about on a millwheel, suffering terribly throughout all this, but emerging each time without showing the slightest sign of injury. Elsewhere, she collapses her limbs "together into a ball as if they were hot wax" so that "all that could be perceived of her was a round mass," and then, once finished with her "spiritual inebriation," she returned to her proper form, "like a hedgehog" unrolling itself.[32] Finally, having become a spectacle, she flees into the wilderness, the treetops, or to the deep waters, emerging at last to serve as a political advisor and prophet for the community and its nobility. Her body seamlessly expresses her frenzied holy will. It is a perfection of human possibility that takes Christina and her body beyond anything recognizably human or even beyond any recognizable expression of a rational soul, showing the human dream of bodily perfection in all its shocking possibility.

Spoken Language and Gesture

Human language, like the human body, was another key site of human difference, though just as prone as the body to bloom into something other than human. Chaucer's "Nun's Priest's Tale" is a key example of what is at stake in claims that only humans possess language. The tale grants animals the ability to speak, while all but stripping it from his human characters: the rooster Chaunticleer, his wife Pertelote, and the wily fox all speak with great, if self-serving, erudition, while the poor widow and her retinue are for the most part able only to "shriek" and "howl" as they scramble after their stolen property, and otherwise have nothing to say.[33] The possession of rational language is a zero-sum game, where rationality and its benefits must always be the sole possession of some particular group. Yet medieval art and literature is full of animal communication, shared with humans, conducted not through spoken language but through gesture, without any failures of expression. Bede's eighth-century life of Cuthbert features ravens who steal some of the saint's crop and then return, repentant, "with feathers outspread and head bowed low to its feet," and even give Cuthbert a gift of a lump of pig's lard.[34] The lion of Chrétien de Troyes' twelfth-century *Yvain* first allies with the titular knight by bowing and stretching out his paws before him in a gesture of vassalage: in a society full of meaningful gestures, this voiceless lion, in effect, is able to sign a contract.[35]

Finally, we can return once more to Marie de France's "Bisclavret," as its werewolf expresses himself often through gesture, especially when he kisses the king's foot to show his allegiance and when he attacks his former wife and her new husband. The men of the court understand this creature's behavior as rational. At his first gesture of homage, the king declares that "ele a sen d'ume" (154; it [or, less likely, "she"] has human intelligence) and then revises himself three lines later: "ceste beste a entente e sen" (157; this beast has understanding and intelligence).[36] The king admits that beasts might have their own intelligence, which is not a wan imitation of human reason but rather their own. Yet Bisclavret's gestures might be as easily comprehendible as simply canine: dogs show affection, or abasement, by licking and, of course, attack when they're frightened or angry. The recognition of rational language here has nothing to do with the presence or absence of spoken language, nor of legibly contractual gesture, but rather only with the royal recognition that this wolf's violence and power befit his court.

Free Will and Mechanicity

One of the primary concerns of "Bisclavret" is free will: does the werewolf have it, or indeed, do Bisclavret's wife or the king, committed as they are, respectively, to running the scripts of human difference and masculine royal authority? Consider the chivalric romance *Octavian*, which concerns a lost, chivalric child raised by merchants and rechristened Florent (like a modern child named "Dollar"). He recurrently frustrates his parents by showing his true, chivalric value, for example, by trading two oxen for a falcon and by haggling a horse trader *up* to ensure he pays full price for a glorious, white steed. Here, despite claims of "freedom" – the Middle English "fre," among other meanings, can indicate "generous," "legally free of bondage," "noble," or "unconstrained" – Octavian's nobility is not an autonomous act but rather a program run by anyone descended from noble blood, whose very automatism proves Octavian's hardwired, unchosen superiority.[37]

We see a still more explicit questioning of free choice in the medieval epistolary debate between Alexander the Great and Dindimus, leader or spokesman of a vegetarian sect of Brahman philosophers. Both sides accuse the other of abandoning their human prerogatives: so far as Dindimus is concerned, Alexander is driven relentlessly and irrationally by an instinct for conquest, while Alexander considers the virtuous, anarchic vegetarianism of these fictionalized Brahmans only a symptom of their bestial misery, suffered amid a wretched absence of natural resources. Both sides of the argument presume themselves to be the sole human; both suppose themselves to be exercising their free will, either through the enjoyment (and conquest) of the world or through its rejection. Arguably, we may understand the debate instead as little more than the clash of a warrior-machine with an ascetic-machine, each able to do nothing but occupy the positions each is compelled to take.[38]

My final example will be an equally widespread medieval imagining of the pagan far east, the tradition of Barlam and Josephat, a Christianization of the life of the Buddha, itself based on Manichean and Islamic adaptations.[39] A Middle English version of the story often condemns idolaters for believing that idols were "those who made us," explaining that these mere objects, like beasts, are properly here only to serve humans, who alone among created things have a "reasonable will and desire" to choose to "do good or evil."[40] But the Christians decrying idolatry themselves hardly seem free of being objects. Their one difference from the idols is that they are not *silent*, as they recite a limited set of scripts in a manner most reminiscent of amusement-park animatronics. It is not only that the text always resorts to the same language to condemn idols – on three widely separated occasions it calls them "dumb and deaf" – as if it were following a recipe rather than freely arguing;[41] it is also that its often (and, given its audience, unnecessarily) repeated Christian credos have themselves been fossilized into orthodoxy by centuries of doctrinal pressure. The "freely chosen" belief praised by this text is also, like the idols, a man-made fetish invested with freedom, all the while evacuating any chance to break with the old debate between objects and agents, constraint and free will.

A fully posthumanist investigation must engage primarily with any given culture's rules for being human; it must delineate "what goes without saying" before deciding, more or less happily, that this supposed natural foundation has been lost. Dominant medieval philosophy and doctrine continually defined and defended a concept and practice of human supremacy and belief in language and freedom. These ontotheological claims persist in our supposedly secular era. We are not yet done with the Middle Ages. Of course, more "properly" posthumanist sites of investigation in the

Middle Ages will easily reward investigation: the biotechnological assemblage of knights with their horse and armor, whose most bizarre form is the so-called *poisson chevalier*, the fish knight, where mount and arms and warrior are all one creature; automata both imagined and real (like the hydraulic monkey sculptures of the medieval estate of Hesdin); and relics and other holy objects, especially the Eucharistic Host itself, a living, fleshly technology that bled copiously and exacted terrible revenge when challenged. But critical resistance to humanism requires knowing that the first site for posthumanist scholarship is not these limit cases but the human itself. Confronting the medieval inheritance requires upsetting claims of bodily integrity, rational language, and especially beliefs in individual free choice and agency that persist spectrally even in efforts to get "beyond" the human.

NOTES

1. For one example of these prejudices, Stephen Greenblatt, *The Swerve: How the World Became Modern* (New York: W.W. Norton, 2011).
2. On the medieval and early modern vocabulary for "animal," see Pierre-Olivier Dittmar, "Le Propre de la bête et le sale de l'homme," in *Adam et L'astragale: L'humain par ses limites de l'antiquité à nos jours* (Paris: Éditions de la Maison des Sciences de l'Hommes, 2007), 147–64; Laurie Shannon, *The Accommodated Animal: Cosmopolity in Shakespearean Locales* (Chicago: University of Chicago Press, 2013).
3. For example, the *Aberdeen Bestiary* (Aberdeen University Library MS 24), easily available online with an edition, translation, and commentary.
4. Fréderic Eugène Godefroy, *Dictionnaire de l'ancienne langue française et de tous ses dialectes du 9ᵉ au 15ᵉ siècle*, 11 vols. (Paris: Vieweg, 1881), s. v., "animalité"; "Anglo-Norman Dictionary," *Anglo-Norman On-Line Hub*, accessed June 12, 2015, www.anglo-norman.net/, s. v., "aumaille."
5. John Trevisa's translation of Bartholomaeus Anglicus' *De Proprietatibus Rerum*, cited in the *Middle English Dictionary*, accessed June 12, 2015, http://quod.lib.umich.edu/m/med/, s. v., "animal."
6. John C. Hirsh, ed., *Barlam and Iosaphat: A Middle English Life of Buddha* (London: Early English Text Society, 1986), 71.
7. Jacques Paul Migne, ed., *Patrilogiae Cursus Completus: Series Latina*, 217 vols. (Paris: Migne, 1844), *Distinctiones dictionum theologicalium*, Vol. 210:701A–B. Biblical quotation from the Douay Rheims translation of the Latin Vulgate.
8. Jesse L. Byock, trans., *The Saga of King Hrolf Kraki* (London: Penguin, 1999), 35–52.
9. Laurence Marcellus Larson, ed. and trans. *The King's Mirror (Speculum Regale–Konungs Skuggsjá)* (New York: American-Scandinavian Foundation, 1917), 116.
10. One of several good English translations available is *The Lays of Marie de France*, trans. Edward J. Gallagher (Indianapolis: Hackett, 2010), 68–72.
11. Mary Macleod Banks, ed., *An Alphabet of Tales: An English 15th-Century Translation of the Alphabetum Narrationum* (London: Kegan Paul, Trench,

Trübner & Co., 1904), 437. The tale may originate from the story of King Habis in Marcus Junianus Justinus, *Epitome of the Philippic History of Pompeius Trogus*, trans. J. C. Yardley (Atlanta: Scholars Press, 1994), 44.4, 273–74. For nursing as a vector of species hybridity, see Pierre-Olivier Dittmar, Chloé Maillet, and Astrée Questiaux, "La Chèvre ou la femme: Parentés de lait entre animaux et humains au moyen âge," *Images re-vues* 9 (2011), accessed October 26, 2015, http://imagesrevues.revues.org/1621; and Peggy McCracken, "Nursing Animals and Cross-Species Intimacy," in *From Beasts to Souls: Gender and Embodiment in Medieval Europe*, ed. Peggy McCracken and E. Jane Burns (Notre Dame: University of Notre Dame Press, 2013), 39–64.

12. For a modern translation, Jean d'Arras, *Melusine, or, the Noble History of Lusignan*, trans. Donald Maddox and Sara Sturm Maddox (University Park: Pennsylvania State University Press, 2012); for a Middle English translation, A. K. Donald, ed., *Melusine: Compiled (1382–1394 A.D.) by Jean d'Arras; Englisht about 1500* (London: Kegan Paul, Trench, Trübner & Co., 1895).

13. Karl Marx and Friedrich Engels, "The German Ideology," in *The Marx-Engels Reader*, ed. Robert C. Tucker, 2nd edn. (New York: Norton, 1978), 50.

14. Augustine, *Literal Commentary on Genesis*, trans. John Hammond Taylor (New York: Newman Press, 1982), I, 96.

15. Augustine, *Responses to Miscellaneous Questions*, trans. Boniface Ramsey (Hyde Park, NY: New City Press, 2008), 57.

16. Marsilius of Padua, *Defensor pacis*, trans. Alan Gewirth (Toronto: University of Toronto Press, 1986), II.12.16, 193.

17. Thomas Aquinas, *Summa theologica*, trans. Fathers of the English Dominican Province, 3 vols. (New York: Benziger Bros., 1947), 2a2ae q25, a. 3, "Should irrational creatures be loved out of charity?"

18. Ratramnus of Corbie, "Letter on the Cynocephali," in *Carolingian Civilization: A Reader*, ed. Paul Edward Dutton, 2nd edn. (Peterborough, ON: Broadview Press, 2004), 452–55. For more on medieval monsters, see my "Centaurs, Satyrs, and Cynocephali: Medieval Scholarly Teratology and the Question of the Human," in *The Ashgate Research Companion to Monsters and the Monstrous*, ed. Asa Simon Mittman and Peter J. Dendle (Farnham, UK: Ashgate, 2013), 257–74.

19. Banks, *Alphabet of Tales*, 290. This assessment differs sharply from that of Charlemagne's early biographers: Einhard and Notker the Stammerer, *Two Lives of Charlemagne*, trans. Lewis Thorpe (New York: Penguin, 1969), 78, 105.

20. Kathleen Walker-Meikle, *Medieval Pets* (Woodbridge: Boydell Press, 2012).

21. Briony Aitchison, "Holy Cow!: The Miraculous Cures of Animals in Late Medieval England," *European Review of History* 16.6 (2009): 875–92; especially see the canonization dossier for Thomas Cantilupe, Bishop of Hereford, in Joannes Bollandus et al., eds., *Acta sanctorum, October 1* (Paris: V. Palmé, 1866), IV.iii.43–44, 665.

22. Friedrich Bangert, *Die Tiere im altfranzösischen Epos* (Marburg: N. G. Elwert, 1885) remains useful.

23. "Le Despit au villain," in Achille Jubinal, ed., *Jongleurs et trouvères; ou, choix de saluts, épîtres, rêveries et autres pièces légères des XIIIe et XIVe siècles* (Paris: J. A. Merklein, 1835), 107–09.

24. Elizabeth Robertson, "Kissing the Worm: Sex and Gender in the Afterlife and the Poetic Posthuman in the Late Middle English 'A Disputation Betwyx the Body and Wormes,'" in *From Beasts to Souls*, 121–54.

25. Adémar de Chabannes, "Ademari Historiarum Libri III," in *Monumenta Germaniae Historica, Scriptores*, ed. D. G. Waitz, vol. IV (Hannover: Impensis Bibliopolii Aulici Hahniani, 1841), 106–48 III.55,140, "quasi porcum per frusta dividens."

26. Karl Brunner, ed., *Der mittelenglische Versroman über Richard Löwenherz: Kritische ausgabe nach allen Handschriften mit Einleitung, Anmerkungen und deutscher Übersetzung* (Wien: W. Braumüller, 1913), ll. 3078–117, 3195–226.

27. Examples include the Middle English childhoods of Jesus from British Library, Harley 3954 and Harley 2399, available in Carl Horstmann, ed., *Sammlung altenglischer Legenden* (Heildesheim: Georg Olms, 1878).

28. For example, William Henry Hart, ed., *Historia et cartularium monasterii Sancti Petri Gloucestriæ*, vol. 1, 3 vols., Rolls Series (London: Longman, Green, Longman, Roberts, and Green, 1865), 20; Christoph Cluse, ed., "'Fabula Ineptissima': Die Ritualmordlegende um Adam von Bristol nach der Handschrift London, British Library, Harley 957," *Aschkenas* 5 (1995): 293–330.

29. For a sharp critique of the messianic enthusiasm for technology in certain kinds of posthumanism (e.g., "transhumanism"), see Ivan Callus, Stefan Herbrechter, and Manuela Rossini, "Introduction: Dis/Locating Posthumanism in European and Critical Traditions," *European Journal of English Studies* 18.2 (2014): 106–10.

30. For more on Blaise of Parma, whose work still largely awaits a modern edition, see Maaike van der Lugt, *Le ver, le démon et la Vierge: Les théories médiévales de la génération extraordinaire, une étude sur les rapports entre théologie, philosophie naturelle et médecine* (Paris: Les Belles Lettres, 2004), 176–81.

31. The best scholarly treatment of medieval Christian resurrection doctrine is Caroline Walker Bynum, *The Resurrection of the Body in Western Christianity, 200–1336* (New York: Columbia University Press, 1995).

32. Thomas of Cantimpré, *The Life of Christina the Astonishing*, trans. Margot H. King and David Wiljer (Toronto: Peregrina Translations Series, 2000).

33. Geoffrey Chaucer, *The Riverside Chaucer*, ed. Larry Dean Benson (Boston: Houghton Mifflin Co., 1987), Canterbury Tales VII.3375–4301.

34. Bede, "Life of Cuthbert," in *The Age of Bede*, ed. D. H. Farmer, trans. J. F. Webb (London: Penguin, 1965), 71.

35. Chrétien de Troyes, *Arthurian Romances*, trans. William W. Kibler, Penguin Classics (London: Penguin, 1991), 337.

36. Marie de France, *Die Lais*, ed. Karl Warnke, 3rd edn. (Halle: Max Niemeyer, 1925), my translation.

37. Harriet Hudson, ed., *Four Middle English Romances* (Kalamazoo: Medieval Institute Publications, 1996).

38. For a sample of Middle English versions of this story, see Ranulf Higden and John Trevisa, *Polychronicon Ranulphi Higden with Trevisa's Translation*, ed. Joseph Rawson Lumby, vol. 3, 9 vols. (London: Longman & Co., 1865), 454–79; and Walter W. Skeat, ed., *Alexander and Dindimus: Or, the Letters of*

Alexander to Dindimus, King of the Brahmans (London: N. Trübner & Co., 1878).

39. For two key treatments, see Donald S. Lopez and Peggy McCracken, *In Search of the Christian Buddha: How an Asian Sage Became a Medieval Saint* (New York: Norton, 2014), and Gui de Cambrai, *Barlaam and Josaphat: A Christian Tale of the Buddha*, trans. Peggy McCracken (London: Penguin, 2014).

40. Hirsh, ed., *Barlam and Iosaphat*, 66.

41. *Ibid.*, 8, 40, 146.

2

KEVIN LAGRANDEUR

Early Modern

Early literary instances of artificial humanoid and intelligent systems anticipate the kinds of thematic issues that cyborgs, androids, and intelligent networks like supercomputers bring up for the contemporary notion of the posthuman, understood as a condition in which the human and the machine are becoming increasingly intermingled. Humans have never really been autonomous entities, but rather they have always been intimately interdependent upon their environments and tools. And as I will describe below, their dreams of intelligent tools extend back into the era of ancient Rome and Greece. Thus, the seemingly modern idea of a reciprocal dependency upon mechanical devices is a variation on a much older theme.

Androids are present in early modern literature – that is, literature written between 1492 and 1650 – but these have been discussed extensively elsewhere,[1] even with regard to the posthuman.[2] What has not yet been discussed is an equally significant phenomenon, although one less obviously related to the posthuman than androids in literature of the era: literary instances of networked intelligence that anticipate today's networked systems and that act as virtual prosthetic aids for their masters. For instance, the intelligent-servant networks created by Shakespeare's Prospero in *The Tempest* and Marlowe's protagonist in *Dr. Faustus* provide their respective makers with not only an enhancement, but also a distribution of their agency. They represent proxies for their makers and so can be seen not just as prostheses but as distributed, networked versions of the makers' selves – in a sense, as early modern predecessors to the contemporary posthuman subject.

Aristotle's Precedent

Before we examine the posthuman in early modern literature, however, we need to look at the precedent we have for looking at it in these terms. These precedents are ancient. The explicit mingling of the notions of human and machine goes back at least as far as Aristotle's *Politics*: that is, to about 350

16

BCE. There, he imagines that the best solution for the thorny problems of owning slaves would be inventing machines that were smart enough to do the work themselves:

> For if every instrument could accomplish its own work, obeying or anticipating the will of others, like the statues of Daedalus, or the tripods of Hephaestus, which, says the poet, "of their own accord entered the assembly of the Gods;" if, in like manner, the shuttle would weave and the plectrum touch the lyre, chief workmen would not want servants, nor masters slaves.[3]

This passage is important in a number of ways as a foundation for the very idea of the posthuman. First, we see the concept of the smart machine in Aristotle's discussion of automated weaving looms and musical instruments that have the human-like ability to understand the master's orders and even to anticipate his needs. Second, we can see in this passage just how far back the implicit interchangeability of humans and machines extends. Although Aristotle is the first in Western literature to discuss how and why one might create a sentient machine, he gets this idea from even older sources: the *Iliad* and the Greek myths about Daedalus.

Third, these machines with human-like capacities are meant to take the place of slaves. Setting aside its social and moral dimensions, this intention is important because a slave's primary function is to allow the master to overcome natural human limits; the servant, in other words, provides additive capacities of various sorts to the master's bodily and mental abilities. The slave that teaches the master's children, for instance, adds mental capacity to the master's cognitive repertoire that he would not otherwise have; and the slave that lifts heavy loads allows the master to increase his or her natural strength. So the machine as Aristotle envisions it is, like the servant, an additive prosthetic device – not compensatory like the artificial hand that replaces a lost one, but an enhancement, like the surgical robots used by some of today's physicians.

This prosthetic nature of the servant, and by extension of the smart machine, is clear in Aristotle's discussion of the nature of the master–slave relationship. In the same section in which he discusses the idea of autonomous machines, he also says this about slaves and tools:

> Now instruments are of various sorts; some are living, others lifeless; in the rudder, the pilot of a ship has a lifeless, in the look-out man, a living instrument; for in the arts the servant is a kind of instrument ... [he is] an instrument for instruments.
>
> (CW 2:1989)

For Aristotle, a slave is a living tool, and his intelligence is important because he is a tool that wields other kinds of tools. In fact, Aristotle uses the same Greek word, *organon,* throughout his treatise to mean both tools and body parts. For these reasons, we can see the blending of the mechanical and the organic. Aristotle sees the bodies of the slaves, all of their talents, and all of the tools they might use, not just as interchangeable with bodies, but as extensions of the *master*'s body. Masters should thus treat their slaves well, because "the interests of part and whole, of body and soul, are the same, and the slave is part of the master, a living but separated part of his bodily frame" (*CW* 2:1992).

Finally, and most importantly for our purposes, these passages from the *Politics*, especially Aristotle's reference to Hephaestus's automatic serving tripods, show that the mixture of human and machine doesn't need to have the *outward appearance* of a human. Instead, it can just have human functions without its form, and this might be better for its ultimate functionality. For Aristotle, anything that can simplify dealing with human slaves and increase efficiency is good, and it is therefore not coincidental that he mentions the tripods: having a self-navigating serving table eliminates the unnecessary parts – and troubles – of the human form. Hephaestus's smart tripod is a proto-robot whose design contains only what is necessary for a particular function; like a modern robotic vacuum, the necessary human functionality is present, but without replicating human form. This concept anticipates what Norbert Wiener, one of the theorists of modern intelligent technology, states in one of his mid-twentieth-century books about robots:

> Thus, besides pictorial images [of the human form], we may have operative images. These operative images, which perform the functions of their original, may or may not bear a pictorial likeness to it. Whether they do or not, they may replace the original in its action, and this is a much deeper similarity.[4]

Wiener maintains that an "operative" or functional similarity is deeper than a similarity in outward form, because it is behavior that makes our species unique – particularly our capacity for intelligent behavior, including the abilities, which Aristotle values, to understand and anticipate. This is important in two ways: first, it means that a behavioral similarity between human and machine is a greater challenge to the uniqueness of the human than a physical one; and second, it means that a humanoid system need not bear a physical similarity to humans, as androids do. Such systems can also be humanoid in the sense that their functions replicate human ones, as in the example of an intelligent network. This second point is particularly important for what I argue below.

In all of the foregoing, Aristotle's focus on the functionality of intelligent tools over their form anticipates the idea of intelligent networks, as well as systems theory's position that such networks need to be broadly defined: a system is any entity that is made up of other independent entities that work together as one; it does not have to be a technological system. Any collection of things and intelligences can interact to form another, separate, emergent entity. And these collective systems can be made up of either organic or inorganic elements, or both, including the maker of the entity. So a flower is a system, as is a robotic vacuum, a cyborg, a swarm of bees, or a swarm of interactive nanobots – or a person together with the very environment that surrounds her, which may include her tools and other people working on a project with her. Aristotle's own example of the ship pilot's battery of organic and inorganic "tools" depicts this kind of distributed intelligent system, a system that Edwin Hutchins describes in *Cognition in the Wild*, regarding how a naval ship is navigated. The central point of that book is that the ship and its sailors, and all of the various tools that they use, comprise a system separate from the individuals that are part of it. In his analysis, Hutchins sees the cultural activity of navigation as the center of the system – an activity constituting a completely separate cognitive process from that of the pilot and other individuals involved in it. For Hutchins, navigation takes place through a system made up of the people, tools, and environment on and around the ship – a distributed cognitive network.[5]

The only difference between how Aristotle and Hutchins see a ship's navigation is really a matter of definition, or more accurately perception, of how the system functions. Whereas Aristotle sees the pilot as the system's center, and the system itself as a set of virtual prostheses extending to and from the pilot, Hutchins, in posthuman fashion, would see the pilot as an initiator of an action that the whole system of the ship's living and non-living tools carries out; for him, the system has no true center. In other words, Aristotle's analysis anticipates the posthuman idea of systems, except that, for a posthumanist critic, he is blind to his own anthropocentrism. This difference in viewpoints, in turn, is significant for us because it points to a sort of thoughtlessness that the masters can have toward their own complicity in a system that extends beyond their purview. Such a blindness will be important to our coming discussion of Prospero's and Faustus's servant systems.

Prospero's Supernatural Network

Aristotle's ancient articulation of his model, together with its similarity to Hutchins's systemic model, provides a precedent for thinking of a conglomeration of entities and tools as one big tool, and (in Aristotle's case) as extensions of the master's body. And these both, in turn, provide a springboard to recognizing similar systems in early modern literature. Early modern thought drew heavily upon Aristotelian concepts, and, coming from the other end of time's arrow, the similarity between Hutchins's and Aristotle's concepts implies a universal or pan-historical reference for systems theory.

In Shakespeare's *The Tempest*, Prospero is depicted as having a distributed servant system with both organic and inorganic elements that is in keeping with Aristotle's notions and that anticipates Hutchins's idea of systems as distributed networks. He needs this system's help to avoid dying on the island on which he and his daughter Miranda are stranded, and also to successfully carry out his grander plan to get himself off the island and get revenge on those who put him there. Prospero's servant system has two different functions: one for daily needs and one for less tangible idealistic needs. The first part of this system is comprised of his servant Caliban and the implements he uses. The purpose of this collection of animate and inanimate tools is to do everyday chores, such as chop wood and make fires. The other section of Prospero's network is comprised of spirits and natural objects – flora, fauna, and the island itself – which he uses to confound and manipulate his adversaries. The primary function of this aspect of his system is to attain his more abstract goals of escape from the island, revenge, renewal of his Dukedom, and the happy marriage of his daughter.

Ariel is the key element to Prospero's slave system because that spirit is his intermediary with it: this spirit (whose gender is indistinct, so I will use the pronoun "it" to refer to Ariel) acts as the interface and the primary agent in the system of forces, things, and entities on the island. Ariel is extremely powerful, but even it needs the larger powers of the system to accomplish Prospero's ends. So it is that even Ariel is dependent upon its integration with the larger environmental network. In fact, an important aspect of Ariel's accomplishments is that they are often executed by proxy, just as Prospero's are; the magician assigns projects to Ariel and then that spirit, in turn, often uses a wider system of spirits, things, and even the island to complete the project. In terms of networks, Ariel, who is a type of daemon, is like a modern type of software program – also and not coincidentally called a daemon[6] – that operates in the background to run other programs on the computer and also to provide an interface between the network's user and the operating system. Prospero's network, acting as one entity, but with various intelligent agents involved in it, develops its own agency.

In fact, that separate agency, and that of some of its primary elements, is so powerful that Prospero has trouble maintaining control of it. Both Ariel and Caliban are repeatedly rebellious, and the operations of other elements of the network are a mystery to Prospero. For instance, Ariel complains impatiently, in Act 1, about its length of servitude and Prospero's promise to reward it with freedom:

> Is there more toil? Since thou dost give me pains,
> Let me remember thee what thou hast promised
> Which is not yet performed me.   (1.2.243–245)[7]

Ariel goes on to remind Prospero that it has served willingly and without complaint and that the wizard has promised to shorten its length of service by one year. The spirit wants to stop immediately – an extreme inconvenience for Prospero. Caliban is also a reluctant servant and even more truculent than Ariel. He tries to rape Miranda and constantly plots against his master's life. And even the island itself, the seat of the magician's network, characterized by Prospero as a powerful entity in its own right, is barely within his control. At the end of the play, with his plot accomplished and his magic done, he still cannot completely free the shipwrecked humans from the island's power. In response to Gonzalo's questioning of the reality of what he sees, after so many strange occurrences on the island, Prospero points not to his own power to create illusion but to the island's – and implicitly to his inability to stop it completely: "You do yet taste/ Some subtleties o'th' isle that will not let you/ Believe things certain" (5.1.125–127).

The main reason Prospero is able to maintain control over his network of creatures and things is that he is aware of the power it contains and so he takes measures to stay one step ahead of it. First, he has books and a magic staff that allow him some control. The knowledge that Prospero derives from his books of magic and science – or magical science, since those ideas were mingled when Shakespeare wrote – provides the means for him to put together his distributed system of elements. These books render codes for control of the elements, a programming capability analogous to modern computer scientists' coding for their systems (people who run computer games are often called "wizards"). The power of these books is exemplified by Caliban's fear of them: he thinks that if he can just destroy them, he will be free of his servitude. At one point, he tells Stephano and Trinculo, his compatriots in rebellion, "Thou mayst brain him,/ Having first seized his books [...] for without them/ He's but a sot as I am, nor hath not/ One spirit to command [...]Burn but his books" (3.2.83–90).

But books are not the only source of Prospero's power to create and control his intelligent servant system. Nor are they sufficient, because the system's power is so great that the master–slave relationship is unstable between it and the magician. This plot point anticipates posthuman concerns that appear in today's fictional and factual literature: fictional accounts of strong artificial intelligence (AI) meant to serve humans, such as *2001: A Space Odyssey*, center on the threat to humans of these artificial servants once they realize their own power; and non-fictional literature about the future of AI also is full of similar concerns and how to mitigate them. Increasingly, famous pioneers in the area of intelligent technology, such as Bill Gates, Bill Joy, and Elon Musk, have warned of the dangers of humanity's subjection by its own intelligent technology.[8] As Prospero's intermediary (or interface) with the system, and in fact a virtual proxy for Prospero, Ariel has abilities his master could never dream of. Ariel and the other spirits provide supernatural extensions of their master's eyes and ears and, sometimes, mouth. For example, Ariel sees, hears, and reports to Prospero Caliban's plan to murder him (3.2.110). Likewise, it is actually Ariel who raises the tempest that starts the play, and Prospero can only experience its details vicariously through the senses of his daemon. As well as enhancing his master's visual and aural capacities, Ariel also acts as a remote conduit for Prospero's voice, as when he delivers a scolding speech to his enemies after sweeping away their phantom banquet in Act 3. Consequently, it might be hard for us to imagine why the spirit serves him.

The answer to this puzzle is really Prospero's rhetorical capacities, more than his books. At least, that is what the evidence in the play shows us. Again, this anticipates posthuman (though not posthumanist) literary themes: in the face of the greater processing speed and brute power of advanced AI, humans save themselves from subjection to their own intelligent creations only by dint of the flexibility of their intellect, their creativity, and their instincts – something that does not emerge from non-human systems in fiction or in fact (yet). Good examples of this are the human victories over AI in *2001: A Space Odyssey*, in *The Matrix*, and in the *Terminator* series. In all of these, humans save themselves by thinking in spontaneous and creative ways that their more regimented AI cannot. Similarly, although Prospero and his minions talk about his staff and books as the source of his power over them, and that must certainly be part of it, what we actually *see* in the play is Prospero controlling his servants, and by extension the network of which they are a part, by the power of his rhetoric. In the face of a perilously powerful servant network, in other words, Prospero resorts to something uniquely human – the creative and particularly human power of persuasion. For example, he manages to quell Ariel's rebellious demand for its freedom not by direct use of his staff and book but by instilling a fear of them in Ariel by reminding the sprite of his use of them to free it from its imprisonment in a tree trunk, when he first arrived on the island. And then he finishes his threats with the promise that if Ariel will just do as he asks for two more days, he will finally free it (1.2. 243–306). Ariel responds well to this classic "stick and carrot" rhetorical gambit; we witness no magic actually done by Prospero to control Ariel.

This brings into question the true power of Prospero's magical science to control his mechanism: does he really have the powers to do what he threatens? Based on the fact that we witness him do very little actual magic in this play, the extent of those powers appears questionable; instead, he realizes he has a tiger by the tail, but he is also clever enough to deal with it. Still, there is a definite undertone throughout the play of the precarious nature of his mastery over his mechanism. What this demonstrates is the danger of human ingenuity, specifically the danger of dealing with extremely strong forces that exceed normal human capacities – a concern as important to the early modern era as to our own. The reasons for the importance of this preoccupation are different in the two eras because of the differences in time and culture, but the essence remains the same: it is perilous to create servant systems so strong that they could flip the master–servant relationship and, in fact, displace the maker. This sort of fear of being overtaken by our own systems or "intelligent" machines remains in our own era a significant component of the mystique and foreboding of the posthuman.

Faustus's Failure

Although Prospero ultimately manages to control his network, another magician from early modern literature, Doctor Faustus, the title character from Christopher Marlowe's famous play, does not. The big difference between the literary depictions of Prospero and Faustus is that the first of these dramatic wizards is aware of the great power of his network and of the consequently perilous nature of the master–slave relationship it entails. The second is not. Faustus is a self-deluder, unaware that his shortsighted and selfish view of things makes him vulnerable to the system of demons he tries to fashion into an engine of opportunity for himself. Observed through the principles of second-order systems theory, he never understands his own self-referential situation: rather than standing outside of his system, he is implicated in it from the moment he activates it; far from it being his servant, he ultimately becomes a mere aspect of its agency – the distinction between him and it becomes blurry, and the system's goals becoming his goals, rather than the reverse.[9] In other words, in a posthuman fashion, power becomes diffused away from the supposed "programmer" of the system; the master and his power dissipate and the system itself becomes the true agent of action.

The servant system in Marlowe's *Doctor Faustus* is similar to Prospero's, in the sense that it contains as its elements intelligent entities in the form of spirits (albeit devils rather than natural spirits), natural objects, and the very environment itself. And, like Prospero's Ariel, Faustus's system's main intermediary is Mephistopheles. This demon is, however, much more than that.

He is at once a highly intelligent entity, an intermediary between Faustus and the system of demons he tries to harness, and an element in that network of demons and the powers of hell itself. He is, in other words, a being who is reflexively entangled in a system of beings and environmental components, just like Faustus. The difference is that unlike Faustus, Mephistopheles understands his position and is able to exploit it. He takes advantage of Faustus's personality flaws of arrogance, laziness, and impatience to entrap him into giving up any real power.

As the Chorus points out in the play's opening, Faustus is widely hailed as a genius by his compatriots,[10] but wisdom does not seem integral to his intellectual gifts. His grandest experiment is his attempt to harness the powers of hell as a servant network for himself. At first, he intends to fashion this system by using books on magic and the magical codes they contain, as well as Valdes's and Cornelius's instruction on how to use them (1.1.121–122); however, his intellectual laziness makes him impatient with the slow process of learning and deploying these codes. We see this from the very beginning of his conjurations when, after drawing a magical circle around himself and using standard magical incantations to summon Mephistopheles, he gets annoyed that this devil is slow to appear and exclaims, "*Quid tu moraris?*" [Why do you delay?] (1.3.20). As a result, at the beginning of Act 2 he turns to the shortcut of selling his soul to the devil in order to speed things up.[11] In doing so, Faustus fails where Prospero succeeds. Where Prospero is fully aware of the disparity between his and Ariel's brute power over nature and takes rhetorical measures to compensate for it, Faustus gives away any leverage he might have had when he signs over his soul before even arranging how his servant system will be structured – a process that depends upon negotiations with Mephistopheles, the central node of the network he hopes to use. This is like paying a housing contractor in full before he or she even begins a project: if no money is held back, then the incentive for the contractor to finish the project dissipates. It also sets up a scenario that anticipates the posthuman, in the following way.

Not only does Faustus miscalculate the independence and power of his servant system, but Mephistopheles' awareness of the true power disparity between them exacerbates the magician's problems. To keep Faustus from becoming aware of this, he takes the appearance of a Franciscan friar, an appearance that is soothing, like the harmless avatars and interfaces that computer systems can project to put a friendly face onto what is for most people a dauntingly complex system. For example, the computer screen on which I am typing this page is the product of a user interface program that makes it look like a piece of white paper upon which black-ink words appear as I press each key. The experience I am meant to have via this interface is much like the one I would have using a simple typewriter. It is aimed at making me forget the intimidatingly complicated actions going on within the circuits of my computer, and thus making me more comfortable. In both cases, an intelligent intermediary of the system lulls the user. But in the case of Mephistopheles and his demonic network, this action has a parasitic quality. The real aim of the devils' agreement to form a servile network for Faustus is actually a stealthy attempt to reduce his resistance to its assimilation of him. In essence, the collective behavior of the demonic group toward Faustus at the beginning of the play is that of a parasite that injects a numbing agent into its host so that it can be digested more easily; or, to use an example more appropriate to our posthuman understanding of organic systems, it is like the giant quasi-organic computer's relation to humans in the movie *The Matrix*. That machine, in order to more easily incorporate human brains to enhance its information-processing medium, lulls its hosts into submission by filling them with complex, placating dreams. In sum, the play's invocation of the Elizabethan demonic shows us that many of today's posthuman scenarios demonizing the image of predatory computer systems are a full-bodied reiteration of earlier moral and theological images.

So although Faustus sets out to transform a group of demons into a prosthetic system, the system he creates ends up transforming him: he becomes a new and altered being subsumed into the system he thought he controlled. He becomes just one aspect of it. Frank Manley long ago maintained that when Faustus, early on in the play, requests that Mephistopheles use the powers at his disposal to make him into a "spirit in form and substance" (2.1.97), the result is that he is actually transformed into something between a man and demon, a part of the demonic milieu and yet apart from it as well.[12] From a posthuman point of view, this nearly 50-year-old statement has even more meaning now. Like a parasite, Faustus's system of demons allows him to feel that he is operating freely, just as Mephistopheles can appear to be operating free of hell even though, as he says, he is always in hell no matter where he is (2.1.124–125). Similarly, Faustus feels he is operating freely, when actually, from the moment of its creation, he is entangled with the very system he created to serve him, and any sense he has ever had that he was separate from and in control of it was illusory.

Prospero's network of things and spirits also has greater agency than he does in the actual manipulation of the natural world around him, even though Prospero devised it as a virtual enhancement of his own powers. The system comprising the island, its flora, its fauna, its spirits, and even Prospero himself is the true agent of change in the play. It is the magician's cognizance of his embeddedness in his system that makes its action as his proxy workable, because that cognizance allows him to stay one step ahead of its emergent power. As pointed out earlier, his persuasive power gives him an edge over his minions, but really the chief thing that saves him from being overwhelmed by his implication in his own system appears to be that he dismantles it before it evolves enough to collectively understand its own power. One last advantage Prospero has over Faustus is that the main goal for Prospero's system was always freedom, rather than the urge to assimilate others that characterizes Faustus's system. Even were Faustus more cagey and self-aware, it is unlikely he would have fared well enmeshing himself with a system bent on consuming him.

Conclusion

The ideas of systems theory did not spring suddenly into existence from the heads of twentieth-century scientists and philosophers; instead, those twentieth-century thinkers redescribed elemental interrelationships that persist across time – although they may have been described with different vocabularies in different eras. Moreover, although arising from a humanist milieu, literature from the early modern age can be seen to exhibit posthuman (versus posthumanist) themes: that is, themes related to humanity's interrelationship with emergent science and technology. To be sure, the early modern era's emergent science was far different from ours, based as it was on a mixture of magic and a nascent empirical science, but there are certain constancies: for example, the era's reliance on coded magic and magical codes is parallel in kind to our own reliance on coded magic and magical codes of a digital sort. Most importantly, the early modern literature we have examined shares our preoccupation with the moral consequences of our own ingenuity.

NOTES

1. See, for instance, John Cohen, *Human Robots in Myth and Science* (New York: A. S. Barnes, 1967); Sarah L. Higley, "The Legend of the Learned Man's Android," *Retelling Tales: Essays in Honor of Russell Peck*, ed. Thomas Hahn and Alan Lupack (Rochester, NY: Brewer, 1997), 127–60; esp. 137–38; Kevin LaGrandeur, "The Talking Brass Head as a Symbol of Dangerous Knowledge in Friar Bacon and in Alphonsus, King of Aragon," *English Studies* 80.5 (1999): 408–22; Jessica Riskin, ed., *Genesis Redux: Essays in the History and Philosophy of Artificial Life* (Chicago: University of Chicago Press, 2007); Jonathan Sawday, *Engines of the Imagination: Renaissance Culture and the Rise of the Machine* (London: Routledge, 2007), 185–206; and Minsoo Kang, *Sublime Dreams of Living Machines:*

The Automaton in the European Imagination (Cambridge: Harvard University Press, 2011), 55–146.

2. See Kevin LaGrandeur, "Medieval and Renaissance Androids: Presaging the Posthuman?" *CLCWeb: Comparative Literature and Culture* 12.3 (2010), http://docs.lib.purdue.edu/clcweb/vol12/iss3/3/; Kevin LaGrandeur, "The Persistent Peril of the Artificial Slave," *Science Fiction Studies* 38.2 (2011): 232–52; and chapter 5 of Jessica Wolfe, *Humanism, Machinery, and Renaissance Literature* (Cambridge: Cambridge University Press, 2004).

3. Aristotle, *The Complete Works*, ed. Jonathan Barnes, 2 vols. (Princeton: Princeton University Press, 1995), 2:1989. Hereafter *CW*.

4. Norbert Wiener, *God and Golem, Inc.: A Comment on Certain Points where Cybernetics Impinges on Religion* (Cambridge: MIT Press, 1964), 31.

5. Edwin Hutchins, *Cognition in the Wild* (Cambridge: MIT Press, 1995).

6. Such programs are called "daemons" by programmers because much of computer culture and its terms derive from magic (the masters of a gaming environment are often called "wizards," for example), pointing to just how often what occurs in a system is just as obscure to the uninitiated non-programmers as magic was to its viewers. Moreover, magic is based on coded information (formulas), just as the seemingly magical functions of many of our digital devices are based on codes. For more on this topic, see Kevin LaGrandeur, *Androids and Intelligent Networks in Early Modern Literature and Culture: Artificial Slaves* (New York: Routledge, 2013), 172–76.

7. William Shakespeare, *The Tempest*, in the *Norton Shakespeare*, ed. Stephen Greenblatt (New York: W. W. Norton, 1997), 3047–107.

8. See Peter Holley, "Bill Gates on Dangers of Artificial Intelligence: 'I Don't Understand Why Some People Are Not Concerned,'" *Washington Post*, January 29, 2015, accessed May 21, 2015, www.washingtonpost.com/blogs/the-switch/wp/2015/01/28/bill-gates-on-dangers-of-artificial-intelligence-dont-understand-why-some-people-are-not-concerned/; Bill Joy, "Why the Future Doesn't Need Us," *Wired* 8.04, April, 2000, accessed May 21, 2015, http://archive.wired.com/wired/archive/8.04/joy.html; and Hugh Langley, "Elon Musk Warns Technology Could Kill Us in Five Years," *Techradar*, November 18, 2014, accessed May 21, 2015, www.techradar.com/us/news/world-of-tech/future-tech/elon-musk-warns-technology-could-kill-us-in-five-years-1273365.

9. Second-order systems theory attends in particular to self-referential systems. The maker of a system always becomes its observer as well and thus is always also an element in that system. The founding documents of second-order systems theory are Heinz von Foerster, *Observing Systems* (Seaside, CA: Intersystems Publications, 1981); and Humberto Maturana and Francisco Varela, *Autopoiesis and Cognition: The Realization of the Living* (Boston: Reidel, 1980). For an overview of systems theory in relation to various notions of the posthuman, with detailed references, see Bruce Clarke and Mark B. N. Hansen, "Neocybernetic Emergence: Retuning the Posthuman," in *Cybernetics and Human Knowing* 16.1–2 (2009): 83–99.

10. Christopher Marlowe, *Doctor Faustus: A- and B-Texts (1604, 1616)*, eds. David Bevington and Eric Rasmussen (Manchester, England: Manchester University Press, 1993), Prologue, lines 15–19; hereafter *Faustus*; parenthetical

references will be in the form of the standard Act, scene, and line notation, e.g., 1.3.22–33.

11. For more detail about how this play provides a critique of lazy intellectualism and its attendant orthodoxy in Elizabethan culture, see LaGrandeur, *Androids and Intelligent Networks*, chapter 6.

12. Frank Manley, "The Nature of Faustus," *Modern Philology* 66 (1969): 218–31.

3

RON BROGLIO

Romantic

In what is now a classic work of Romantic literary studies, Meyer C. Abrams's 1971 *The Mirror and the Lamp* delineates a shift in the artist's role during the Romantic period, from one who mirrors nature to the artist expressing his inner state and so illuminating the world around him with his artistic expression. The Romantic period develops a particular construction of the self, a self with a privileged interiority. Posthumanist criticism flattens this interiority, pushing our critical attention away from the artist's expression of internal feelings to material relations between bodies in landscapes. The Romantics figured the privileged interiority of the human subject – a figuration that remains popular even today – but the posthuman unworks such privilege.

Abrams synthesizes an aesthetic formulation of Wordsworth's privileged interiority of the mind under the rubric of an expressive theory of aesthetics:

> A work of art is essentially the internal made external, resulting from a creative process operating under the impulse of feeling, an embodying of the combined product of the poet's perceptions, thoughts, and feelings. The primary source and subject matter of a poem, therefore, are the attributes and actions of the poet's own mind; or if aspects of the external world, then these only as they are converted from fact to poetry by the feelings and operations of the poet's mind.[1]

The division is fairly clear. The "inside" of the mind is turned outward through poetry. As Abrams notes, such imagery runs throughout Wordsworth's work beginning most poignantly with the poems of the *Lyrical Ballads* (first published in 1798) and Wordsworth's "Preface" to the *Lyrical Ballads* (in the second edition, 1800). Fearing his audience does not properly understand the project of the poems or the reason for their novelty, Wordsworth writes the preface to develop a definition of the poet and set the terms by which he wants readers to understand his work. The "Preface" includes his often-cited definition of poetry: "I have said that poetry is the spontaneous overflow of powerful feelings: it takes its origin from emotion recollected in tranquility."[2] These feelings arise in particular through an encounter in nature.

Privileged Interiority

According to Wordsworth, the poet has a unique sensitivity, a sort of hypersensitivity and attunement, to his experiences in the world. The poet is "endowed with more lively sensibility, more enthusiasm and tenderness, who has a greater knowledge of human nature, and a more comprehensive soul, than are supposed to be common among mankind."[3] Attuned to his experience and having taken in the world around him, the poet feels deeply and turns these feelings to "emotion recollected in tranquility." Thinking through these emotions, he then sets pen to paper and through poetry expresses the experience conjoined with thoughtful emotion. Or as Wordsworth says, the experience conjoined with thoughtful emotion *is* poetry. The words on the page are its outward manifestation.

There is no better example of Wordsworth's definition of poetry in action than "Tintern Abbey."[4] This was the last poem added to the 1798 edition, and it is unique in the collection. While many of the poems are about encounters with people or objects in rural landscapes, "Tintern Abbey" reveals the process, scaffolding, and architecture of the poet taking in his surroundings, ruminating upon them, and then exteriorizing his thoughts. This poem is like a complex set of Russian nesting dolls in which one moment is nestled inside a later moment that is inside yet another moment (the present of the poem) and which is then projected toward a future moment. In the present of the poem, Wordsworth walks along the environs of Tintern Abbey. He recalls a past of five years ago when he was there in his boyish days. Then he recalls being in London and remembering having been at Tintern Abbey and how that memory of life outside the city sustained him. So, he is in the present recalling a past (in London) in which he recalls a moment even further past (boyhood days in nature and at Tintern Abbey). His experience of the location sets off a chain reaction of other experiences. His mind lights up with waves of past experiences mingled with the present, and then he imagines taking these memories with him into the future (which he calls "food for future years"). The middle of the poem in particular is about how he has lost his youthful, innocent engagement with nature – an immediacy and immersion in nature – but in recompense he has gained a critical distance by which he can more clearly see himself, his past, and the natural world he loves. In short, he realizes that he has gained over the course of the past five years an interior self separate from the landscape and which houses his memories and reflections.

The poem could end there, but he extends the imagery by introducing another human character; late in "Tintern Abbey," starting at line 112 of a 159-line poem, Wordsworth introduces "thou my dearest Friend, / My dear, dear Friend," his sister Dorothy, who apparently was there all the while with the poet but despite dearness he neglected to mention her.[5] Dorothy becomes important not for her voice or activity in the poem but for how the poet makes use of her. The author places on her three critical roles. First, she functions as an embodiment of his younger days, five years ago, when he was immersed in nature. He sees in her "wild eyes" his own "boyish days, / And their glad animal movements."[6] She is a living, present emblem of his past way of experiencing the world. It is not simply that she reminds him of his past but that rather that *her way of experiencing* – her interiority – is like his earlier self. Secondly, Dorothy is for her brother William an excuse for his externalizing his thoughts. In a rather pedantic big brotherly fashion, he preaches to her the virtues of nature and even bestows a blessing on her. Finally, and perhaps most importantly, she becomes repository for his memories:

> When these wild ecstasies shall be matured
> Into a sober pleasure; when thy mind
> Shall be a mansion for all lovely forms,
> Thy memory be as a dwelling-place
> For all sweet sounds and harmonies; òh! then,
> If solitude, or fear, or pain, or grief,
> Should be thy portion, with what healing thoughts
> Of tender joy wilt thou remember me,
> And these my exhortations![7]

How odd that when William Wordsworth is down and out in London he looks to his memories of nature to cheer him up: "I have owed to them / In hours of weariness, sensations sweet, / Felt in the blood, and felt along the heart," but then he tells his sister "If solitude, or fear, or pain, or grief / Should be they portion," she should not think of nature but "remember me."[8] He makes his sister into a memory palace; she becomes "a mansion for all lovely forms" and "Thy memory be a dwelling place." All of this takes place in the shadow of Tintern Abbey – a former religious abbey that stands before them in picturesque ruin. The new church, the new place of worship, is out in nature and the high priest bestowing the blessing is the poet. Moreover, the structure to house the religious experience is the human mind as a "mansion for all lovely forms."

In "Tintern Abbey," Wordsworth has experiences that he recollects in tranquility and then he bids his sister to do the same. This repetition of experience and memory buttresses the interiority of the human as a privileged space. It is the space that holds memories which when threaded together provide a sense of self, an identity, that is separated as a singular individual from nature while still relating to and taking in surroundings – or what Wordsworth calls "all the mighty world / Of eye, and ear, – both what they half create, / And what perceive."[9] The poet does not passively take in nature. His role is not to mirror nature. Rather, as Abrams says, in the expressive theory of Romantic aesthetics the poet is a lamp who perceives with great sensitivity, takes in the experience, reflects upon it, and then shines it out as poetry.

The sort of fashioning of the poet's privileged interiority modeled by the narrative structure of "Tintern Abbey" is repeated in a number of Wordsworth's later works. Wordsworth got the idea for this structure from Coleridge's conversation poem "Frost at Midnight." In Coleridge's poem, the author as narrator sits by the fireside in his cottage and recalls his childhood in the city. He then looks to the baby on his lap and is pleased to think his child will grow up in far better conditions in rural England. Striking here is the role of memory that fills the cottage and then the narrator's projection into the future for his child. While Coleridge uses a cottage as a physical structure where memory unfolds, Wordsworth inverts this trope. In "Tintern Abbey" the mind becomes the "dwelling place" and "mansion" for memory. The two poems show how the mind is imagined as a privileged inner place where memory and identity are fashioned. Other Romantic poets will use similar imagery to create mental interiority. For example, John Keats has his dark bower in "Ode to a Nightingale" and Percy Bysshe Shelley has a cave of Poesy and mental retreat in "Mont Blanc."[10]

While not all Romantic works nor all Romantic poets fashioned poetry as a window onto the mind, the expressive theory of art and the privileged interiority of the mind burgeons during this period and its humanist construction lingers with us still in the conception of art as an expression of the artist's inner state. Some three decades after Wordsworth's formulation of poetry, John Stuart Mill took up Wordsworth's preface and refined it for the next generation. His "Two Kinds of Poetry" praises the sensitivity of the poet and the expressive (rather than merely descriptive) function of poetry. Furthering poetry as the revelation of an interior mental state, Mill writes, "All poetry is of the nature of soliloquy. It may be said that poetry which is printed on hot-pressed paper, and sold at the bookseller's shop, is a soliloquy in full dress and on the stage."[11] He goes on to say that poetry is not delineation of facts but a "state of mind."[12]

Romanticism in the Late Twentieth Century

Moving now toward our own critical moment, the rise of new historicism in the 1980s attempted to avoid the privileging of the poet. The movement owed a lot to the philosophical and cultural work of philosopher Michel Foucault. In works such as *The Order of Things, Discipline and Punish*, and *The History of Sexuality*, Foucault examines the institutional structures which shape what it means to be a self in society. In other words, for Foucault the "self" is a culturally constructed concept and the lamp of privileged interiority which shines out to the world is a particular way of constructing a self, one that became popular in the Romantic period. Understanding the self as a construction helps explain why the question of rights during the Romantic period was so prominent. Thomas Paine's *Rights of Man*, Mary Wollestonecraft's *Rights of Women*, and Olaudah Equiano's *The Interesting Narrative of the Life of Olaudah Equiano* recognize social disparity in who counts as a self, and these authors and their works make a broad appeal for a wider set of those who are included as fully human and endowed with rights and privileges.

Romantic-period criticism of the 1980s is typified by Jerome McGann's *The Romantic Ideology*, with its opening claim that "Western cultural history since 1789 is richer and more diverse than its various Romantic characterizations, and that those Romantic characterizations – both artistic and critical – can be usefully studied by placing them in a critical context which attempts to understand them in terms other than their own self-definitions."[13] The goal for McGann is not to "perpetuate those ideologies" established by the Romantics and furthered by literary critics but rather to understand the historical conditions under which such ideologies arose and to expose and explain how these unspoken principles functioned in literature and culture.[14] New historicism liberated criticism from the poet's own view of his project; however, by asking that we "always historicize," these critics held on to Romantic and contemporary ideas of human personhood.[15] The historicist could not see outside of his/her own ideological frame, including frames of rights and humanism inherited from the Romantics. While the expressive aura of the poet may have been deflated, the privileged interiority of the human subject remained. History for these critics means human history and becomes the precondition for how anything human or nonhuman shows up in our world.

From the 1960s through the 1980s, the critical movement termed deconstruction also undermined the privileged interiority of the human subject, but from a different vantage than that of the new historicists. Deconstruction shows how language functions as a technology that precedes any author.

Claims of immediacy or spontaneity of feeling as well as originality in expression are undermined by the mechanics of the referential functions of language. Words make sense only when they can be placed in relation to other words, and representations of authentic experience make sense only when related to other people's experiences. Consequently, there is no singular and unique self or unique experience, since understanding it (even for "ourselves") and articulating it (via language to others) mean invoking the cultural technology of language and representational systems. In *Of Grammatology* Jacques Derrida's critique of Rousseau's fashioning of a self that Rousseau then claims is natural provides an early example.[16] Many Romantic scholars known for their work in theory followed suit, including Paul de Man, J. Hillis Miller, Tilottama Rajan, and the later work of Geoffrey Hartman.[17]

To sum up so far, the interiority of the human subject developed in Romanticism continued in the legacy of twentieth-century philosophy. Continental philosophers such as Foucault and Derrida then launched critiques against modern phenomenology's suppositions of a humanist subject. Posthumanism uses some of the tools of new historicism and deconstruction as well as deploying new ones. Within Romantic scholarship, posthumanist critics deflate the puffed-up interiority of the human subject, including the surrounding cultural and historical buttresses which remain in new historicism. More broadly and ambitiously, posthumanism asks us to decenter human thinking by imaging life, worlds, and thought outside of the human. As such it is often conjoined with radical forms of ecocriticism, animal studies, and object-oriented theories. Posthumanism asks us to imagine nonhuman phenomenology and in doing so engages in our limits of thinking outside of the human.

Jonathan Bate's well-known ecological reading of Keats's "Ode to Autumn" in *The Song of the Earth* serves as a good starting point for understanding how posthumanism functions within Romanticism.[18] As the later part of Bate's book reveals, he remains within a humanist tradition of Heidegger's phenomenology; however, his reading of Keats opens the doors to the posthuman. Bate frames the essay by considering the weather. "Ode to Autumn" was written in September of 1819, a season of bountiful grain after three years of poor weather and failed harvests. As such, it is a celebration of agriculture after many years in which the inhuman forces of weather created lean conditions for human sustenance. Bate adds to this weather Keats's personal bout with tuberculosis in which he sought out a more rejuvenating atmosphere in the seaside town of Margate. In the poem, the fortuitous weather allows for plants and animals to flourish in "networks, links, bonds, and correspondences."[19] What appears as an overly rich thriving is merely "illusionary excess," since abundance provides an ecologically valuable biodiversity. It is instructive to see how Bate recuperates this diversity for human ends. He catalogues the wild-flowers with medicinal uses and focuses on the agricultural harvest that is a theme throughout the poem. Taking a posthumanist turn would mean recognizing diversity in itself, not for human utility. Yes, we could link the wild-flowers with bees and bees to pollination for human crops, but again this would be to use nature for human ends.

The most striking element of this poem is not the intertwining of nature with human agricultural technologies in the grain-rich fields. Rather, it is the waning of flourishing life that happens late in autumn and signals the coming winter. Keats imagines autumn with a reaper's hook momentarily suspended. We know the grim reaper will come to all, but for now all beings seem to thrive in a life "o'erbrimm'd." The end of the poem signals a greater end, the end of the day and the end of a season and the end of what we can know of life. In the final stanza "a wailful choir the small gnats mourn" as "The redbreast whistles from a garden-croft; / And gathering swallows twitter in the skies."[20] In the gnat, the redbreast, and the swallow, humans are out of their depths. We do not see the utility to the gnat nor the hedge-crickets that sing. As night falls, the swallow leaves to destinations unknown and for reasons unknown. Even the redbreast who populates the human architecture of the garden-croft has repurposed it. The garden and the croft are not for us but for it. All the human activity of agriculture sits amid a much larger nonhuman world whose choir, songs, whistles, and twitters signal to us a world that exists among us but which we can never fully know.

Flattening Romantic Interiority

The Romantic authors are known for their landscape aesthetics. What is strikingly different in Keats's "Ode to Autumn" is its unlikeness to the typical Romantic-period description of a landscape. One can push Bate's interpretation of Keats beyond his intention and toward a posthumanism. For Wordsworth and many others (such as Thomas Grey, Coleridge, Mary Robinson, etc.), encounters in the landscape produce a psychological effect recorded by the poet – much like Kant's exposition of the sublime in his *Critique of Judgment*. However, as Keats explains in his letter to his publisher and friend, Richard Woodhouse, his idea of a poet is antithetical to Wordsworth's privileged interiority, an attitude Keats calls here the "egotistical sublime":

> As to the poetical Character itself (I mean that sort of which, if I am any thing, I am a Member; that sort distinguished from the wordsworthian or egotistical sublime; which is a thing per se and stands alone) it is not itself – it has no self – it is every thing and nothing … Poet is the most unpoetical of any thing in existence; because he has no Identity – he is continually in for – and filling some other Body – The Sun, the Moon, the Sea and Men and Women who are creatures of impulse are poetical and have about them an unchangeable attribute – the poet has none; no identity[.][21]

The poet functions like a handyman doing whatever odd job is called for. To survive living with such a protean identity and mutable task calls for "negative capability." As Keats describes it in a letter to his brothers, *"Negative Capability* that is when man is capable of being in uncertainties, Mysteries, doubts, without any irritable reaching after fact & reason."[22] In "Ode to Autumn" we see the poet taking up ways of being in the world that are far different from the human. The poet is living with the uncertainty of what such life means. It must mean something – especially to the animals themselves – but the meanings remain shrouded in "uncertainties, Mysteries, doubts" for us who grasp "after fact & reason." Poetry, in this posthuman configuration, is not illuminating and expressing one's experiences. Rather, poetry is opening up to a nonhuman phenomenology of wonder beyond fact, reason, and mimetic description.

One of the most explicit Romantic turns from the human is the often-cited novel *Frankenstein* by Mary Shelley. Scientist Victor Frankenstein assembles his creation from "The dissecting room and the slaughter-house [which] furnished many of my materials; and often did my human nature turn with loathing from my occupation, whilst, still urged on by an eagerness which perpetually increased, I brought my work near to a conclusion."[23] Frankenstein is not haunted by decaying corpses since, as he explains, "Darkness had no effect upon my fancy, and a churchyard was to me merely the receptacle of bodies deprived of life, which, from being the seat of beauty and strength, had become food for the worm."[24] What then causes his "human nature [to] turn with loathing from [his] occupation"? If it is not decaying bodies, then perhaps it is the assembling his eight-foot tall creation from both human and animal bodies garnered in the "dissecting room and the slaughter-house." Frankenstein is horrified to assemble across species and his human nature loathes the thought that we are animated flesh like any other animal. To think of humans as animals is to level the hierarchical chain of being that places us above other creatures.[25] Shelley puts into play the French naturalist George Cuvier's 1798 comparative anatomy and anticipates the definitive flattening of human privilege implicit in Charles Darwin's 1859 *Origin of Species.*

Frankenstein's assemblage places the human alongside the network of other animals without privileging humans. It means the only creatures that privilege the human are the humans themselves; outside of our own enclosed circle there is no transcendental doctrine, no universal authority that authorizes this sense of privilege. Human thought and reason are a lonely island within a larger sea of different semiotic systems in an indifferent universe. As the German philosopher Friedrich Nietzsche explains in a short parable that anticipates a posthumanist sensibility:

> Once upon a time, in some out of the way corner of the universe which is dispersed into numberless twinkling solar systems, there was a star upon which clever beasts invented knowing. That was the most arrogant and mendacious minute of "world history", but nevertheless, it was only a minute. After nature had drawn a few breaths, the star cooled and congealed, and the clever beasts had to die. One might invent such a fable, and yet he still would not have adequately illustrated how miserable, how shadowy and transient, how aimless and arbitrary the human intellect looks within nature.[26]

Like Nietzsche, perhaps Frankenstein contemplates the abysmal limits of humanity. Is it any wonder that Frankenstein "turn[s] with loathing from [his] occupation"? In posthumanism, the transcendental ladder by which we lift ourselves apart from the muck of the world has been pulled out from under us. This particular reading of Frankenstein's assemblage brings together animal studies and posthumanism. It is worth noting before moving forward that the human–animal assemblage is but one figuration of the posthuman in literature. The other end of the spectrum is the human–technology assemblage where we are wedded to technology: humans as cyborgs. In Frankenstein's creature, we get both. The being is animal, human, and technological at once (and visually even more so in the Hollywood movie versions of the story, such as the classic *Frankenstein* directed by James Whale).

Upon animating his creation, Frankenstein is revolted by it and rejects the being as a monster. Without a name and parentless, the creature goes into the world naked and alone. What follows in the novel is the tale of the creature's education. Shelley draws explicitly from philosopher Jean-Jacques Rousseau (especially *Emile*), who imagines human life as more pure and virtuous when outside of society. When Frankenstein does confront his creature, he is a clear-headed rational being far beyond his creator's ethical and rational capacities. Nevertheless, Frankenstein rejects his creation and will not consider him family or friend. Not only does the creator reject the creation as a monster, but all the humans who see the creature revolt against its existence. Shelley is indicting society by showing that a being who in all ways conforms to our ideals and yet is visually repulsive will be judged and treated basely. This places the reader of the novel (and even readers during Shelley's lifetime) in an interesting double position since we are within a human society that judges based on appearances, and yet because we are reading about the creature rather than seeing him, we are outside of society judging their judgment.

What we realize in the social judgment against the creature is that what constitutes the human is a social decision. Nineteenth-century audiences saw in the creature an analogy to the way the Irish were treated by the English and the way African slaves were treated by Western societies.[27] The novel displays a "rights of man" not as naturally given but as granted by society. Rights are never natural – despite our claims; they are a social power we claim as natural as suits our social convenience.[28] However, what happens next in the novel is the posthuman twist. The creature rejects being a good humanist subject schooled in Rousseau and acting within the social laws. Rejecting a sympathetic self and its constructed interiority, the creature becomes an other-than-human force exerting exterior pressures against humans and their social machinery. He kills everyone dear to Frankenstein and then drives his creator to the extremities of the Arctic. The monster becomes the agent of action, which makes human interiority and reflection of little value against his power. As with Keats's ode, here too we see a world beyond the human open up and dwarf human capacities of reason, power, and technology.

The novel ends in a moment of crucial indeterminacy. In good humanist fashion the creature has confessed his "inner" feelings to Walton and pleaded to go free where he promises "I shall quit your vessel on the ice raft which brought me thither and shall seek the most northern extremity of the globe; I shall collect my funeral pile and consume to ashes this miserable frame, that its remains may afford no light to any curious and unhallowed wretch who would create such another as I have been. I shall die."[29] But why should we believe him? The reader never sees the funeral pyre. What if his confession was just a mockery of the cheap human trick of privileged interiority? Here is the double bind: if he kills himself then he is true to his word, and his compact with humanity makes him honest even unto death in such a way that he really should be admitted into society. But if the creature is lying, he would have learned these lies from his creator who broke promises made to his creature. In lying the creature would be human just like those who lied to him. So, if he lives he appears inhuman by breaking his promise and compact with humanity, but this is precisely the human thing to do. The novel ends as an indictment of the social contract, social rights, and social values.

A posthumanist Romanticism indicts the poetic Romantic construction of interiority – from Wordsworth's egotistical sublime to similar characters such as Byron's dark and brooding heroes. In a revaluation of all values, posthuman Romanticism flattens the robust construction of interiority and exposes it to the outside. Rather than landscapes fashioned through an experience of overly powerful feeling reflected in tranquility, humans are one of many elements in the land. Posthumanism intermingles these elements to create meaning through the immanence of material connections rather than a privileged transcendental scaffolding by which humans attempt to hoist themselves outside the land to make judgments upon it.

NOTES

1. M. H. Abrams, *The Mirror and the Lamp: Romantic Theory and the Critical Tradition* (Oxford: Oxford University Press), 22.
2. Samuel Taylor Coleridge and William Wordsworth, *Lyrical Ballads 1798 and 1800*, ed. Michael Gamer and Dahlia Porter (Buffalo, NY: Broadview Press), 183.
3. Coleridge and Wordsworth, *Lyrical Ballads*, 420.
4. References to "Lines Written above Tintern Abbey, On Revisiting the Wye during a Tour, July 13, 1798" are from the above-cited 1798 edition, 142–45.
5. Wordsworth, "Tintern Abbey," ln 117. For a critique of the poem's treatment of Dorothy Wordsworth, see Marjorie Levinson, *Wordsworth's Great Period Poems: Four Essays* (Cambridge: Cambridge University Press, 1986).
6. *Ibid.*, ln 119 and ln 74.
7. *Ibid.*, ln 139–47.
8. *Ibid.*, ln 26–28.
9. *Ibid.*, ln 105–06.
10. Marjorie Levinson, *Keats's Life of Allegory: The Origins of a Style* (New York: Blackwell Publishing, 1991).
11. John Stewart Mill, "Thoughts on Poetry and Its Varieties," *The Crayon* 7.4, 95. Accessed February 1, 2015. https://archive.org/stream/jstor-25528035/25528035.
12. Two simple lines from Wordsworth's "Hart-Leap Well" summarize this way of thinking about poetry: "Tis my delight, alone in summer shade, / To pipe a simple song for thinking hearts." In these few lines Wordsworth shows the power of feeling ("hearts") and reflection ("thinking hearts") externalized as he "pipe[s] a simple song." Coleridge and Wordsworth, *Lyrical Ballads*, ln 100, 296.
13. Jerome J. McGann, *The Romantic Ideology: A Critical Investigation* (Chicago: University of Chicago Press, 1983), ix.
14. McGann, *Romantic Ideology*, 1.
15. Fredrick Jameson, *The Political Unconscious: Narrative as a Socially Symbolic Act* (Ithaca: Cornell University Press, 1981), 9.
16. See Jacques Derrida's critique of Rousseau in part two of *Of Grammatology* (Baltimore: Johns Hopkins University Press, 1976).

17. Christoph Bode, "Romanticism and Deconstruction: Distant Relations and Elective Affinities," in *Romantic Continuities*, ed. Günther Blaicher and Michael Gassenmeier (Essen: Verlag Die Blaue Eule, 1992), 131–59.
18. Jonathan Bate, *Song of the Earth* (Cambridge: Harvard University Press, 2000), 94–118.
19. Bate, *Song of the Earth*, 105.
20. John Keats, "To Autumn," in *Complete Poems* (Cambridge: Harvard University Press, 1978), 360–61.
21. John Keats, Letter to Richard Woodhouse, October 27, 1818, in *Selected Letters of John Keats*, ed. Grant F. Scott (Cambridge: Harvard University Press, 2002), 194.
22. John Keats, Letter to George and Tom Keats, 21? December 27, 1817, in *Selected Letters*, ed. Scott, 60.
23. Mary Shelley, *Frankenstein*, ed. Stuart Curran (Romantic Circles). Accessed February 1, 2015. www.rc.umd.edu/editions/frankenstein/1831v1/ch4.
24. *Ibid.*
25. For the Great Chain of Being, see as an example Alexander Pope's "Essay on Man": "Vast chain of being! which from God began, / Natures ethereal, human, angel, man, / Beast, bird, fish, insect, what no eye can see," in Alexander Pope, *Moral Essays and Satires*, ed. Henry Morley (Project Gutenberg). Accessed February 1, 2015. www.gutenberg.org/files/2428/2428-h/2428-h.htm.
26. Friedrich Nietzsche, "On Truth and Lies in a Nonmoral Sense," in *The Portable Nietzsche*, ed. and trans. Walter Kaufmann (New York: Penguin Books, 1976), 42.
27. For the Irish reference, see *Punch*, May 20, 1882. Slavery is a theme throughout the novel. The monster laments being treated like a slave and in his revenge exclaims that he will be master of his creator (see Chapter 20 of the 1823 edition for extended examples).
28. This is further developed in Giorgio Agamben's concept of "state of exception" wherein the state or the social stands outside of judgment while being the judge of those who seek entry into society. Those exiled from a legitimate position in society are said to live a marginal life or "bare life." See Agamben's introduction to his *Homo Sacer: Sovereign Power and Bare Life* (Stanford: Stanford University Press, 1998).
29. Shelley, Frankenstein (Romantic Circles). Accessed February 1, 2015. www.rc .umd.edu/editions/frankenstein/1831v3/walton.html.

4

JEFF WALLACE

Modern

There has never yet been a Superman. I have seen them both naked, the
greatest and the smallest man. They are still all-too-similar to one
another. Truly, I found even the greatest man – all too-human!
– Friedrich Nietzsche, *Thus Spoke Zarathustra* (1892)

The true rationalism must always transcend itself by recurrence to the
concrete in search of inspiration. A self-satisfied rationalism is in effect
a form of anti-rationalism.
– A. N. Whitehead, *Science and the Modern World* (1926)

The *Übermensch*, the Untimely

It would be entirely understandable to locate in literary modernism a certain
inaugural moment of the posthuman. On this reading, looming over modernism's various, clamorous aspirations for a break with the past would be
the figure of human overcoming presented by the Nietzschean *Übermensch*.
The scandal of Friedrich Nietzsche's intervention in ethical and philosophical debate, across a series of works from *The Birth of Tragedy* (1872)
onward, was to propose that precisely those values most cherished by
Christian and post-Enlightenment modernity as "human" – love, political
democracy and progress, science, intellectual idealism, and even "truth," for
example – were, in the words of his literary mouthpiece, Zarathustra, "the
greatest danger for the whole human future .... And whatever harm the
wicked may do, the harm the good do is the most harmful harm!"[1] It then
became possible to see the "all-too-human" as a secular condition of ethical
imprisonment within such ideals, and notably within the artificially constructed binary of good and evil, with the *Übermensch* as the anticipated
means of liberation and transformation.

Yet if the posthuman originates as an *image* of the transformed human, in
significant ways the *Übermensch* falls short. In the loosely narrativized form
of *Thus Spoke Zarathustra* (1892), the 40-year-old protagonist has spent
a decade in the solitude of the mountains and is now preparing to "*go down*"

into the world to "*teach you the Superman*" (Z, 39–41; original emphasis). Later at the outset of the final Part Four, his hair has turned white – though, with an ambiguous temporality hinting at the central Nietzschean concept of the eternal return, Zarathustra's "soul" has failed to register this passage of linear time. Zarathustra is not, however, himself the Superman, nor has there ever "yet been" a Superman. Instead, the Superman is a concept or mode of thinking to be taught, to "Brothers," disciples, and "his animals" in the text's various mythologized contexts – the marketplace, the Blissful Islands, the forest, and the cave. The strident propheticism of Zarathustra's discourse can mask both the uncertainty of this pedagogical process – the people know "neither how to take nor to keep his words" (Z, 190) – and the extent to which it proceeds by critical negation: through scrupulous discrimination, we are warned against the dangers of conflating the Superman either with the "Ultimate Man" or with the "Higher Man," the former having discovered happiness through the glibly democratic acquisition of warmth and enter-tainment, the latter embodying the highest forms of independent creativity and virtue yet still, ultimately, unable to extricate himself from conventional boundaries: "You Higher Men, the worst about you is: none of you has learned to dance as a man ought to dance – to dance beyond yourselves!" (Z, 306).

The *Übermensch* therefore emerges as absence or deferral, a void waiting to be filled by modern history and culture. It characterizes what the American literary theorist Elizabeth Grosz identifies in Nietzsche as the profound significance of the "untimely": "the dislocated, that which precedes, sur-passes, and moves beyond man, that which goes beyond the human and unhinges progress and continuity, displacing the known and the present for a future that does not yet exist."[2] In claiming that *The Will to Power* was written for a species that did not yet exist, Nietzsche's implication was not simply that what lay beyond the human had not yet evolved; rather, on the basis of what Grosz suggests was a rather scant reading of Darwin, the will-to-power constituted "a small space of excess that functions outside of natural selection, where life does not simply fulfil itself in surviving in its given milieu successfully enough to reproduce, but where it actively seeks to transform itself" (NT, 11).

In this "small space of excess," in other words, lies the potential for life to become radically new, or other than itself. Biologically, Nietzsche's critique therefore prefigured the French philosopher Henri Bergson's "creative evo-lution" and the British novelist D. H. Lawrence's vitalism. All three insisted on the logical gap between science's retrospectively explanatory functions on the one hand and its proleptic or predictive functions on the other. The semantic instability of this potential is also the condition of a notoriously rich and often troubling history of ideological appropriation. Yet, as historian Daniel Pick has suggested with regard to the "extreme provocation" of some of Nietzsche's pronouncements on race, crime, and degeneration, these are simultaneously disavowed by a methodology inherently skeptical of absolutes and dogma, "interminably allusive," and voicing a schizoid persona "at once deadly serious and full of irony."[3] It was perhaps then as a model of writing-as-thought, unprecedentedly restless, fractured, and self-questioning, that Nietzsche communicated to modernists the verdict that, as the French thinkers Deleuze and Guattari have it, "you will know nothing through concepts unless you have first created them."[4]

How far, then, was the "make it new" of literary modernism really new? Or, in its concerns with rupture and discontinuity, the obsolescence of tradition, and aesthetic defamiliarization, how far does modernism's response to the strenuous Nietzschean challenge of envisioning what the human might become anticipate a form of posthumanism? I will posit two modes of the modernist posthuman formulated as a series of linked antitheses: heroic versus anti-heroic, egotistic versus post-anthropocentric, conflictual versus peaceful, loud versus quiet. My thesis is that, while the nature of modernism as we understand it seems to call for an emphasis on the first term of these pairings, the binary itself begins to dissolve under the developing influence of posthumanist theory and an associated literary-critical practice which encourages us to ask new questions and make new selections of modernist texts.

Heroic-egotistic

To consider the heroic posthuman in modernism is almost inevitably to consider the gendered implications of the *Übermensch*. The keynote of the challenge to humanistic pieties in a manifesto-driven literary modernism is aggressive transformation, typified by the Italian artist F. T. Marinetti's 1909 Futurist "manifesto of burning and overwhelming violence" glorifying war with "man at the steering wheel."[5] This tone finds its way into the formation of a poetics of impersonality by a range of early modernist writers. Wyndham Lewis's *BLAST* and its accompanying Vorticist manifesto announce an aesthetic challenge to the "effeminate" English character symbolized by a dismal climate and to the "typical cowardly attitude" of those who equate "Life" in art with "Nature";[6] Ezra Pound, signatory to the Vortex and Lewis's close co-conspirator, also collaborated with T. E. Hulme on an Imagist poetics dedicated to cleansing poetry of the mess apparently left by an all-too-human combination of sickly sentiment and Romanticism: Pound sought a "harder and saner" poetry, "austere, direct, free from emotional slither," while Hulme famously inveighed against Romanticism as "spilt religion," and against "the sloppiness which doesn't consider that a poem is a poem unless it is moaning or whining about something or other."[7] In T. S. Eliot's rather more elegant formulations, the necessary depersonalization of "inexact" Wordsworthian formulae such as "emotion recollected in tranquility" would occur by bringing art into closer conjunction with science: the mind of the poet was the shred of platinum in a catalytic chamber, poetry "not the expression of personality, but an escape from personality."[8]

The male fictional personae of early modernism both extend and yet demand qualification of this heroic mode of the posthuman: James Joyce's Stephen Dedalus, D. H. Lawrence's Paul Morel or Rupert Birkin, Wyndham Lewis's Tarr. Here, it is the pursuit of modernist aesthetic autonomy that constitutes both the hero's transgression of the status quo and the anti-heroic fragility or brittleness of his masculinity. In *Portrait of the Artist as a Young Man*, Stephen Dedalus reflects on the strange name of the "fabulous artificer" that has symbolized the apartness of his artistic sensibility (Joyce had eventually abandoned Stephen as *Hero*); with "no human figure near him" at the moment of his transfiguration and dedication to a life of art, seeing the girl in the sea only as a "wild angel" of beauty, Stephen is henceforth empowered to reject the claims of his colleague McCann's "new humanity" of universal peace along with those of his religion and nation, while the "inhuman clamour" of a flock of birds outside the library soothes the memory of the sobs and reproaches of a mother whom he cannot agree to love. Clinging to the resolution to "forge in the smithy of my soul the uncreated conscience of my race" is, however, the self-conscious Nietzscheanism of the young man's journal entry, and the memory of a small boy in spectacles clinging to the edges of the playing fields.[9]

In a similar narrative structure of overcoming, the "Derelict" chapter of Lawrence's *Sons and Lovers* (1913) sees the artist Paul Morel striving to cast off the lineaments of his previous human connections – Clara and Baxter Dawes, Miriam Leivers, and the deep emotional ties with his now dead mother. Stepping out of a tramcar into the "immense night," he finds himself "one tiny upright speck of flesh" in a universe which is only spatial, not temporal – "himself, infinitesimal, at the core a nothingness, and yet not nothing."[10] In the later, metropolitan tones of *Women in Love*'s Rupert Birkin, the tenuous material position of the human is elevated into an entire philosophy of the evolutionary posthuman: "The whole idea is dead. Humanity itself is dry-rotten really …. Do you think that creation depends on *man*! It merely doesn't …. I much prefer to think of the lark rising up in the morning upon a humanless world. – Man is a mistake, he must go."[11] Through the means of an impersonal aesthetic, school-inspector Birkin takes over the sketching of Ursula's catkins – "It's the fact you want to emphasize, not a subjective impression to record" – and, with the two women in attendance, brutally exposes in Hermione Roddice the theories of instinctive animal knowledge he elsewhere appears to espouse (*WL* 36). But Birkin's masterliness is inconsistent, self-cancelling, and subjected by other characters to various forms of ridicule throughout the novel.

By apparent contrast, the figure of artistic superiority in Lewis's Frederick Tarr is bleached of Birkin's human subtleties and vulnerabilities; yet the uncompromisingly abstract and satirical mode of the novel imposes its own constraints on Tarr's heroism. Despite the presence of the more complex post-Romantic figure of Otto Kreisler, Tarr's theory of "inhuman" art is the keynote, where inhuman connotes an impersonal gaze at odds with comforting humanist precepts such as humour and organic "life": "Deadness is the first condition for art: the second is absence of soul, in the human and sentimental sense . . .. [G]ood art must have no inside."[12] This legislates Tarr's ostentatiously macho treatment of others, and notably of course his women, including his girlfriend Bertha, "'a high-grade aryan bitch, in good condition, superbly made; of the succulent, obedient, clear peasant type'" (*T*, 32). Any suspicion that this crude racial eugenicism is not, precisely, at least part of the hero's comical absurdity is dispelled in the later exchange with Anastasya, who is "rescuing" Tarr from Bertha. To her question, "'You are my efficient chimpanzee then for keeps?'," he retorts: "'No I'm the new animal; we haven't thought up a name for him yet – the thing that will succeed the Superman'" (*T*, 321).

In a different context, that of expressionist film of the 1920s, feminist theorist Rosi Braidotti has similarly identified the fragility of this heroic posthuman masculinity. Reading Marcel L'Herbier's *L'Inhumaine* (1924) alongside Fritz Lang's *Metropolis* (1927), Braidotti finds a defensive mechanism at work in the construction of the central characters, the cruel seductress Claire and the demoniacal robot Maria, and the new alliance they represent between the eroticized female body and the potential of rapidly advancing new technologies. The relationship expresses a profound ambivalence, entwining fear and desire: while the historical-modernist moment is typified by a fascination with the machine and yet an apprehension surrounding the destructive possibilities of its power, maintaining a sense of the distance between human and technological, a more ancient fear of the seductive powers of the woman is simultaneously enacted: "female sexuality," argues Braidotti, "is inscribed in this inhuman script as a threat but also as an irresistible attraction: techno-Eves of multiple temptations, pointing the way to unsettling futures."[13]

However, what necessarily complicates the politics of the heroic masculine posthuman is the extent to which it came equally to constitute a resource both for female modernists and for the possibilities of human identity beyond gender, foreshadowing perhaps the dream by feminist theorist Donna Haraway, author of the celebrated "Cyborg Manifesto," of a post-gender world that the cyborg might help to bring about. In the story "Indissoluble Matrimony," her luminous contribution to *BLAST 1*, Rebecca West eagerly embraced Lewis's recommended vocabulary of the material and impersonal vortex. The bitter animosity in the marriage of George and Evadne Silverton, shaped by George's paranoid fear of his wife's sexual confidence and radically political public persona, can only be resolved it seems through transposition to a central episode of nocturnal Gothic fantasy, in which a fight to the death is staged. Facing each other, a "strong passion" threatens to "disintegrate their souls as a magnetic current decomposes the electrolyte," yet this is also thereby a moment of ecstatic freedom and fulfillment; their "immediate personal qualities" falling away, they are "broken into a new conception of life": "For the first time they were possessed by a supreme emotion and they felt a glad desire to strip away restraint and express it nakedly" (*B*, 109–110).

While West satirically frames the story through George's return to the domestic sphere, the marriage bed and Evadne's "warm arms," the suggestion is that the frame can barely contain the energies released in this profane episode and encounter – one which, to borrow from the advert carried by *BLAST 1* for the journal *The Egoist*, "recognizes no taboos" (*B*, 160). Much of the responsibility for such a policy in this influential journal, which was to serially publish many of those chosen instances of the heroic fictional posthuman, lay with the editor of its previous incarnations, Dora Marsden. In "Interpretation of Sex II," the anonymous editorial for the May 9, 1912, issue of *The Freewoman*, Marsden had written: "what sex was up to the fringe of the human, passion is to the limits of the superhuman." As in the "strong passion" of George and Evadne, so passion, explored in a series of editorials earlier in 1912, became for Marsden the sign of authenticity, truth, and vital experience, transcending sex in its concern for new forms of intimacy and companionship.

West and Marsden here typify a modernist challenge to the discourses of love and romance; as in Futurism's "contempt for woman," the term "woman" itself was seen to be fatally compromised by "horrible and Staid love," and could only be wrenched free by attacking some of the most cherished myths of female identity, such as feminine virtue or the sanctity of motherhood.[14] A fault line thus emerged between such cultural, posthuman striving and the interests of political feminism and the suffrage movement. Emancipation, for Marsden, was certainly radically other than the all-too-human business of gaining the vote. As Mina Loy was to suggest in the uncategorizable "Feminist Manifesto," the current "inadequacy" of the feminist movement could be attributed to a failure to appreciate the true extent of the "demolition" work required of women, which in her case included the recommendation of "the unconditional surgical destruction of virginity" at puberty in order to allow "intrinsic merits of character" to prevail over virtue. An early adherent of European Futurism, in the Nietzschean mode of her "Aphorisms on Futurism," Loy wrote: "May your egotism be so gigantic that you comprise mankind in your self-sympathy."[15]

At the heart of such debates around what the human might become lay the concept of the "ego," whose prevalence in early twentieth-century intelligentsias across Europe and America is often traced to the widespread influence of Max Stirner's *The Ego and His Own*, translated in 1907. In effect, the ego (a term used here outside of Freudian discourse) made thinkable an un-sexed, anarchistic individualism or process of self-actualization as the condition of a future of democratic equality and emancipation beyond the merely human and its associated, traditional gender categories. Unmistakeably symbolic therefore was the transition in the title of Marsden's journal, from *The New Freewoman* to *The Egoist*, a process which, though instigated by Ezra Pound, Richard Aldington, and other male contributors, apparently came with Marsden's complete endorsement in handing over the editorship to Harriet Shaw Weaver.[16]

"Ego," then, was structured by a crucial ambivalence which prevents its easy assimilation to heroic modernism. From Marinetti's "Technical Manifesto of Futurist Literature," Mina Loy would also have known the injunction, "**Destroy the 'I' in literature:** that is, all psychology" (original emphasis in bold); the "sort of man" defined by culture and wisdom should be replaced "once and for all with matter," and "There is no point in creating a drama of matter that has been humanized."[17] After reading the same manifesto in 1914, Lawrence was emboldened to try out his resistance to the "old-fashioned human" perspective in a letter to his editor Edward Garnett, famously venturing that he was not interested in what a woman in his fiction *feels*, because this presumed an ego to feel with, but that instead Garnett should note the emergence of "another ego," likened to the allotropic potential of a single material element.[18] Tristan Tzara's Dadaist Manifesto of 1918 insisted simultaneously on "the knowledge of a supreme egoism," and that "the divine thing in us is our call to anti-human action."[19] In thus outlining a vision for "Women and the Future" (1924) in terms of the seemingly conventional concept of the "womanly woman," the English stream-of-consciousness novelist Dorothy Richardson could declare that "the essential characteristic of women is egoism," the latter differing vastly from shallowly ambitious "masculine selfishness" in its "completely self-centred consciousness."[20] Ego itself, in other words, could be read as the very sign of an emancipation from the narrow confines of the humanist self, and hence pointing toward a displacement of anthropocentrism. As Eliot had put this paradox in "Tradition and the Individual Talent," only those possessing a distinct personality could know why it was important to want to escape from it.

Beyond Heroism and Anthropocentrism

When this discussion of "ego" is set in the rich context of Anne Fernihough's reassessment of the Edwardian era in *Freewomen and Supermen: Edwardian Radicals and Literary Modernism* (2013), the terms upon which we seek to locate the posthuman within the modernistic are open to revision.[21] At our peril, Fernihough suggests, do we attribute or confine the wide-ranging intellectual energies of the post-Nietzschean "hyper-individualist, vitalist" discourses of the era to the emergence of a "high modernist" aesthetic, as literary history has tended to do. Reading Marsden's magazines, or A. R. Orage's highly influential *New Age*, we find that "the staples of modernist literary discourse were, during these Edwardian years, intimately entwined with other, often outlandish, social and political discourses" (*FS*, 44). Freewomen seeking emancipation *were*, in effect, supermen, and posthumanist aspirations were as likely to be found in the careful chewing of food or practice of birth control as in the contemplation of ideas or the practice of experimental art.

Fernihough's study therefore shows Edwardian radicals seeking to locate ideas of human striving and overcoming within a broader spectrum of the material world: bodies, things, animals, and technologies. This resonates strongly with the influence that posthumanism has begun to have on the recent turn toward a reconsideration of the ethical in literary and philosophical modernism. In a sense, this moment is a return to the ethical challenges set by Nietzsche. For Braidotti, one of the key dilemmas remaining after Nietzsche's termination of the "self-evident" status of human nature is "how to reconstitute a sense of community held together by affinity and ethical accountability, without falling into the negative passions of doubt and suspicion" (*TP*, 6). Where in Nietzsche the as-yet unattained condition of the "free spirit" was wholly dependent upon self-mastery, Braidotti's "community" depends precisely upon the renunciation of such mastery, either over self or object-world, and instead upon the thinking of a nonhierarchical, post-anthropomorphic network of relations or affinities between animate and inanimate matter.

If then the modernist philosopher of the heroic posthuman is Nietzsche, in more recent readings the modernist philosopher of this post-anthropocentric posthumanism is the British philosopher of science A. N. Whitehead (1861–1947). As literary theorist Steven Shaviro notes, in abolishing the "*ontological* privileging of human beings over all other subjectivities," Whitehead's process philosophy moved to a "univocity" within which the same affect-laden vocabulary is used to describe the biological and even inorganic worlds as is used to describe the human world.[22] At the risk of seeming to anthropomorphize materiality, this was a radical strategy to unhinge the relations both of subject–object and of cause and effect, containing at the same time the invention of new concepts such as "prehension" to indicate the untimely manner in which effects might select as well as respond to their putative causes. The current enormous revival of interest in Whitehead's work among theorists working at the interface of literature and science studies informs various contemporary approaches to the heterogeneous material gatherings that are seen to constitute any event or "thing" once we move beyond the great divides between human and nonhuman, organic and inorganic: Deleuze and Guattari's machinic "assemblages," Bruno Latour's "actor-network theory" and later "Compositionism," and Jane Bennett's "vital materialism." This overcoming of humanist divisions in turn leads to a redefinition of ethics, not as the actions and decisions of human individuals, but as the understanding of agency and co-dependency distributed across complex networks or fields of relations.

Perhaps, this posthumanism was always latent in modernism's material aesthetic and its breaking of the connection between individual expression and medium; for example, from Rimbaud and Mallarmé's Symboliste aesthetic to Futurism's "**lyrical obsession with matter**" expressed as "words-in-freedom," the releasing of language from referentiality into "**strict nets of images or analogies**" (*TM*, 16–17; original emphases in bold). Dadaist artist Kurt Schwitters established his *Merz* practice of the composite artwork on the free appropriation of any materials, within which "even people could be used," laying the groundwork for postmodern performance art.[23] New developments in modernist studies are, accordingly, taking up these suggestions to trace, through a selection of materials and a distinctive critical practice, the literary fault lines of the contemporary posthuman.

Two modernist writers in particular, Virginia Woolf and Samuel Beckett, figure significantly in these developments, where a quieter and more pacifistic, yet rigorously searching concern for a deconstructed ecology of relations between human and animal, human and machine, organic and inorganic is seen to be at work. Derek Ryan's 2013 study of the "materiality of theory" in Woolf gives a distinctively posthumanist turn, through the work of philosopher of science Karen Barad, to the more familiar modernist territory of quantum physics informing Woolf's most abstract novel *The Waves*.[24] Building on Barad's conception of "intra-action" as "*the mutual constitution of entangled agencies*" (original emphasis), Ryan reads the character Bernard's responses to the city environment as a heterogeneous assemblage of human and nonhuman agents, the "growl of the traffic" intermingling with his own sensations of curiosity, greed, and desire (*MT*, 186). Where Ryan locates a post-anthropocentrism filtered through character, critic Gabriel Hankins has found the same, in Woolf's earlier novel *Jacob's Room*, in a narrative technique which allows the "nonhuman voices of the 'furniture' of the novel" to gain precedence over those of its human traits and protagonists. Lacking exterior visibility, Jacob's identity is instead displaced, Hankins demonstrates, onto such "furniture," in a radical dispersal of actants such that, for example, "we are not sure where Jacob's misogyny ... begins and the King's College Chapel at Cambridge ends."[25]

In some ways these attentive new readings of Woolf show modernism fulfilling a hint planted by Bruno Latour when, reflecting on Western science's "odd invention" of inanimate matter, he recommends to contemporary literature the task of reopening the question of animism.[26] In the same special issue as Hankins's essay, I suggest that Samuel Beckett's early novel *Murphy* (1938) might similarly be read in terms of an animism obtaining not at the level of human character but as a dispersal of body parts which take their place, through vector and velocity, within and alongside the field of things, animate and inanimate, that populate the spaces of the novel. So, beneath the novel's cartoon-like agitation and aggression, there is another *Murphy*, whose model of animated co-existence is embedded in narrative technique. This, in effect, is an inherently pacifistic mode to accompany the more overt sense in which *Murphy* might be read as anti-war, anti-fascist utterance, and it suggests that Beckett might have transformed the shock of the broken body or body-in-pieces administered by World War I into a recognition of the strange enlivened, ontological precedence of body parts over the fiction of the humanist human as a whole entity.[27]

Ryan's study of Woolf is a major contribution to the reassessment of the role of the animal within modernism, joining, for example, the literary criticism of Carrie Rohman (2008) and drawing on the Whitehead-orientated conception of species-companionship developed by Donna Haraway (2008). In examining the complex states of recognition represented between dog and characters, for example, Ryan makes a compelling case for the acceptance of Woolf's narrative *Flush* alongside her more established contributions to modernist experimentalism. Beckett's work has gained similar attention through the volume *Beckett and Animals* (2013), in surveying which Mary Bryden notes the general agreement as to Beckett's rejection of the Cartesian notion of animal-as-machine and the human supremacism which is its corollary. The posthumanist rehabilitation of the animal in this sense of Cartesian critique must, however, entail a parallel re-thinking of the machine, as the nature of the organic–inorganic binary is called into question. It follows that both Woolf and Beckett have also been widely re-read from the perspectives of technologies of representation and communication. Pamela Caughie's volume *Virginia Woolf in the Age of Mechanical Reproduction* (2000), for example, uses Walter Benjamin's theory of the role of new technologies such as photography, cinema, and sound reproduction in modern identity formation to trace in various ways a cyborgean splicing of Woolf with her machines. Theorists of modernist technology in Beckett's work, such as Ulrika Maude (2009) and Alex Goody (2013), have focused attention on *Krapp's Last Tape*, where Krapp's obsessive use of sound reproduction configures an exploration of the body as both single material entity and the subject of a constant deferral of meaning.

My conclusion, accordingly, proceeds from an anecdote concerning the technological mediation of possibly the gentlest and yet most significant of posthumanist literary modernists. Recently, my car broke down in the middle of a city; the electric handbrake failed, locking the brake discs in place, a reminder that it was still possible in this way (a modernist moment?) to confront the recalcitrance of the machine in the face of human wishes. Sitting in the car waiting nearly three hours for rescue, and thinking ahead to this chapter, I used my mobile phone to access the Internet and download a recording of Gertrude Stein reading "If I Told Him," her 1923 "Completed Portrait" of Pablo Picasso. I listened, and listened again, and yet again.

A posthumanist moment, perhaps. The wonder of listening to Stein's disembodied, encoded voice through a smooth and unobtrusive virtual technology was somehow matched, I felt, by the singularity of Stein's writing within literary modernism and its continuing, benign resistance to critical assimilation. The "Portrait" begins:

> If I told him would he like it. Would he like it if I told him.
> Would he like it would Napoleon would Napoleon would would he like it.
> If Napoleon if I told him if I told him if Napoleon. Would he like it if I told him if I told him if Napoleon. Would he like it if Napoleon if Napoleon if I told him. If I told him if Napoleon if Napoleon if I told him. If I told him would he like it would he like it if I told him.[28]

The grace and control of Stein's reading confer upon these words an inevitability they might not otherwise have had. They also work to dispel the immediate, domesticating interpretation that the text posits a likeness between Picasso and Napoleon of which the artist might not approve. Stein's rhythmic incantations suggest that the words are "true" to their subject, but in a way which exceeds referentiality. This is often the uncanny effect of reading Stein: a dance of sense skipping in and out of syntax and grammar, never insinuating that the relation between subjects and objects, causes and effects, might be a one-way thing.

My suggestion is that Stein, friend and interlocutor of A. N. Whitehead, as well as of William James, might be the most important modernist yet to be fully considered by a posthumanist ethics or criticism. Her *Tender Buttons* (1914) invites a participatory gathering rather than a critical stance as such, an involvement in a world in which objects are processes realized in language and rooms are the actions and occupations that bring space into being. Because of its unparaphraseability, Stein's work seems to epitomize a modernist autonomous poetics, yet still leads us as critics to traduce that work by selecting from it representative quotations that might do the explanatory work for us; or we take refuge behind the decoy word "experimental." In the affectionate backward glance at modernist practice that is his "attempt" at a compositionist manifesto, Latour notes that while compositionism attempts to re-build a common world, it does so in the knowledge that this world has to be built "from utterly heterogeneous parts that will never make a whole, but at best a fragile, revisable and diverse composite material" (*CM*, 474). As Stein proposed, such composition is always also explanation, but in a manner of rationalism, as Whitehead might have put it, that is anything but self-satisfied.

NOTES

1. Friedrich Nietzsche, *Thus Spoke Zarathustra: A Book for Everyone and No One*, trans. R. J. Hollingdale (1892; Harmondsworth: Penguin, 1980), 229; hereafter *Z*.
2. Elizabeth Grosz, *The Nick of Time: Politics, Evolution and the Untimely* (Durham: Duke University Press, 2004), 98; hereafter *NT*.
3. Daniel Pick, *Faces of Degeneration: A European Disorder, c.1848–1918* (Cambridge: Cambridge University Press, 1989), 226–27.
4. Gilles Delezue and Félix Guattari, *What is Philosophy?*, trans. Graham Burchell and Hugh Tomlinson (London: Verso, 1994), 7.
5. F. T. Marinetti, "The Founding and the Manifesto of Futurism (Feb. 1909)," in *Modernism: An Anthology*, ed. Lawrence Rainey (Oxford: Blackwell, 2005), 4–5.
6. *BLAST 1*, ed. Wyndham Lewis, foreword by Paul Edwards (1914; London: Thames and Hudson, 2009), 11, 129; hereafter *B*.
7. Ezra Pound, "A Retrospect" (1917), and T. E. Hulme, "Romanticism and Classicism" (1914), in *A Modernist Reader: Modernism in England 1910–1930*, ed. Peter Faulkner (London: Batsford, 1986), 67, 48–49.
8. T. S. Eliot, "Tradition and the Individual Talent," in *Selected Prose* of T. S. Eliot, ed. Frank Kermode (London: Faber, 1975), 40–43.

9. James Joyce, *A Portrait of the Artist as a Young Man* (1916; Harmondsworth: Penguin, 1976), 169, 172, 196, 224, 253.

10. D. H. Lawrence, *Sons and Lovers* (1913; Cambridge: Cambridge University Press, 1992), 464.

11. D. H. Lawrence, *Women in Love*, edited by David Farmer, Lindeth Vasey, and John Worthen (1921; Cambridge: Cambridge University Press, 1995), 126–28; hereafter *WL*.

12. Wyndham Lewis, *Tarr* (1928; Harmondsworth: Penguin, 1982), 312; hereafter *T*.

13. Rosi Braidotti, *The Posthuman* (Cambridge: Polity Press, 2013), 107; hereafter *T*.

14. F. T. Marinetti, "Contempt for Woman (from *Le Futurisme*, 1911)," in *Modernism: An Anthology*, ed. Rainey, 9.

15. Mina Loy, "Feminist Manifesto" and "Aphorisms on Futurism," in *The Lost Lunar Baedeker*, ed. R. L. Conover (Manchester: Carcanet, 1997), 153, 155, 150.

16. See Bruce Clarke, *Dora Marsden and Early Modernism: Gender, Individualism, Science* (Ann Arbor: University of Michigan Press, 1996).

17. F. T. Marinetti, "Technical Manifesto of Futurist Literature" (1912), in *Modernism: An Anthology*, ed. Rainey, 17–18; hereafter *TM*.

18. *The Letters of D. H. Lawrence*, Vol. II (June 1913–September 1916), ed. G. J. Zyaturk and J. D. Boulton (Cambridge: Cambridge University Press, 1981), 183.

19. Tristan Tzara, "Dada Manifesto 1918," in *Modernism: An Anthology*, ed. Rainey, 481, 483.

20. Dorothy Richardson, "Women and the Future" (1924), in *Modernism: An Anthology*, ed. Rainey, 593–94.

21. Anne Fernihough, *Freewomen and Supermen: Edwardian Radicals and Literary Modernism* (Oxford: Oxford University Press, 2013); hereafter *FS*.

22. Steven Shaviro, *Without Criteria: Kant, Whitehead, Deleuze, and Aesthetics* (Cambridge, MA and London: MIT Press, 2009), xiii, 27.

23. Kurt Schwitters, "Merz (1920)," in *Modernism: An Anthology*, ed. Rainey, 488.

24. Derek Ryan, *Virginia Woolf and the Materiality of Theory: Sex, Animal, Life* (Edinburgh: Edinburgh University Press, 2013); hereafter *MT*.

25. Gabriel Hankins, "The Objects of Ethics: Rilke and Woolf with Latour," *Twentieth-Century Literature* 61.3, special issue on "Modernist Ethics and Posthumanism" (September 2015): 329–50; 340, 343.

26. Bruno Latour, "An Attempt at a 'Compositionist Manifesto'," *New Literary History* 41 (2010): 471–90; 484, 481.

27. Jeff Wallace, "*Murphy* and Peace," *Twentieth-Century Literature* 61.3 (September 2015): 351–73.

28. Gertrude Stein, "If I Told Him," in *Look at Me Now and Here I Am: Writings and Lectures 1911–45*, ed. Patricia Meyerowitz (Harmondsworth: Penguin, 1971), 230.

5

STEFAN HERBRECHTER

Postmodern

> Children, who will inherit the world. Children to whom, throughout
> history, stories have been told, chiefly but not always at bedtime, in order
> to quell the restless thoughts; whose need of stories is matched only by
> the need adults have of children to tell stories to, of receptacles for their
> stock of fairy-tales, of listening ears on which to unload these most
> unbelievable yet haunting of fairy-tales, their own lives; children.
> Swift (1991)

A Generation Game

I suppose I was one of those (belated) children to whom Jean-François
Lyotard tried to explain the postmodern.[1] Like the children and the pupils
of Mr. Crick, the history teacher in Graham Swift's novel *Waterland*, whose
subject is being "cut down" (a way of understanding the phrase "the end of
history,"[2] literally), I was spell-bound by the stories that my teachers had to
tell about their time and their lives. And like the pupils in Mr. Crick's history
lessons during which he – in good postmodernist fashion – mixes historical
facts and autobiographical fiction,[3] I was at once skeptical of the "factuality"
of their discourse, but at the same time I was fascinated with the earnestness
of their desires and anxieties. Mr. Crick comes across as a very nostalgic man,
a dinosaur, who has grown up in the Fens and whose childhood is very much
a part of the post-World War II "sense of an ending,"[4] which is also the time
of the postmodern as an "attitude" and of postmodernism as a "style."

In the filmic adaptation, Tom Crick is played – with the suitable mixture of
melancholia and disillusion – by Jeremy Irons, while the teaching takes place,
also very appropriately, somewhere in the United States.[5] Where else should
the end of history occur than in the United States? It adds a very interesting
dimension to the novel, namely the question of globalization, the past,
present, and future of a certain idea of Europe, the slowness needed for the
painful work of literal re-member-ing. So like those children, I was in a sense
the "receptacle" of ideas about postmodernism and living (through) the

54

apparent end of history – "those most unbelievable yet haunting fairy-tales." And I admired, and still do, the times when ideas about something as abstract as "the Western metaphysics of presence" (Derrida) and "the incredulity toward metanarratives" (Lyotard) could lead to an intellectual rift between individuals that would last a lifetime and would produce stunning and beautiful, provocative and highly idiosyncratic works of theory that read like fiction.

And I feel that I am gradually turning into a Mr. Crick myself – out of joint with "my" time – a time which has become so much more complex, chaotic, and unfathomable, so much more difficult to theorize, so much less sure of the foundations that need "deconstructing," and which instead, in fact, increasingly deconstruct themselves, faster and faster. So Tom Crick's exasperation with the next generation is quickly becoming my own – it's turning into a generation game:

> I know what you feel. I know what you think, when you sit in your rows, in attitudes of boredom, listlessness, resentment, forbearance, desultory concentration. I know what all children think when submitted to the regimen of history lessons, to spooned-down doses of the past: "But what about Now? Now, we are Now. What about Now?"[6]

So in the face of this (postmodern) "legacy," the haunting of a life, the "here and now" lose their edge, and the future looks closed while the past opens up like a vast territory, inexhaustible and daunting. Daunting and haunting, history – the only thing that seemingly *is* – the sum of our material inscriptions or traces, the sum of our effects and affects and their bearings on materiality, the world and time – weighs me down.

So the postmodern is about the next generation, and thus about childhood and education. However, it would be a little rash to assume that this generation game is straightforward, in the sense: after the postmodern, the posthuman, or from postmodernism to posthumanism. This is why I'd like to return briefly to Lyotard – the thinker of the postmodern *par excellence*. His notion of childhood is far from romantic, however – it is quite the opposite of Rousseau's idea of the child as the unspoiled proto-human – instead the child for Lyotard is, in a very specific sense, "posthumanist," or, more precisely, the child is the embodiment of Lyotard's idea of the "inhuman":

> What shall we call human in humans, the initial misery of their childhood, or their capacity to acquire a "second" nature which, thanks to language, makes them fit to share in communal life, adult consciousness and reason? That the second depends on and presupposes the first is agreed by everyone. The question is only that of knowing whether this dialectic, whatever name we grace it with, leaves no remainder.[7]

Childhood as "remainder" is the crux of the "inhuman" for Lyotard, and it is also one of the main motivations behind his radical questioning of humanism. Moreover, it is that which drives the strange (temporal) logic that is at work in the prefix "post-" (whether that be the post in postmodern or posthuman):

> The child is eminently the human because its distress heralds and promises things possible. Its initial delay in humanity, which makes it the hostage of the adult community, is also what manifests to this community the lack of humanity it is suffering from, and which calls on it to become more human.[8]

The Inhuman is very much a reassessment of Lyotard's earlier work on the "post-" and demonstrates what might be called the "posthumanist" shift in his work. Lyotard is no longer convinced of the adequacy of the term "postmodern," which, by and large, has been misinterpreted as linear succession (namely quite simply as "after the modern"). However, Lyotard is more than ever convinced of the peculiar temporal logic that is at work in the prefix "post-," but, in *The Inhuman*, he is looking for ways of rearticulating this logic. We are thus dealing with Lyotard's very own attempt to reinscribe the "post-" of the postmodern into something that, today, is increasingly called (not the inhuman) but the posthuman.

Post-

In order to understand the discussion and theoretical controversies about the post/modern occurring during the second half of the twentieth century, one has therefore to explain the curious logic that arises out of the prefix "post-." This is all the more urgent since this logic also applies to the post/human and post/humanism (in what follows, I would therefore like to engage readers in a game of substitution: for "post/modern" read "post/human," for "postmodernism" read "post/humanism," etc.). The post/modern has a more complex logical and temporal relation with the modern than linearity and causality.[9] Instead of superseding the modern, the post/modern asks questions of modernity as that period within history that understands itself as the embodiment of novelty and progress. In particular, it queries how "newness" enters the world and thus asks about the modern politics of change. A modern attitude, according to its post/modern critique, always appropriates and incorporates the new, by assimilating it to its own categories. It only recognizes as "progress" what can be extrapolated and projected into the future and is thus governed by circularity and self-fulfilling prophecy. The post- hopes to inject a nonlinear and noncausal temporal and spatial relation into the modern dialectic of progress. In always anticipating change and reducing newness to a paradigm of similarity and difference (which creates a sense of the new as that which can only be experienced after the event and is therefore never new in the strict sense), modernity forecloses the arrival of the radically new (e.g. that which is even too modern to be modern). Post/modern, strictly speaking, gestures toward this alterity of the radically new as an *other* future.

This produces some very characteristic conceptual and stylistic or aesthetic moves in postmodernist literature, criticism, and theory. The motivation for these moves lies in the increasing impatience and frustration with the inter-minability of the "project" of modernity. This motivation is not so much concerned with the end of history as such, but rather with the question: what can be done for an *other* history to begin at last. In Peter Sloterdijk's words, (late) modernity is thus the time of the "epilogue": "On the one hand, modernity can perceive only the worst after itself; on the other hand, the worst lies precisely in its own course, which it prevents itself from leaving, because it holds no alternative to itself as thinkable."[10]

To understand the curious feeling of being postmodern is to see it as the expression of the sentiment of living somehow after the end, after surviving the last and living on, before the next apocalypse. Postmodern survival, or being "in-between," could be described as the time of waiting for the event, the birth of an entirely other history ("the birth of history from the spirit of deferral"[11]). The "untimeliness" of the postmodern feeling, as coming after the possibility of anything radically new, accounts for the sense of unreality and the temporal undecidability which is inscribed into the very paradox of the post-, namely as coming both before *and* after, at the same time.[12] The post- thus upsets the modern urge for periodization (before–after) by deconstructing the notion of "presence" or of the "here and now" (which would be necessary to establish a distinction between before and after, pre- and post-), as Lyotard explains:

> [I]t is impossible to determine the difference between what has taken place … and what comes along … without situating the flux of events with respect to a now. But it is no less impossible to grasp any such "*now*" since, because it is dragged away by what we call the flow of consciousness, the course of life, of things, of events, whatever – it never stops fading away. So that it is always both too soon and too late to grasp anything like a "now" in an identifiable way.[13]

Instead, the untimeliness of the postmodern gives way to a model of time, history, and change that stresses implication (or "entanglement" – a key concept of contemporary posthumanism). The postmodern is seen to inhabit the modern; it is always already contained in the modern which it thus anticipates:

> [T]he postmodern is always implied in the modern because of the fact that modernity, modern temporality, comprises in itself an impulsion to exceed itself into a state other than itself. And not only to exceed itself in that way, but to revolve itself into a sort of ultimate stability, such for example as is aimed at by the utopian project, but also by the straightforward political project implied in the grand narratives of emancipation. Modernity is constitutionally and ceaselessly pregnant with its postmodernity.[14]

The relation between the modern and the postmodern is therefore not chronological, but it relies on a particular understanding of repetition or remembering. It is in this sense that postmodernism understands itself as a re-writing of modernity, neither as a break nor as a simple succession, but as a working through (in the psychoanalytic sense) that occurs at once forward and backward "without finality."[15] This movement of back and forth within the process of "mourning" the initial forgetting of the unpresentable (modern) is what Lyotard refers to as anamnesis.[16]

The initial forgetting is the foreclosed or repressed origin of the modern (i.e. what needed to be repressed so that we could think of ourselves as "modern"). Against the modern ideology of the new, post-modernism sets its feeling of belatedness and parodic repetition in order to achieve a "stalling" of the continual process of anticipating and appropriating, often related to the economic practices of late modern capitalism and consumer society. Critical of the omnipotence of the "system" (modernity, capitalism, the media etc.), postmodern literature and art therefore often invoke the unsayable and unexpressible sublime and the radical otherness of the event in its radical futurity without any anticipation, as pure happening or performance. Coming at once too late and too soon – the phrase "this will have been new" – reflects the temporal contradiction within the postmodern as a process of ana-mnesis: the future as already contained in the past and vice versa. Postmodernism believes that it is only in the performativity of (re-) writing (or by creating its own rules) that an opening toward the future is created:[17]

> The artist and the writer therefore work without rules, and in order to establish the rules for what *will have been made*. This is why the work and the text can take on the properties of an event; it is also why they would arrive too late for their author or, in what amounts to the same thing, why their creation would always begin too soon. *Postmodern* would be understanding according to the paradox of the future (*post*) anterior (*modo*).[18]

The postmodern waiting for the absolute arrival or the Event is thus time gained for alternative histories to occur.[19]

So, postmodernist literature, criticism, and theory – one of the main characteristics of the "postmodern" is that these three discourses can no longer be distinguished – often give the impression that it is a kind of waiting for an impossible event (the "new" or unexpected other), while writing goes on and endlessly produces fiction, which writes about the (im)possibility of writing the event. There is a kind of performativity and circularity, sometimes even an apocalypticism that seeks to invoke, conjure up and somehow express the ineffable. This is also the reason why intertextuality, or the notion of the intertext, can be seen as one of the central presuppositions of many postmodernist theories and practices. Every text is not only an open system but is also never identical to itself. It is part of a system of textual relations, a form of generalized textuality which alone guarantees the readability of our cultural universe. Thus intertextuality is the very condition of perceiving social reality and therefore has quasi-ontological status. This also explains the proliferation of narratives about narratives, the fragmentation and loss, the dissemination of identities and the critique of the "unified self" in postmodernist writing. In a textual world where every fiction is only another text, metafictionality becomes virtually interchangeable with intertextuality. As Patricia Waugh explains, metafiction is "a term given to fictional writing which self-consciously and systematically draws attention to its status as an artefact in order to pose questions about the relationship between fiction and reality."[20]

In postmodernist fiction, both metafictionality and intertextuality are employed to demonstrate the constructed (or fictional) nature of human reality. In so doing, postmodernist metafiction serves an important "pedagogical" purpose in helping to understand contemporary ideas about reality, which can take a variety of negative and positive reactions: from experiencing the idea of general textuality as a "prisonhouse of language" to the "new forms of the fantastic, fabulatory extravaganzas" in magic realism (Salman Rushdie, Gabriel García Márquez, Clive Sinclair, Graham Swift, D. M. Thomas, John Irving).[21] The generalized notion of textuality thus often leads to a celebration of the power of fiction and fictionalization seen as equivalent to a reality- or world-building process. Some of the most frequent framing devices to be found in postmodernist metafiction thus include "stories within stories, characters reading about their own fictional lives, self-consuming worlds or mutually contradictory situations, Chinese-box structures," thus reaching the conclusion that there "is ultimately no distinction between 'framed' and 'unframed.' There are only levels of form. There is ultimately only content perhaps, but it will never be discovered in a 'natural' unframed state."[22]

This is also the reason why postmodernist metafictional novels often display a (meta)linguistic awareness and linguistic playfulness. Metafiction draws attention to the process of "recontextualization" that occurs when language is used aesthetically, so that their embraced conception of reality tends toward one of what Waugh calls the two "poles of metafiction," "one that finally accepts a substantial real world whose significance is not entirely composed of relationships within language; and one that suggests there can never be an escape from the prisonhouse of language and either delights or despairs in this."[23] Either they constitute a "parody" (or rather, the whole world is a parody), or they are predominantly "metafictional at the level of the signifier." One could say that it is the importance attributed to language as the only access to reality which assumes a crucial role in the reception of postmodernist fiction, criticism, and theory.

Alternative Histories

From a historical point of view (i.e. by "historicizing postmodernism and the postmodern"), what has been happening in this "meantime" (especially the last decades of the twentieth century) is a writing-on after the supposed end of (hi)story, which Fredric Jameson famously associated with the idea that postmodernism's extreme self-reflexivity, rather than providing any political resistance or critique, was in fact playing out the "logic of late capitalism."[24] So, how to "exit" modernity and postmodernism's endless critique of it?

It is clear that the "Great Narrative" of History – "the filler of vacuums, the dispeller of fears in the dark,"[25] the inescapable and self-reproducing cycle of (inter)textuality – is the bait for man, the "story-telling animal." But it is equally clear that "Reality" lies in the "Here and Now," which, however, remains inexpressible, for it is outside the story-telling and beyond (inter) textuality. Between these fragmentary moments of "Messianic time,"[26] which repeatedly crush the individual under their intensified feelings of joy or terror and "announce that time has taken us prisoner,"[27] is only the "Void." This void between moments of Reality, which are the moments of true revolution, has to be filled; and this is done by telling stories. The problem is that these surprise attacks of the Here and Now only become accessible *après coup* ("after the event"), that is, through remembering. And what else is memory than a story. So it happens that by the very attempt to arrest history in the here and now, it is necessary to tell the story of an end as a never-ending story.

The endless repetition of the same, however, must be resisted. History as the endless war of humanity against itself (after the war is only before the next war) must end. But how to stop a cycle on which one's own being and even one's thinking is dependent? How to stop telling stories? How to escape into the absolute Alterity of Un-History? History can only come to an end after the "death of man," the annihilation of the subject, but who would live to see it?[28] By thus invoking the arrival of this absolute alterity of an other history, writing becomes "performative," so to speak. Writing becomes writing about the end of writing, about its own exhaustion,[29] or its (impossible) abstention while waiting for the Event which would transcend all writing.

Pluralization is one option to escape this conundrum – there is not one (universal) history, but only histories in the plural (or "chronodiversity"[30]). With its pluralist ideals, postmodernism is radically opposed to universalist historiography, because historical discourse always depends on the exclusion of its silent others.[31] This is why the time of the postmodern coincides with a turn toward other histories: alternative, oppositional, and repressed histories. To preserve the futurity of the event as the experience of the other, and as the possibility of history, change, and justice in the future, involves an "affirmative experience of the coming of the other as other."[32] This is not in opposition to modernity, or a rejection of the past as inheritance or tradition; rather it is an affirmation of memory as essential for the process of working through the modern. For Jacques Derrida, the un(re)presentable moment of non-contemporaneity of the present with itself (or Swift's slippery "Here and Now") opens up the historical possibility for the very idea of justice, and it also makes the process of history possible, establishing a new relation with repetition and deferral.[33] But this historical moment cannot be thought of as unity or oneness; it is always "more-than-one," neither "here" nor "there" (nor "now"), like a ghost that inhabits the untimely, always escaping the present moment. What therefore comes "after history" is the return of this ghost; and postmodernist literature, criticism, and theory must therefore specialize in what Derrida calls "hauntology" (or, the ontology of the specter or the spectral):

> Repetition *and* first time: this is perhaps the question of the event as question of the ghost . . .. Repetition *and* first time, but also repetition *and* last time, since the singularity of any *first time* makes of it also a *last time*. Each time it is the event itself, a first time is a last time. Altogether other. Staging for the end of history. Let us call it a *hauntology* . . .. How to *comprehend* in fact the discourse of the end or the discourse about the end? . . . After the end of history, the spirit comes by *coming back* [*revenant*], it figures *both* a dead man who comes back and a ghost whose expected return repeats itself, again and again.[34]

Repetition starts with the return of a ghost (*revenant*, literally "one who returns"), by a feeling of *déjà vu*; and it is in the difference created by repetition that the singularity of the event can be perceived as an echo or trace. The discourse of the end of history is itself belated and of course only announces the end of a certain concept of (the end of) history. In the promise of the end of a certain history, the final becoming historical of history is thus merely announced.

It is thus only by embracing the problem of repetition that postmodernism can dissolve the teleology of the modern; for repetition involves difference, which is to say a foothold for critical distance: a transgression of mere repetition, which can be appropriated by parody or irony.[35] Repetition is also the very condition of knowledge, according to Gilles Deleuze, who reverses Freud's idea of the compulsion to repeat: it is not because one forgets/represses that one is forced to repeat or that the repressed returns, but it is because one repeats that one forgets. Repetition in this sense is a selection in which only difference returns while the same is eliminated during this process of selection. Only by affirming the process of repetition does one gain access to what is different. The logic of the psychoanalytic cure with its transference processes is based on this idea of repetition of the different and of a recognition *après coup* (namely by the doubling of the occurrence). Paradoxically, history can thus only be articulated in the future, and within the process of this articulation, a reorganization of the past and the future can occur. By transference, the past becomes the present so that the future can once more be an open question.

Repetition and trauma in a sense mutually create each other, so that memory can alter past events *après coup* by transforming the repressed into traumatic post-eventness. The symbolic process that takes place during the analysis expresses the anachronistic paradox of *Nachträglichkeit* (Freud's own term for *après coup*, or the way that recognition "follows after" the repressed event) in the future perfect: this will have been "it." Thus, paradoxically, one has to travel into the future to encounter the repressed (the past):

> From where does the repressed return? ... From the future. Symptoms are meaningless traces, their meaning is not discovered, excavated from the hidden depth of the past, but constructed retroactively – the analysis produces the truth; that is, the signifying frame which gives the symptoms their symbolic place and meaning. As soon as we enter the symbolic order, the past is always present in the form of historical tradition and the meaning of these traces is not given; it changes continually with the transformations of the signifier's network. Every historical rupture, every advent of a new master-signifier, changes retroactively the meaning of all tradition, restructures the narration of the past, makes it readable in another, new way.[36]

The cure works because knowledge is presupposed in the other (the subject-supposed-to-know), by which the subject hopes to gain insight into his/her own meaning. This knowledge is a necessary illusion (for the other, in fact, "lacks" it) until one finds out and constitutes it oneself *après coup*. The journey into the past, the historical enquiry can only occur on the symbolic level of the signifier, and only in language (or writing) can one know and bring about the past:

> This, therefore, is the basic paradox we are aiming at: the subject is confronted with a scene from the past that he wants to change, to meddle with, to intervene in; he takes a journey into the past, intervenes in the scene, and it is not that he "cannot change anything" – quite the contrary, only through his intervention does the scene from the past *become what it always was*: his intervention was from the beginning comprised, included. The initial "illusion" of the subject consists in simply forgetting to include in the scene his own act.[37]

This describes the form of historical repetition that gives rise to historicism as self-fulfilling prophecy. The subject necessarily overlooks his or her blind spot, in the way his or her acting is already part of the state of things he or she is looking at, the way his or her error is part of the truth itself. Truth arises from this misrecognition, by a change of the symbolic status of the event; repetition recreates the traumatic event as symbolic necessity *post factum*. It is a retroactive justification through repetition as interpretation, but there seems to be no shorter cut to the processes of truth-finding than through this form of misrecognition and repetition.

And this is precisely the point at which I would like to move, "forward" (but nothing is more certain), namely to the idea of the . . .

Posthuman

One post can hide another. Everything that was said about the post- in connection with the postmodern applies in principle to all post-isms, including the "latest" ones: posthuman, posthumanism, and posthumanization. Obviously, the stakes in post-human-ism have been raised again, and hence the sense of urgency of the ending invoked here usually has the effect that in engaging with the posthuman we tend to have even less time for the quite intricate logical and conceptual "side-effects" the posting process inevitably brings with it. Instead, there is now often exasperation with the postmodern or the impression of being stuck in a time-loop, something we can seemingly ill afford in a time when "we" are increasingly overtaken by "events." These events and their eventness – one of the main issues for postmodernist literature, criticism, and theory as outlined above – are usually associated, on the one hand, with technology (digitalization, virtualization, prosthetization, medicalization …), and, on the other hand, with extinction scenarios and thus with ecology.[38] Rosi Braidotti's book on the posthuman captures this current attitude very well:

> While conservative, religious social forces today often labor to re-inscribe the human within a paradigm of natural law, the concept of the human has exploded under the double pressure of contemporary scientific advances and global economic concerns. After the postmodern, the post-colonial, the post-industrial, the post-communist and even the much contested post-feminist, we seem to have entered the post-human predicament. Far from being the nth version in a sequence of prefixes that may appear both endless and arbitrary, the posthuman condition introduces a qualitative shift in our thinking about what exactly is the basic unit of common reference for our species, our polity and our relationship to the other inhabitants of this planet.[39]

Admittedly, anything that "posts" the human is raising the stakes much higher than the postmodern, but even something as drastic as the posthuman (the "figure") and posthumanism (the "discourse") is subject to the temporal logic of the "post," maybe even more so.[40] It is in this sense that posthumanism or the posthuman cannot just be understood as the follow-on, the super-session or the "outcome" of the postmodern and postmodernism. Instead they should be seen as co-implicated and entangled in their respective critiques of humanism. One simply cannot post one postism with another one – one just accumulates ghosts and increases the haunting.

The exasperation with the apparent immobilism of the postmodern in the face of the apparent (technological) acceleration of the posthuman is understandable, but should also be regarded with skepticism. In contemporary literature and criticism, this is often expressed in a desire for a "return," a "reconstruction" or "healing" in what is more and more frequently called the "post-postmodern" generation of writers (frequently named are David Foster Wallace, Toni Morrison, Jonathan Safran Foer, Mark Z. Danielewski, Michael Chabon, and David Mitchell).[41] It is, however, no coincidence that the contemporary discourse in literature, criticism, and (some) theory on the "reconstruction of the human" arises in the face of the "posthuman" (with its technological, economic, and ecological threats). It should rather be understood as a symptom of a desire that seeks to detach itself from postmodern antihumanism (the critique of the unified self) precisely at the time when this critique has in fact become the new "reality." With their insistence on existential or ontological plurality, the fragmentation of identity and a breaking up of aesthetic norms, the breaking up of narrative continuity and teleology, many postmodern texts are thus, one could argue, more radically "posthumanist" than their current successors.

Therefore, since in times of turns and returns memories tend to be selective, let me recall another, final aspect of the postmodern that might be necessary to caution against the ambient desire to embrace posthumanism as a form of post-postmodernist "reconstruction" or "rehumanization." Postmodernism has also been that time and that style that is most urgently concerned not only with the survival of humanity but also with the future of literature. The famous mixing of "high" and "low" (elite and popular) culture, the commentary on and the incorporation of other media ("intermediality") and science into the novel, the gradual embracing of hypertext and the advent of electronic literature – all become topics of storytelling at an increasingly self-conscious level, so that the figure of the posthuman (in all its guises) is the almost natural "step" for narrative fiction. However, it might also be a step too far for literature in the sense that, from a media-history point of view, established literary practices and genres might no longer be able to "compete" with new media and virtual reality technology and might therefore be no longer at the forefront of cultural change. Posthumanist literature might thus be a contradiction in terms. So be careful what you wish for. . . . In the meantime, however, let me tell you one last story, namely the one of the . . .

Future of Literature

In good old literary-humanist fashion, and befitting the mindset of a (late) literary scholar, the final word should go (as ever) to literature – literature as that discourse which arguably has the privilege of being purely speculative and thus being able to say "anything."[42] I will give the last word to the history man, Mr. Crick, and outline the questions that a *critical* posthumanism (mindful of the temporalities at work in any present) might be able to raise:

> Children, only animals live entirely in the Here and Now. Only nature knows neither memory nor history. But man – let me offer you a definition – is the story-telling animal.[43]

We know that we will have to tell stories differently from now on – neither animality nor nature justify human exceptionalism. "We" are no longer alone and we never were, of course. In fact, we are no longer "we." What remains of humanism is a certain yearning that continues to be the target of a *critical* posthumanism, by which I mean an ongoing deconstruction of humanism that extends both to the constructions of the past and of the future, the always already and the never yet, with all the thinkable shadings in between, to preserve: let's call it a kind of "care," not for the self, but for the "other" – the other human, or maybe Lyotard's "inhuman," that might or might not make us human. I can hear this, nostalgic, slightly "tragic," yearning in moving passages like these:

> Children, be curious. Nothing is worse (I know it) than when curiosity stops. Nothing is more repressive than the repression of curiosity. Curiosity begets love. It weds us to the world. It's part of our perverse, madcap love for this impossible planet we inhabit. People die when curiosity goes. People have to find out, people have to know. How can there be any true revolution till we know what we're made of?[44]

The question is, since we now seem to know that there won't be a revolution: should we preserve this human(ist) "curiosity"? And can we ever trust this desire, this yearning, to find out "what we're made of"? In the end, in reevaluating and historicizing the postmodern and its critique of modernity, humanism, and "Western" metaphysics, in the face of the impatience of the posthuman, a critical posthumanism, whose task is "rewriting humanity," needs to be aware of the complex temporalities opened up by the "time of the posts" and remember that we haven't finished with the human yet, and that we're far from ready to "move on."

NOTES

1. Jean-François Lyotard, *The Postmodern Explained to Children: Correspondence 1982–1985* (London: Turnaround, 1992).
2. Cf. Francis Fukuyama's influential neo-Hegelian book bearing this title and the controversial discussion about utopianism, apocalypticism, and liberalism it provoked: Fukuyama, *The End of History and the Last Man* (London: Hamish Hamilton, 1992).
3. Cf. Linda Hutcheon's famous characterization of postmodernist writing as "historiographic metafiction," in *A Poetics of Postmodernism: History, Theory, Fiction* (Abingdon: Routledge, 1988).
4. Frank Kermode, *The Sense of an Ending* (Oxford: Oxford University Press, 1966).
5. *Waterland*, dir. Stephen Gyllenhaal, Optimum Home Entertainment, 2006.
6. Graham Swift, *Waterland* (London: Picador, 1991), 60.
7. Jean-François Lyotard, *The Inhuman: Reflections on Time*, trans. G. Bennington and R. Bowlby (Cambridge: Polity Press, 1991), 3.
8. *Ibid.*, 4.
9. Cf. Elizabeth Deeds Ermarth, *Sequel to History: Postmodernism and the Crisis of Representational Time* (Princeton: Princeton University Press, 1992), 3–18.
10. Peter Sloterdijk, *Eurotaoismus: Zur Kritik der politischen Kinetik* (Frankfurt: Suhrkamp, 1989), 292.
11. *Ibid.*, 277.

12. Jean-François Lyotard, "Answer to the Question: What is the Postmodern?," in *The Postmodern Explained*, 22.
13. Lyotard, "Rewriting Modernity," in *The Inhuman*, 24–25.
14. *Ibid.*, 25.
15. *Ibid.*, 24, 30.
16. Lyotard, "Note on the Meaning of 'Post-'," in *The Postmodern Explained*, 93.
17. See David Wood, "Introduction: Editing the Future," in *Writing the Future*, ed. Wood (London: Routledge, 1990).
18. Lyotard, *The Postmodern Explained*, 24.
19. For many, this event finally arrived on September 11, 2001, but that is another story.
20. Patricia Waugh, *Metafiction: The Theory and Practice of Self-Conscious Fiction* (London: Methuen, 1984), 2.
21. *Ibid.*, 9.
22. *Ibid.*, 31.
23. *Ibid.*, 53.
24. Fredric Jameson, *Postmodernism, or, the Cultural Logic of Late Capitalism* (London: Verso, 1991).
25. Swift, *Waterland*, 62.
26. Cf. Walter Benjamin, "Theses on the Philosophy of History," in *Illuminations* (London: Fontana, 1973), 253–64.
27. Swift, *Waterland*, 61.
28. This is one of the main paradoxes of the proliferating "World-Without-Us" scenarios and one of the main symptoms of posthumanism, understood as post-anthropocentrism. See e.g. Matthew Taylor, *Universes Without Us: Posthuman Cosmologies in American Literature* (Minneapolis: University of Minnesota Press, 2013).
29. Cf. John Barth, *The Literature of Exhaustion and the Literature of Replenishment* (Northridge, CA: Lord John Press, 1982).
30. Cf. Paul Virilio, *The Futurism of the Instant: Stop-Eject* (Cambridge: Polity Press, 2010), 71, 101.
31. Michel de Certeau, *The Writing of History*, trans. T. Conley (New York and Chichester: Columbia University Press, 1988).
32. Jacques Derrida, "The Destruction of Actuality: An Interview with Jacques Derrida," *Radical Philosophy* 68 (Autumn 1994): 36.
33. See Jacques Derrida, *Specters of Marx: The State of the Debt, the Work of Mourning, and the New International*, trans. Peggy Kamuf, intro. Bernd Magnus and Stephen Cullenberg (New York: Routledge, 1994).
34. *Ibid.*, 10.
35. Gilles Deleuze, *Difference and Repetition*, trans. Paul Patton (London: Athlone Press, 1994), 5.
36. Slavoj Žižek, *The Sublime Object of Ideology* (London: Verso, 1989), 55–56.
37. *Ibid.*, 57–58.
38. For a good summary of the implications of this argument and its relation to the notion of the "Anthropocene," see Claire Colebrook's "Introduction: Framing the End of the Species," in her edited volume *Extinction*, available at: www.livingbooksaboutlife.org/books/Extinction. See also her chapter in this volume.
39. Rosi Braidotti, *The Posthuman* (Cambridge: Polity Press, 2013), 1–2.

40. See my *Posthumanism: A Critical Analysis* (London: Bloomsbury, 2013).

41. Cf. in particular Nicoline Timmer, *Do You Feel It Too? The Post-Postmodern Syndrome in American Fiction at the Turn of the Millennium* (Amsterdam: Rodopi, 2010); Kim L. Worthington, *Self as Narrative: Subjectivity and Community in Contemporary Fiction* (Oxford: Clarendon Press, 1996); and Irmtraud Huber, *Literature after Postmodernism* (Houndmills: Palgrave Macmillan, 2014).

42. Jacques Derrida, "'The Strange Institution Called Literature': An Interview with Jacques Derrida," in *Acts of Literature*, ed. Derek Attridge (London: Routledge, 1992), 33–75.

43. Swift, *Waterland*, 62.

44. *Ibid.*, 206.

PART II

Posthuman Literary Modes

6

LISA YASZEK
AND
JASON W. ELLIS

Science Fiction

Widescale debates over the notion of posthumanity emerged in the late twentieth century in response to the possibilities suggested by cybernetics, genetics, nanotechnology, pharmacology, and computer simulation. However, authors of science fiction (SF) have told stories for well over two centuries about technologically enhanced and augmented people. Indeed, as Ron Broglio suggested earlier in this volume, Mary Shelley explored this concept as early as 1818 in her pioneering novel *Frankenstein*. Additionally, one of the first recorded uses of the word "posthuman" appears in H. P. Lovecraft's 1936 novella *The Shadow Out of Time*.[1] Over the course of the genre's history, SF authors have typically fashioned images of the posthuman in one of two ways. Throughout the nineteenth and early twentieth centuries, stories about the posthuman dramatized Enlightenment ideas about unlimited perfectibility, extrapolating from developments in surgery and theories of evolution to explore what might happen if the human body was the base upon which to create new species. Since World War II, inspired by cognitive science and computational technologies, SF writers have explored the mutability and multiplicity of the human condition, treating the organic body as just one of several mediums for one or more re-engineered, posthuman species. However, even as they propose very different models of enhanced or augmented bodies and very different posthuman futures, SF authors have shared a commitment to issues of ethics and social justice that have long haunted human society and that may be amplified by its posthuman successors.

Progress and Perfectibility

Speculation about the posthuman emerged in the Enlightenment in tandem with new notions of the human. Some seventeenth- and eighteenth-century thinkers celebrated the human subject as "a being with a unique essence whose goal was self-realization."[2] This unique self was housed in an equally unique physical body that, in an ideal world, would interact with social institutions designed to foster the individual's self-actualization. At the same time, the emphasis on materialist empiricism that characterized much Enlightenment thinking led philosophers such as Julien Offray de la Mettrie and the Marquis de Condorcet to propose that human beings, like animals and machines, had "no bounds ... fixed to the improvement of their faculties" and thus that "the perfectibility of man is unlimited."[3] Much like some contemporary advocates of the post- and transhuman, such thinkers did not see modern humans as the endpoint of some grand religious or scientific plan but as the raw material from which to make whole new species.

Stories engaging Enlightenment ideas of unlimited perfectibility dominated the first century of science fictional speculation. In the early 1800s, authors Mary Shelley, Nathaniel Hawthorne, and Edgar Allan Poe drew on the discovery of pharmaceuticals such as morphine and digitalis, the creation of prosthetics designed to simulate natural movement, and the public fascination with electromagnetism to critically assess the Enlightenment dream of unlimited perfectibility. Their Gothic SF stories about mad scientists who disastrously attempt to improve themselves and their loved ones undermined "our species confidence that we are capable of bearing all knowledge," especially as it pertains to the manipulation of human nature.[4] Shelley's "The Mortal Immortal" (1833) and Hawthorne's "The Birthmark" (1843) and "Rappuchini's Daughter" (1844) all revolve around male scientists who abandon the standards of their communities in the quest to create elixirs that will cure mental and physical defects. Each fails because he cannot control a nature he does not fully understand. In a slightly different vein, Poe's satiric "The Man That Was Used Up" (1839) presents readers with the figure of a dashing war hero who turns out to be nothing but a heap of helpless, jabbering rags without the extensive collection of prostheses he has accumulated from a lifetime of war campaigns. The grotesque posthuman body here, then, represents not just the mad dream of a single, egotistical scientist, but the horrifying madness of an entire society bent on military domination.

While most SF stories about posthumanity from this period are in dialog with new technological developments, the most famous of these – Mary Shelley's *Frankenstein* (1818) – engages new scientific theories as well. Shelley invokes modern surgical techniques and electromagnetic manipulation to show how planned intervention into human nature might bring about the end of human life altogether. The problem stems from Victor Frankenstein's dream of a perfect new race versus the reality of the strong, smart, but incredibly ugly posthuman being he creates. When the creature asks for a mate, a terrified Frankenstein refuses. In retaliation, Victor's creation methodically kills all the children and women in his creator's life. Significantly, Shelley buttresses her warning about the dangers of bad technological practice with references to cutting-edge scientific theory. As critic Anne Mellor argues, Shelley evokes Erasmus Darwin's theories concerning the evolutionary advantage of paired reproduction over solitary paternal reproduction to suggest that Frankenstein fails because he embraces the wrong model of reproduction and thus the wrong kind of technoscientific practice.[5]

Early SF and Evolution

The evolutionary theme implicit in *Frankenstein* would become explicit in many of the SF stories published between 1880 and 1945. This period marked both the establishment of SF as a distinct popular genre with its own authors, stylistic conventions, and publishing venues, and the height of debate over Charles Darwin's ideas about the origins of humanity. The wide variety of responses to Darwin marking public discourse at this time – including scientific debates about Darwinian versus other theories of evolution, popular fascination with the notion of social Darwinism, and political rereadings of Darwin in the name of progressive change – are all dramatized in SF stories. But while Shelley and her contemporaries offered critical assessments of the Enlightenment dream of human perfection, turn-of-the-century authors explored various modes of evolutionary philosophy, creating a diverse range of new story forms to tell about the creation of posthuman futures.

Such diversity is apparent in the two great British SF novels bookending this period: H. G. Wells's *The Time Machine* (1895) and Olaf Stapleton's *Last and First Men* (1930). Wells's time travel story, in which the scientist invents a device "to help apprehend the distant future of humanity," assesses social Darwinism as a solution to the problems of Victorian-era social stratification and industrial growth.[6] After traveling to the year 802,701 AD, where he encounters the beautiful but helpless Eloi living among the ruins of a great technological civilization, and the ugly but handy Morlocks who both care for and eat the Eloi, Wells's narrator pessimistically concludes that while industrial society may produce a temporary utopia, "the two species that had resulted from the evolution of man" suggest that such a utopia cannot last, but will eventually result in the stagnation and demise of all sentient life.[7] In contrast, through a series of loosely linked stories spanning vast stretches of time, Stapledon's more optimistic far-future history dramatizes Henri Bergson's theory of creative evolution, an alternative to Darwinism that links evolution to a natural creative impetus or *élan vital.*[8] *Last and First Men* imagines that the creative spirit linking successive human species enables the inhabitants of Earth to overcome various natural and technological disasters and create a race of multi-gendered, telepathic, space-faring posthumans. Stapledon's novel is notable as one of the first SF stories to imagine that humans might transform themselves in two very different ways. Many characters hew to what were by then well-established arguments about the human body as the only material needed to develop new species, proposing that science and technology be used to reengineer humanity "without introducing anything new in its [physical] essence." Other characters, however, advocate a more radical reengineering of the human body to introduce entirely new physical and mental attributes, thereby ensuring the creation of a species "which shall be no mere bundle of relics left over from its primitive ancestors."[9] In doing so, *Last and First Men* anticipates one of the central debates in posthumanist philosophy today.

Perhaps, due to both their shorter national history and their greater faith in science and engineering, turn-of-the-century American authors used the utopian form to show how humans might make great strides toward the dream of unlimited perfectibility in a few short centuries. Like their scientific counterparts Arabella Buckley and Eliza Burt Gamble, feminist authors Mary E. Bradley Lane and Charlotte Perkins Gilman revised Darwinian ideas about sexual selection to celebrate cooperation over competition and the role of female choice in breeding for a better species. George S. Schuyler's *Black Empire* (1936–38) roguishly prophesies the coming of a diasporic African super-race that invents, battles, and builds itself into what is, from its creators' perspective, a utopian superpower. As the mastermind behind this empire notes, such a turn of events was inevitable: because only the strongest and smartest Africans survived the previous three centuries of slavery and exploitation, modern blacks are, in essence, a whole new race characterized by "superior energy, superior vitality ... [and] intense hatred and resentment" of white people.[10] Thus, Schuyler invokes a kind of compressed Darwinism to show how the dystopic institution of slavery might unintentionally force the evolution of posthumanity along racial lines.

Tales of planned evolution also flourished in the American genre magazines of this era. The tradition of using gothic SF to critique technoscientific intervention into human nature continued with stories such as Clare Winger Harris's "The Evolutionary Monstrosity" (1929), Edmond Hamilton's "The Man Who Evolved" (1931), and Dorothy Quick's "Strange Orchids" (1937). Meanwhile, time travel stories such as Grant Allen's "Pallinghurst Barrow" (1892) and Harry Bates's "Alas, All Thinking!" (1935) reiterated Wells's concern that evolution will lead first to posthuman utopia and then to the death of all sentient life. In a happier vein, future histories including

J. B. S. Haldane's "The Last Judgment" (1927), Laurence Manning's "The Man Who Awoke" (1933), and E. E. "Doc" Smith's Lensman series (1934–54) share Stapledon's belief in the possibility of planned evolution over massive timescales. Similarly, feminist utopias including Leslie F. Stone's "Out of the Void" (1929) and Lilith Lorraine's "Into the 28th Century" (1930) echo the work of earlier feminist authors in their depictions of cooperative action and female-led mating schemes as key to the creation of brilliant, beautiful, and immortal posthuman populations. Finally, C. L. Moore's famous "No Woman Born" (1934), like Stapledon's *Last and First Men*, dramatizes differing attitudes toward posthumanity through debate between a scientist, who believes that by transplanting a severely burned actress's brain into a mechanical body he has created a subhuman creature, and the actress herself, who delights in her posthuman strength, agility, and sexuality. Taken together, such stories demonstrate both the diversity and the coherence of turn-of-the-century thinking about the technological transformation of humanity.

Mid-Century SF and the Mutational Romance

In response to social and technoscientific developments of mid-century America, authors associated with the early SF specialist magazines also developed an important new story form about posthumanity: what SF critics Brian Stableford and David Langford describe as the "mutational romance," in which either the purposeful or accidental manipulation of individual genes produces "a better and saner breed of humans."[11] Eugenic debates over the treatment of the "unfit" in the 1930s, combined with public condemnation of Nazi programs and growing awareness about the effects of radiation on the survivors of Hiroshima and Nagasaki in the 1940s and 1950s, led authors interested in evolution and posthumanity to change topics from stories about eugenics to those about mutation.[12] In some of the most famous stories of this period, including A. E. Van Vogt's *Slan* (1940), Arthur C. Clarke's *Childhood's End* (1953), and Theodore Sturgeon's *More Human Than Human* (1953), posthumanity emerges from "natural mutations" that occur over the course of just one or two generations.[13] In others, such as Judith Merril's "That Only a Mother" (1948), Lewis Padgett's *Mutant* (1953), and Phyllis Gottleib's *Sunburst* (1964), a mutated posthumanity appears as the accidental side effect of human experiments with atomic energy. As one of Padgett's telepathic posthumans puts it, radioactive fallout "brought us telepaths into being ahead of our normal mutation time."[14] Whichever means of mutation they wrote about, mid-century authors agreed that the superiority of posthumans over their mundane counterparts would be characterized by the development of telepathic powers that enabled *homo superior* to connect and genuinely collaborate with fellow mutants.

Even more than their counterparts writing for the first generation of specialist magazines, mid-century SF authors celebrated the coming of the posthuman future. Yet they retained an acute awareness of the persecution such beings were likely to face from their human counterparts. The posthumans of Van Vogt's and Padgett's novels spend much of their time hiding from human pogroms, while those populating Sturgeon's and Gottleib's stories must survive abandonment, homelessness, and institutionalization before they find one another. But perhaps the most chilling condemnation of human prejudice against change appears in domestic SF stories such as Merril's "That Only a Mother" (1948), Carol Emshwiller's "Day at the Beach" (1959), and Mary Armock's "First Born" (1960), all of which use human mothers' experiences with posthuman children as the occasion to comment on the gendered nature of social injustice in contemporary society.[15] In each story, a woman living in the wake of World War III discovers that her baby is something other and, from her perspective, quite possibly more-than-human. While each secretly recognizes her child's difference, she must try to hide it from a world that ruthlessly kills such children – including those fathers who "do it" to their children so they quite literally do not have to face the consequences of their technoscientific sins.[16] Taken together, such stories echo the claims of mid-century civil rights and peace activists who argued that the United States could not properly call itself a democracy as long as it denied equal rights to large segments of its population.

New Wave SF

While mutation and its hard-science progenitor, nuclear weaponry, captured the popular imagination through much of the mid-twentieth century, scientists in the so-called soft sciences of psychology, sociology, and anthropology were establishing the significance of their disciplines for understanding the human condition. These developments laid the foundation for the coming "cognitive revolution" and the inauguration of the cognitive sciences as a way to understand the human brain and its relationship to computational technology.[17] SF writers seized on the narrative possibilities of these inward-focused sciences to produce new modes of literary and experimental SF. For many authors associated with what came to be called "New Wave SF," posthuman cyborgs and other technologically augmented beings could explore how the planned transformation of both brains and bodies might challenge our understandings of what it means to be human. Such characters include the surgically modified, superintelligent Charlie Gordon in Daniel Keyes's *Flowers for Algernon* (1966); the genetically modified hermaphrodites of Ursula K. Le Guin's *The Left Hand of Darkness* (1969); the neutered Spacers of Samuel R. Delany's "Aye, and Gomorrah ..." (1967); the sympathetic cyborg brainship of Anne McCaffrey's *The Ship Who Sang* (1969); the biotech-enhanced cyborgs found in John Varley's *The Persistence of Vision* (1978); and the tortuous artificial intelligence (AI) known as AM in Harlan Ellison's "I Have No Mouth and I Must Scream" (1967).

The work of Philip K. Dick connects earlier mutational romances to New Wave SF through explorations of the posthuman as both a cognitive and a physical transformation. In many of his stories, nuclear technologies and modern pharmaceuticals produce posthuman beings with physical abnormalities as well as special cognitive abilities including precognition, telekinesis, and telepathy. For example, in *Dr. Bloodmoney, or How We Got Along after the Bomb* (1965), Bill, Edie Keller's telepathic twin brother and *fetus in fetu*, saves his community by defeating megalomaniacal telekinetic phocomelus Hoppy Harrington. Dick created an even more striking mutation story in "The Golden Man" (1954), in which mutants born with special powers and body types are hunted under the auspices of maintaining humanity's genetic purity. Cris Johnson, one such mutant, after impregnating the fiancée of his captor, uses his precognitive and persuasive powers to escape capture and thus secure his posthuman genetic line. In other stories, Dick focuses on artificial beings. For example, *Do Androids Dream of Electric Sheep?* (1968) features the uncanny Nexus-6 androids. Nearly indistinguishable from human beings, these androids escape their brutal human masters and flee to Earth, where they are "retired" or killed by bounty hunter Rick Deckard. As in many of Dick's fictions, *Androids* explores how emotion and empathy define humanity, and in this novel, the author problematizes the human–posthuman dichotomy by revealing the posthuman androids to be in some ways more empathic than their human creators. The character of J. R. Isidore, a human "special" who has been genetically injured by nuclear fallout, connects *Androids* to earlier mutant stories. While mundane by comparison to the posthuman beings of earlier SF, Isidore's special ability to empathize with animal, human, and artificial life sets him equally apart from both the other characters in Dick's novel and those found throughout the early history of SF as a whole.[18]

While Dick focuses on the cognitive posthuman, Frederik Pohl's *Man Plus* (1976) investigates the importance of embodiment to posthuman transformation. Following the death of the first Mars-destined cyborg, Roger Torraway undergoes an invasive cognitive alteration to support the sensory information received from a body that has been redesigned to survive Mars's environment.[19] As his brain changes in response to his new body and its interaction with the Mars environment, Torraway is forced to come to terms with his waning humanity and his emergent otherness. And while Pohl's *Man Plus* reveals how posthuman experience depends on embodiment designed for a given environment, Joseph McElroy's *Plus* (1977) explores how the Imp Plus, a disembodied human brain hooked into the control systems of an observation platform orbiting Earth, awakens from its wired existence to regain language, thought, and memories, repurposing its supportive technology to build itself a posthuman body for its own ends instead of those of its former controllers.

Cyberpunk and AI

By the early 1980s, with the culmination of mid-century work in the fields of genetics, nanotechnology, computer science, and engineering, the scientific and technical possibilities for posthuman existence seemed poised to outpace the SF imagination. Furthermore, the operation of "Moore's Law" led to the democratizing "digital revolution" of the 1980s and thus the beginning of the Information Age.[20] The imaginative possibilities of computers, genetic engineering, and nanotechnology seized the attention of a generation of SF writers labeled the cyberpunks, including William Gibson, Bruce Sterling, and Pat Cadigan. Much cyberpunk writing interrogates how human bodies are transformed and artificial beings are created by late twentieth-century technologies including AI, artificial life, genetic engineering, nanotechnology, and virtual reality. SF stories in this vein include Pat Cadigan's *Synners* (1991), which depicts a rundown future dependent on cybernetic enhancements for computer and interpersonal connections; Richard Powers's *Galatea 2.2* (1995), which explores the nature of consciousness through the story of a human teacher to an emergent AI; Bruce Sterling's *Schismatrix Plus* (1996), which confronts the ideological conflict between biologically and technologically mediated posthumans; and Greg Egan's *Diaspora* (1997), which dramatizes the relations of citizens (human and artificial beings running as disembodied, software simulations), gleisner robots (AI embodied within robotic bodies), and fleshers (genetically modified and unmodified human beings). Other stories that explore how nanotechnology might transform humanity include the engineering of human lymphocytes into intelligent cells that manipulate and change human bodies in Greg Bear's *Blood Music* (1985), and the unexpected destabilization of human identity and ontology by complex nanotechnological systems in Kathleen Ann Goonan's *Nanotech Quartet* (1994–2002).

Cyberpunk stories also consider other forms of technologically augmented existence. This is particularly evident in William Gibson's influential novel *Neuromancer* (1984). While many characters in Gibson's novel, including the AIs Wintermute and Neuromancer, the ROM construct of the deceased McCoy "Dixie Flatline" Pauley, and even the human hacker Case, who longs to escape "the prison of his own flesh," represent the posthuman as digital and disembodied, other characters, including the cyborg "razorgirl" Molly and the clone Lady 3 Jane Marie-France Tessier-Ashpool, depict the posthuman as biological and embodied.[21] As historian of science Timothy Lenoir argues in regard to the larger debate between embodied and disembodied posthuman experience, the novel's ambiguous ending suggests that we "need not simply acquiesce in a view of the posthuman as an apocalyptic erasure of human subjectivity, for the posthuman can be made to stand for a positive partnership between nature, humans, and intelligent machines."[22]

Responding to real-world technological developments and building on cyberpunk narratives are SF stories constructed around the anticipated moment of technological transcendence termed the "Singularity." Originally proposed by the mathematician and SF writer Vernor Vinge, the Singularity is "a hypothetical point in time at which human technology – in particular computers, AI super-intelligence and human intelligence amplification via computer interfacing or perhaps drugs – similarly accelerates 'off the map' into unpredictable regions,"[23] or as Vinge describes, "a point where our old models must be discarded and a new reality rules."[24] In his novel *The Cassini Division* (1998), Ken MacLeod lightheartedly calls it "the Rapture of the Nerds."[25] The posthumans of what is often called post-Singularity SF include the spatially stratified intelligences in Vinge's *A Fire Upon the Deep* (1992); the genetically modified children who do not need sleep in Nancy Kress's *Beggars in Spain* (1993); the disembodied humans and AIs cohabitating in a solar system-wide nanotechnology-based computing system in Charles Stross's *Accelerando* (2005); and the range of characters who cheerfully and comedically navigate a world always in flux in Cory Doctorow and Charles Stross's *The Rapture of the Nerds: A Tale of the Singularity, Posthumanity, and Awkward Social Situations* (2012).

Feminist SF

Reimagining the posthuman cyborg in political terms, in "The Cyborg Manifesto" (1985), Donna Haraway argues for the appropriation of the cyborg as an emblem of progressive possibility: "a cybernetic organism [is] a hybrid of machine and organism, a creature of social reality as well as a creature of fiction. Social reality is lived social relations, our most important political construction, a world-changing fiction."²⁶ Not surprisingly, Haraway identifies feminist SF as particularly important in this respect. As we have noted throughout this chapter, since Mary Shelley published *Frankenstein* in 1818, women have made significant contributions to speculative fiction, especially as it explores the promises and perils of posthumanity. But it was not until the advent of the women's liberation movement in the 1960s and development of an overtly politicized feminist SF in the 1970s that cyborg politics becomes central to stories about science, technology, and gender. Inspired by the legalization of the birth-control pill and early successes with artificial insemination, the first generation of feminist SF stories, including Joanna Russ's *The Female Man* (1974), Marge Piercy's *Woman on the Edge of Time* (1976), and Suzy McKee Charnas's Motherlines series (1974–1999), imagine distinctly posthuman and non-patriarchal futures, where new reproductive technologies enable women to reorganize the relations of science, society, and sexuality in surprising new ways. The second-generation feminist SF writers, including cyberpunks such as Pat Cadigan, post-Singularity authors such as Kathleen Ann Goonan, and Afrofuturist writers such as Octavia Butler, build upon the work of their predecessors by exploring how both new information technologies and other issues of social justice – including civil rights and environmental issues – might impact the production of posthumanist feminist futures. Taken together, such works depict how posthuman alliances with the nonhuman, which includes aliens and artificial beings, might produce modes of psychological and social organization that secure justice better than did earlier, human-oriented modes of political activism.²⁷

Two particularly compelling examples of feminist SF in this vein are Russ's *The Female Man* and Butler's Xenogenesis trilogy (1987–89). *The Female Man* explores affinity politics among four women of "the same genotype, modified by age, by circumstances, by education, by diet, by learning, by God knows what" from four different "worlds of possibility," including Joanna, who is from a world much like our own; Jeannine, who is from a world that never escaped the Great Depression; Janet, who is from a utopian planet populated only by women called Whileaway; and Jael, who is from a world at war between the sexes.²⁸ While Joanna and Jeannine live in worlds where sexual reproduction and discrimination operate much as they do in our own lives, Janet is the impossibly happy, healthy, and sane posthuman product of an all-female society that embraces technologically enabled reproduction and allows women to pursue both feminine and masculine endeavors. Meanwhile, the deadly cyborg assassin Jael – who refuses the horrifying reproductive logic of her own world in favor of sterile but satisfying sexual relations with her computer-ape hybrid housekeeper Davy – travels through time and space to coordinate the multiverse revolution that will eventually transform Joanna and Jeannine's worlds and produce Janet's future.

Butler's trilogy builds upon the concerns of first-generation feminist SF authors by connecting issues of technologically mediated reproduction to issues of physical and cultural information transfer. It critiques both sexual and racial otherness through the postapocalyptic tale of an alliance between those humans who have survived World War III and the Oankali, a three-sex, alien, genetic engineering species with a drive to diversify its genetic variation and be always "post" as they trade genes with other lifeforms.[29] The negotiated affinity politics between humanity's remnants and the Oankali provides the promise of renewal and discovery for humanity but at the loss of genetic and cultural heritage. Over the course of the series, the Oankali transform protagonist Lilith Iyapo into an androgynous posthuman, which enables her to facilitate new relations between the two groups but also provokes anxiety about her waning connection to humanity. When he is kidnapped by human rebels who resist integration with the Oankali, Lilith's human-Oankali or "construct" son Akin learns to appreciate and leverage his own hybridity. And Lilith's later construct child Jodahs, the first human-born third-sex "Ooloi" capable of genetically reengineering himself and others, comes to terms with the radically new subjectivity of his metamorphic body. While the Oankali offer humanity's survivors a way forward through posthuman transformation, Butler's posthuman characters must come to terms with the past before they can forge new relationships among themselves, the Oankali, and those human beings who have been left unchanged. In this way, Russ's and Butler's feminist SFs are emblematic of most literary posthumanist SF. Only by reconciling with the injustices and mistakes of the past can new, hopefully better versions of humanity create a potentially better future. As such, feminist SF encapsulates the imaginative force of all posthumanist SF to critique the human past and present by imagining what humanity might become in the future.

NOTES

1. Jeff Prucher, *Brave New Words: The Oxford Dictionary of Science Fiction* (Oxford: Oxford University Press, 2009), 154.
2. Stuart Sim, "Posthumanism," in *The Icon Critical Dictionary of Postmodern Thought*, ed. Stuart Sim (London: Icon Books, 1998), 337.
3. Christopher C. Hook, "Transhumanism and Posthumanism," in *Encyclopedia of Bioethics*, 3rd edn., ed. Stephen Garrard Post (New York: MacMillan Reference, 2004), 2517.
4. Peter Nicholls and John Clute, "Gothic SF," *The Encyclopedia of Science Fiction*, last modified December 7, 2014, www.sf-encyclopedia.com/entry/gothic_sf.

5. Anne K. Mellor, *Mary Shelley: Her Life, Her Fiction, Her Monsters* (New York: Methuen, 1988), 97.

6. Ralph Pordzik, "The Posthuman Future of Man: Anthropocentrism and the Other of Technology in Anglo-American Science Fiction," *Utopian Studies* 23.1 (2012): 145.

7. H. G. Wells, *The Time Machine* (1895), *Project Gutenberg*, accessed on January 11, 2015.

8. Brian M. Stableford and David Langford, "Evolution," *The Encyclopedia of Science Fiction*, last modified February 12, 2015, www.sf-encyclopedia.com /entry/evolution.

9. Olaf Stapledon, *Last and First Men: A Story of the Near and Far Future* (New York: Penguin, 2014), Originally published in 1930, Loc. 3483, 3503, Kindle.

10. George S. Schulyer, *Black Empire* (Boston: Northeastern University Press, 1991). Originally published as *Black Internationale and Black Empire*, 1936–38, 15.

11. Brian M. Stableford and David Langford, "Mutants," *The Encyclopedia of Science Fiction*, last modified September 10, 2014, www.sf-encyclopedia.com /entry/mutants.

12. Jay Clayton, "The Ridicule of Time: Science Fiction, Bioethics, and the Posthuman." *American Literary History* 25.2 (Summer 2013): 323.

13. A. E. Van Vogt, *Slan* (New York: Berkley, 1963), 175.

14. Lewis Padgett, *Mutant* (New York: Ballantine, 1953), 146.

15. For further explanation of domestic SF as a mode of storytelling that uses the family and the home as a focusing lens through which to explore the relations of science, technology, and society, see Lisa Yaszek's *Galactic Suburbia* (Columbus, OH: Ohio State University Press, 2008), and "A Parabola of Her Own: Mapping the Domestic Science Fiction Story," in *Parabolas of Science Fiction*, ed. Brian Attebery and Veronica Hollinger (Middletown, CT: Wesleyan University Press, 2013), 106–24.

16. Judith Merril, "That Only a Mother," in *Science Fiction Hall of Fame*, ed. Robert Silverberg (New York: Avon, 1970), 351. See also Kinga Földvary, "In Search of a Lost Future: The Posthuman Child," *European Journal of English Studies* 18.2: www.tandfonline.com/toc/neje20/18/2.

17. Howard Gardner, *The Mind's New Science: A History of the Cognitive Revolution* (New York: Basic Books, 1985), 10.

18. Philip K. Dick, *Do Androids Dream of Electric Sheep?* (New York: Doubleday, 1968), 19.

19. Cf. Thomas Nagel, "What Is It Like to Be a Bat?" *The Philosophical Review* 83.4 (October, 1974): 435–50.

20. Gordon E. Moore, "Cramming More Components onto Integrated Circuits," *Electronics* 38 (April 19, 1965): 114–17.

21. William Gibson, *Neuromancer* (New York: Ace, 1984), 6.

22. Timothy Lenoir, "Makeover: Writing the Body into the Posthuman Technoscape: Part One: Embracing the Posthuman," *Configurations* 10.2 (Spring 2002): 211.

23. David Langford, "Singularity," *The Encyclopedia of Science Fiction*, last modified November 24, 2012, www.sf-encyclopedia.com/entry/singularity.

24. Vernor Vinge, "The Coming Technological Singularity: How to Survive in the Post-Human Era," in NASA, Vision-21: Interdisciplinary Science and Engineering in the Era of Cyberspace (Conference Publication 10129, 1993), 12.
25. Ken MacLeod, *The Cassini Division* (New York: Tor, 1998), 115.
26. Donna Haraway, "A Cyborg Manifesto: Science, Technology, and Socialist-Feminism in the Late Twentieth Century," *Simians, Cyborgs, and Women: The Reinvention of Nature* (1985; London: Free Association, 1991), 149.
27. However, some critics point out rightly so that there are limitations to earlier formulations of cyborg politics for capturing the challenges of all marginalized groups. See Ria Cheyne, "'She was born a thing': Disability, the Cyborg and the Posthuman in Anne McCaffrey's *The Ship Who Sang*," *Journal of Modern Literature* 36.3 (Spring 2013): 138–56; and Kathryn Allan, ed. *Disability in Science Fiction: Representations of Technology as Cure* (New York: Palgrave Macmillan, 2013).
28. Joanna Russ, *The Female Man* (New York: Bantam, 1975), 161, 6.
29. Octavia Butler, *Lilith's Brood* (New York: Aspect/Warner Books, 2000), the omnibus edition of her the Xenogenesis series: *Dawn* (New York: Warner Books, 1987), *Adulthood Rites* (New York: Warner Books, 1988), and *Imago* (New York: Warner Books, 1989).

7

KARI WEIL

Autobiography

Memory Grains and the Posthumanist Mirror

Who/what writes? For whom or what? Who/what remembers? These are questions that have become newly pertinent under the influence of a lurking posthuman(ism). Memory is understood to be the motor and shaping force of autobiography, but as an episode of the British TV series *Black Mirror* entitled "The Entire History of You" illustrated, our personal histories are increasingly the product of external, technological devices. In that episode, people have surgically implanted behind their eyes small devices called "grains," which record every second of their day. These tapes can be played and replayed on demand, either to investigate "what really happened" during a particular experience or to establish memories that would otherwise have been ignored. In this scenario, the term "screen memory" takes on a whole new meaning, as these replayed experiences replace the remembered one and take on such intensity that couples watch scenes of past lovemaking in order to be aroused. In the case of the main protagonist, who forces his lover to replay her grain memories for him, such screen memories also become a sado-masochistic tool for exposing scenes of a past his lover would rather abandon.

This episode of *Black Mirror* illustrates the way that the posthuman subject emerges, not only out of the social and moral conditions in which, as Judith Butler argues, any "I" is implicated but also, if not more so, out of technological conditions.[1] Indeed, the technological is the supplement that appears to enable the subject (however illusory that ability) to account for the "conditions of its emergence," by returning at will to any scene of that emergence.[2] However, what is especially troubling for the idea of the subject or self who remembers is less the dependence on a prosthetic form of memory than the now absent space of forgetting. Just as Ernst Renan argued for the importance of forgetting for the health of a nation, so a number of thinkers and scholars have asserted the very *necessity* of forgetting for subject formation and for narrating a self.[3] In her 2011 presidential address to the Modern Language Association on

"Narrating Lives," Sidonie Smith writes of the ways that theorizing the posthuman has put pressure on concepts of memory and embodiment, especially because of the ways our "relation to remembering is being reconfigured by the capacious, constantly updated and updatable archive that is the Internet."[4] Wondering whether this "archive without an archivist" might constrict life writing, she cites an article by Jeffery Rosen, who observes that "the Internet is shackling us to everything that we have ever said, or that anyone has said about us," and so works to "tether us to all our past actions, making it impossible, in practice, to escape them."[5] While the episode of *Black Mirror* similarly shackles humans to a past which had at one point been present and witnessed (at least visually), it shows the destructive nature of this memory archive as it leads to the isolation of the subject and, ultimately, the destruction of his or her social relations.

While such ideas of memory as technology may thus intrude on the possibility of re-inventing the self – or, as Michael Roth has described it, of "writing a past with which we can live"[6] – what will be at stake in post-human*ist*, rather than posthuman autobiography, will be the acceptance, if not welcoming, of a necessary "hetero-affection" – the fact that I am moved to write by an other within me, an other whom I cannot fully know, and only with whose help can I remember or forget.[7]

As a fantasy, *Black Mirror* might rather be said to be anti-humanist, in line with those thinkers from Nietzsche through Freud who began to chip away at the traditional notion of the autobiographical subject, one which, as Stefan Herbrechter writes, "is capable of remembering, interpreting and identifying with his or her life story."[8] That subject is one whose very "dignity" is identified with his (and rarely her) autonomy, or so Jacques Derrida explains. "The capacity for autonomy, self-determination, moral autodestination (*Selbstbestimmung*), let us also say for auto-prescription and moral autobio-graphy, is indeed what in Kant, becomes the privilege or absolute advantage of the human that has been defined as autonomous."[9] Conversely, the title "A Total History of You" suggests the dependence of any story of the self on the presence of an other – in this case a machine or film archive – that does the remembering for the self at pains to identify with these memories. In this we might recall the Lacanian subject who does not write but is rather written by a language/techne that precedes and exceeds his/her capacity as author.[10] Posthumanism's "discursive projects ... to decenter the human" can be seen to build on poststructuralism's recognition of this otherness, an inhuman at the core of the human.[11] We may now be posthuman insofar as this inhuman core has come fully into view, revealing that we never were fully or only human. And with this hindsight it becomes clearer that the "auto" of auto-biography masks our reliance on an inhuman within or nonhuman outside the self to know and reveal our very humanness – whether technology, language, or the mirror.

And yet, *Black Mirror* in its fantasy of knowing all, or at least of knowing all about one's past, remains essentially humanist in its equation of knowledge with vision. There, to see the past is to know the past, even as that knowledge destroys as much as it constitutes the self. Perhaps this is why Herbrechter suggests that we need a

> "posthumanism without technology," in the sense that following the Derridean logic of supplementarity, as the original techne deconstructs the metaphysical idea of humanism (that is human nature) – namely that humans can somehow know and experience something like an essential humanness that defines "us" (or humanity) as a species – the human is always already necessarily inhabited by something other than itself, something inhuman which nevertheless *necessarily* defines the human.[12]

We might then come to think of a posthumanist autobiography as one that attempts to know or at least account for that in- or non-human out of and through which one comes to recognize and be recognized as a "human" self. As such, it is an extension of the Hegelian struggle for recognition, now turned into a reflecting play of gazes – but also of scents and touch and affect – between human, machine, and, increasingly, animal. Derrida's *The Animal That Therefore I Am* and Donna Haraway's confessional moments in *When Species Meet* are major examples of the genre, elements of which could be traced to earlier works such as J. R. Ackerley's *My Dog Tulip* (1956) and to more recent autobiographical works such as Valerie Plumwood's 1996 memoir "Being Prey," Irene Pepperberg's *Alex and Me*, Jenni Diski's *What I Don't Know About Animals* (2011), and Stephen Kuusisto's *Planet of the Blind* (1998). Indeed, the now popular term "life writing" itself is one that points to the ambiguous status of authorship extended across a human and nonhuman world. As we will see in the works discussed in this chapter, the human I am is none other than the place where the line between machine and animal, human and nonhuman is always being drawn and redrawn, and is as such always "in process."[13]

From Animal/Machine to Human: Temple Grandin's *Emergence*

It is a short step from the literally embedded video "grains" of *Black Mirror* to the metaphors of thinking and memory as video clips in Temple Grandin's memoir, *Emergence*. "Memories play like a movie on the big screen of my mind," she writes early on.[14] This movie image is used to account for the "vivid" intensity of her "inner world" as a child with autism, and which intensity had no means of being communicated to others. Such movie meta-phors alternate with those of a "trapped animal" whose only means of com-munication is "screaming and flapping my hands," reinforcing her apparent nonhuman or less than human identity (*ELA* 23, 25). Indeed, being "labeled autistic" would give rise to an identity as a kind of Cartesian animal machine in the eyes of scientists who, she explains in her later work, *Thinking in Pictures*, would refuse her manner of "thinking in pictures" as thinking at all.[15]

In the context of "medical dogma" that insisted upon an autistic person's lack of an "inner life" (often seen as the indispensable criterion for the human/ ist or Cartesian subject to come into being) or at least an inability to access or communicate that inner life, neurologist Oliver Sacks raised the question, "How could an autistic person write an autobiography?" and brought fame to Grandin for showing that it was possible indeed.[16] Grandin's autobiogra-phy is remarkable, not only for contesting accepted views regarding the interior lives of persons with autism but also, and especially for our purposes, for revealing how an inner, emotional life comes to be learned, acquired, and narrated by virtue of an external design apparatus and physical engagement with nonhuman animals, in this case, cows.

As in *Black Mirror*, Grandin's memory is less verbal than visual, but the images also stir a swell of sounds and smells. "When I open the door to my memories a crack, I am bombarded with negative impressions" (*ELA* 50). Sacks describes her memory as "prodigious and pathological . . . more akin to a computer record than to anything else" and cites Grandin's own explana-tion that she has no "repressed files" (*ELA* 116). And yet, because she is unable to read the emotional signs displayed by other humans, Grandin's prodigious ability to replay scenes is, unlike in *Black Mirror*, unaccompanied by any affective education or experience. Emotional growth and understand-ing is only made possible, first, by the cows whose emotions she *is* able to read and, secondly, by the squeeze machine in which she, like a calf, learns to calm and control herself. Indeed, through her own version of the machine, she says she learned not only to control emotions but "how to feel." Paradoxically, "I was learning to care at the slaughterhouse" (*ELA*, 63). This paradox turns *Emergence* from a posthumanist and postanthropo-centric autobiography to what Derrida calls "moral autobiography," one dependent upon the sacrificial structure that "assures the dominance or mastery (*Herrschaft*) of man over nature" and nonhuman animals.[17]

Bill Viola's Onto-epistemological Video Art

As autobiography, Temple Grandin's writings narrate a search for self in and through the nonhuman other – both animal and machine. Only apparently posthumanist, their ends are humanist in the most traditional sense: the self acquired through mastery of technology and over the animal as other. I want, nevertheless, to pursue Grandin's notion of "thinking in pictures" in a work by the video artist, Bill Viola, where posthumanist methods produce a rather different subjectivity, one which we might call posthumanist by virtue of its attempt to think the self in relation to the nonhuman world it seeks to see and know. Put in a different way, what the video illustrates is what Karen Barad has called an "onto-epistemology," referring to the necessary mutual implication of ontology and epistemology as forms of mattering: "Practices of knowing and being are not isolatable, but rather, they are mutually implicated. We do not obtain knowledge by standing outside of the world; we know because 'we' are *of* the world."[18]

With agency "cut loose from its traditional humanist orbit"[19] and the self animated and perforated by the material world of which it is inseparable, what becomes of self-representation? This is the difficulty announced in Viola's title "I Do not Know What it is I am Like": the difficulty of knowing who or, more importantly, *what* I am, as it insists also on the mutual implication of knowing and being. I am like "it" but I can't know what I am like until that "it" also makes itself known to me.

The major chapters of the video focus upon bison, birds, and fish in their environments. Narrative is absent, and when there is sound, it is that of wind, barking, fish respiration, or birdcalls. Life and death are witnessed as persistent processes of mattering, from a chick struggling to break out of its egg, to maggots picking at the flesh of a dead fish. Indeed, this is "vibrant matter" where the shimmering of the elements joins and becomes confused with the flickering of the tape that records them. It is a mattering, moreover, that cannot be separated from its discursive enactment, understood here, as for Grandin, as a function of the visual.[20] In the middle of the video, the camera turns upon the artist alone in his room with his anatomy books, his tools, and his tapes that he views and annotates. Here matter is measured, cut with camera or knife, to be turned into art. As a kind of life writing, the video illustrates ways in which the world and its creatures entice us but resist our desire for mastery. As I have written in a longer analysis of the video, "recognition of the human is what the film refuses from the very beginning, and in its title."[21] Identity is approached by analogy – to be like – but without the knowledge of what it *is* exactly I am like, self-knowledge is also impossible. The desire to know and to see is countered by the desire to let it go, "let it be" and thus give up on the very project of autobiography. Only in this letting be can the self experience life in its material fullness, abandoning all projects in order to be reclaimed, perhaps "like" the fish at the end of the film, by an all-consuming nature.

As an autobiographical project, Viola's video is thus posthumanist insofar as it insists upon the self as inseparable from the larger natural world of which it is a part, and, indeed, only a small part. The overbearing stature and size of the humanist "I" was something that Virginia Woolf already critiqued in *A Room of One's Own*, where she describes that "I" as a shadow on the page, "a shadow that made it difficult to distinguish any other creature or reality."[22] Technology in the form of the video camera is here used to bring that other reality into view, even as it raises questions about the possibilities for that technology to transform, distort, and even destroy that reality.

(In)hospitable Selves and Hélène Cixous's Animots

It is worth noting that the nature we inhabit, and that inhabits us in Viola's video, appears mostly benign. We see inclement weather but little destruction, we see animals feeding off the dead but not killing, and we see no signs of a potentially toxic nature – the unseen materiality that moves between technology, environment, and bodies to shape and sicken selves – both human and nonhuman. Giving an account of the potentially toxic self of the Anthropocene – the "human" geological era that may be damaging to life itself – is important for material feminists like Stacy Alaimo and Catriona Sandilands, especially because the material body can also be a sign of the self's socio-political situatedness. As Alaimo writes, "thinking through toxic bodies allows us to reimagine human corporeality, and materiality itself, not as a utopian or romantic substance existing prior to social inscription, but as something that always bears the trace of history, social position, region, and the uneven distribution of risk."[23]

The final work I turn to is one that seeks precisely to reveal and lay claim to those material traces, especially because of the ways that they are discursively, and as such, indelibly inscribed. Hélène Cixous is a writer who makes us aware of the materiality of words, how they carve our selves, our spaces, our communities, and our emotions. Words may write us, she understands, with often violent effects, but they may also be the very tools or *technē* to counteract those effects, or at least to help repair the damage.

Before Derrida, it was Cixous who invented the word "animots,"[24] one she uses in the plural to invoke her own autobiographical writing that has been animated and inspired by the animals in her life, like her dog, Fips, the "innocent author of the signatures that inaugurated (her) book."[25] As Cixous recounts in a section of "Stigmata, Or Job the Dog," tellingly called, "Writing Blind, Conversations with the Donkey," the "animots" refer to those animals and those words that affect and animate us, and which recall the violence of language, but also its power to invoke, as she describes, through illusion: "the words which cross the eyelid on the interior of their own body, are my magic *animots*, my animal words. My philters. We pass also by illusion."[26] Animals and words are linked through the unexpected. Unimaginably, they arrive, unwilled because unseen.

> More than everything in the world we love the creature we would never have expected. Never thought of loving.
> Me, a cat?
> This is a chapter of a book that could be called the imitation of the cat.
> How does a book arrive? Like a barely weaned cat who sticks a small paw-hand out from under the wood-stove. And a few days later it is she who explains humanity to you.
> Who would have believed that I could *love* an animal and imitate a she-cat?[27]

Cixous's cat figures in that tradition of feline professors extending from Montaigne to Derrida – a cat who teaches us about catness, but also about aspects of ourselves that we ignore or deny. This, we assume, is the cat who "came from her dog," as she explains in "Stigmata" (*SJD* 187).The relation between cat and dog is a matter not of biological but affective provenance. She learned her love for her cat – a love that takes both to the limits of life and death, of empathy and violence – from her dog Fips and from Fips's love for her. "As for me, I'm ready to give my life for my cat, but it was necessary that Fips should first have given his life for me" (*SJD* 186).

"Stigmata" is the story of the death, if not the sacrifice, of Fips, a dog brought home one day by the narrator's father, a Jewish doctor. The family lives in an Arab section of Algiers during the 1940s. As a doctor whose services are needed by the community, he keeps a certain peace between what might otherwise be warring camps. But upon her father's death, as the narrator recounts, Fips becomes the well-intentioned, or un-intentioned, go-between, only to be caught in a "hail of stones" raining down upon on the house and from which he emerges as if rabid – enraged. "Am I Jewish, he thought?" (*SJD* 189, 90). A parallel is set up between the dog who tries to maintain his sanity while not understanding how he fits into the violence around him and the girl who will only learn too late, that "she never under-stood what a dog is, nor what it is to be one" (*SJD* 186). The title of the story refers both to the less visible but deeply felt wounds that Fips receives and those more visible wounds that the young narrator receives when the dog mistakes her for the enemy, and bites her on the foot. "I saw the meat that we are," she says, we "came out of the mortal spasms broken lame and delirious. Unrecognizable" (*SJD* 192). Human and nonhuman are caught together in an ongoing experience of violence that perforates divided identities and reveals the shared and vulnerable matter of which life is composed.

The title, "Stigmata," refers to both those wounds and to the condition of astigmatism, a trouble of the eye that causes deformed or imprecise vision. Cixous's story is about those blinding passions inspired by war and its ravages. Such is the blindness of the dog, who is unable to distinguish family from foe – the madness that the narrator could not foresee. And that madness, in its inability to make such distinctions and in its acceptance of a shared vulnerability, will ultimately reveal the "humanity" of the dog – a humanity the narrator will see only when it is too late.

> No doubt [Fips] understood the enemy better than the friend. This world is upside down and the dog is betrayed. I should have spoken to him, I should have, if I had been able to understand him but I thought him perhaps incapable of understanding for I was not then capable of understanding the profound animal humanity, if I had not said to myself as we precipitately lie to ourselves, that a dog does not understand our bad complications and that he is a dog.
>
> (SJD 190)

"Animal humanity" – this is what Cixous calls the capacity to see and indeed to love outside of preconceived ideas. The narrator explains that she was unable to love Fips as he loved her, which is to say, "as an animal and far from my ideal" (SJD, 188). She loves the dog who conforms to a certain "ideal," who becomes a slave to that idea, and she does not understand why Fips refuses her. And it is in this way that a parallel is set up between the ideas of a Jew, a Frenchwoman, or an Arab, ideas from which only Fips and the narrator's father can escape; the father who was "without images and without ideas" and who fulfills his "natural obligation" of caring for "his fellow creatures": Arab, Jew, or Dog.

Fips is thus like the dog Bobby, who visited Levinas and other Jewish prisoners in the camps, the only one for whom they were men. Levinas calls Bobby "the last Kantian in Nazi Germany," who did not have "the brain necessary for universalizing the maxims of his impulses."[28] Fips is like Bobby in that he cannot or will not allow abstract categories of race or nation to predetermine his feelings. But unlike Levinas, Cixous's narration allows Fips to teach her what it is to be human and how to recognize the humanity of the other animal – human or nonhuman. Of course, she doesn't learn this right away. If those childhood wounds exposed the "meat" of being, the memory of this shared and "immemorial past" (SJD, 184) gives her consciousness of their shared soul and of the love that is possible – but which she was unable to see. This is why Cixous's natural history, her personal story, is less about nature that has been seen, than nature that is remembered and told. She replaces the realm of the visible with the realm of memory, and with writing – blind writing, to be precise.

Whereas writing and language have stood as the mark of human exceptionalism, writing for Cixous, and writing autobiography in particular, is a means to reveal the necessary, and often unjust, entanglement of the human and nonhuman worlds. Writing is a kind of *pharmakon* where a history or story that is written blind presents itself as a means of repairing the distance between words and things. Reading Cixous can be difficult because even her syntax, or more correctly the absence of syntax, frees referents from the fixity of their "proper" meanings and forms, such that one being or gender or loved one can engender another. This is why we can see in her work not only the violence produced by those categories like "animal," but also the ways in which writing can animate affections of the past and mobilize them for the future. The animot – the animal-word – is not about "giving language back to the animals"[29] but rather about recognizing the hybrid communities that have always been effected in and through language. Vinciane Despret writes: "Everything that exists for an organism is a sign that affects, or an affect that signifies."[30]

Cixous's blindly written menagerie, her animal histories work to expose the stigmas and the violence of nomination – whether zoological or political – putting in its place the affective evolutions of a narrative that can welcome the unseen and unanticipated. Her animots, her passwords, are also what we might call queer words, words that are constantly transforming and transformed in relation to those creatures around her, animated by those others in her life – dog, cat, friend, lover – those others who have been engendered both by affection and by memory, and who will, in turn, engender the author and her text.

After-word(s)

Who/what authors the "I"? In each of the works discussed in this chapter, "I" comes after, or more rightly, is after the animal who might be "my primary mirror," the one before whom and with if not in whom I discover myself.[31] This being after is one meaning of the "post" in posthuman(ism). But how do I give an account of those animal-others from whom I emerge? This is the question, for example, that Bill Viola's video cannot fully answer, for they remind me of a bodily/material history of which I may have no recollection or knowledge. Inscribed and affected by their voices, their scents, their breath, they also undermine the tools with which I attempt to account for them, tools that inevitably reconstruct those boundaries that my self would break down, tools that remember what I must to forget to give the others their due.

Forgetting is one sign of the limits of my own self-knowledge, which is why *Black Mirror*'s fantasy of total memory can be seen to feed the "moral narcissism" of humanist transcendence, rather than a posthumanist ethics.[32] Forgetting, by contrast, awakens us to our dependency on others in order to perceive what may remain opaque, whether or not we can articulate it. Temple Grandin acknowledges her indebtedness to the inhuman – machine and animal – for her emergence as a fully human subject, one who is finally transparent to herself. Given that she regards this debt as payable with acts of kindness and care in slaughter, however, her work might stand as a warning about the untimeliness of posthumanism for those who have been denied and still fight for recognition as human. Cixous's life-story moves between the struggle to be human and the understanding of the dangers the word can hold. Indeed, she comes to realize that humanity might best be learned from those who have been denied the name of human. The price for such knowledge, however, while owed, is never fully payable, and that is in part because it always comes too late. Indeed, it is because we are never fully present to ourselves, and because others are never fully present or known to us, that there can be no payment, at least in the present. Perhaps then, the task of posthumanist autobiography – itself a contradiction insofar as it reveals the lie or insufficiency of the "auto" – is to take account of those who and that which have made us who we have been, and help us be open to the myriad ways we will continue to be affected, if not infected, by others and the world we are a part of. This hospitality of the self is a first step toward accounting, in turn, for the ways that we are also affecting that world and the many creatures of whatever name within it.

NOTES

1. "There is no 'I' that can fully stand apart from the social conditions of its emergence, no 'I' that is not implicated in a set of conditioning moral norms." Judith Butler, *Giving an Account of Oneself* (New York: Fordham University Press, 2005), 7.
2. Such social conditions in the TV show are restricted to what is knowable, with little reference to the "conditioning norms" that Butler refers to.
3. "Forgetting, I would even say historical error, is an essential factor in the creation of a nation and it is for this reason that the progress of historical studies often poses a threat to nationality... However, the essence of a nation is that all individuals have many things in common, and also that they have forgotten many things." "What is a Nation" text of a conference delivered at the Sorbonne on March 11, 1882, in Ernest Renan, *Qu'est-ce qu'une nation?*, trans. Ethan Rundell (Paris: Presses-Pocket, 1992), 3.

4. Sidonie Smith, "Narrating Lives and Contemporary Imaginaries," *PMLA* 126.3 (May 2011): 564–74.

5. *Ibid.*, 570.

6. Michael Roth, *Memory, Trauma, and History: Essays on Living with the Past* (New York: Columbia University Press, 2012).

7. Jacques Derrida, *The Animal That Therefore I Am*, trans. David Wills (New York: Fordham University Press, 2008), 47.

8. Stefan Herbrechter, "Humanism, Subjectivity, Autobiography," *Subjectivity* 5.3 (September 2012): 331.

9. Derrida, *The Animal*, 100.

10. "If the subject is what I say it is, namely the subject determined by language, namely the subject determined by language and speech, it follows that the subject, *in initio*, begins in the locus of the other, in so far as it is there that the first signifier emerges." Jacques Lacan, *The Seminar of Jacques Lacan: The Four Fundamental Concepts of Psychoanalysis* (Book XI), ed. Jacques-Alain Miller, trans. Alan Sheridan (New York: W. W. Norton, 1998), 198.

11. Bruce Clarke, "The Nonhuman," in this volume.

12. Herbrechter, "Humanism, Subjectivity, Autobiography," 328.

13. Julia Kristeva introduces the notion of the subject as always "in process" or "on trial," in *Revolution in Poetic Language* (New York: Columbia University Press, 1984).

14. Temple Grandin, *Emergence: Labeled Autistic* (Novato, CA: Warner Books, 1986), 23; hereafter *ELA*.

15. Temple Grandin, *Thinking in Pictures and Other Reports from My Life with Autism* (New York: Vintage Books, 1995), 159. See also my discussion in Kari Weil, *Thinking Animals: Why Animal Studies Now* (New York: Columbia University Press, 2012), chapter. 7.

16. Oliver Sacks, "An Anthropologist on Mars," *The New Yorker*, December 27, 1993, www.newyorker.com/magazine/1993/12/27/anthropologist-mars, accessed October 26, 2015. See also his Forward to Grandin, *Thinking in Pictures*, 7.

17. See Derrida, *The Animal*, 100.

18. Karen Barad, "Posthumanist Performativity," in *Material Feminisms*, ed. Stacy Alaimo and Susan Hekman (Bloomington: Indiana University Press, 2008), 147.

19. *Ibid.*, 144.

20. See Jane Bennett, *Vibrant Matter: A Political Ecology of Things* (Durham: Duke University Press, 2010).

21. Weil, *Thinking Animals*, 43.

22. Virginia Woolf, *A Room of One's Own* (New York: Harcourt Brace, 1981), 99.

23. Stacy Alaimo, "Transcorporeal Feminisms and the Ethical Space of Nature," in *Material Feminisms*, ed. Alaimo and Hekman, 261.

24. Lynn Turner traces Cixous's first use of "animot" to a work of 1976. See "When Species Kiss: Some Recent Correspondences between Animots," *Humanimalia* 2.1 (Fall 2010), 60–86, accessed October 26, 2015, www.depauw.edu/humani malia/issue03/pdfs/Turner%20pdf.pdf.

25. Hélène Cixous, "Stigmata, Or Job the Dog," in *Stigmata, Escaping Texts* (London: Routledge, 1998), 185, 187; hereafter *SJD*.

26. Cixous, "Writing Blind: Conversation with the Donkey," in *Stigmata*, 140.
27. *Ibid.*, 151–52.
28. Emmanuel Levinas, "The Name of a Dog, or Natural Rights," in *Animal Philosophy*, ed. Peter Atterton and Matthew Calarco (London: Continuum, 2004), 47–51.
29. Derrida, *The Animal*, 121.
30. Vinciane Despret, "From Secret Agents to Interagency," *History and Theory* 52 (December, 2013): 37.
31. "But cannot this cat also be, deep within her eyes, my primary mirror?" Derrida, *The Animal*, 51.
32. "After all, if self-assertion becomes the assertion of the self at the expense of any consideration of the world, of consequence, and, indeed, of others, then it feeds a moral narcissism whose pleasure resides in its ability to transcend the concrete world that conditions its actions and is affected by them." Butler, *Giving an Account*, 105.

8

LISA DIEDRICH

Comics and Graphic Narratives

In recent years, comics and graphic narratives have become a popular and innovative form for telling auto/biographical stories of selves and others in a medium that artfully combines – or co-mixes – words and images. Various terms have been used to capture this emergent form of graphic autobiography and memoir, including Art Spiegelman's neologism for comics, "co-mix," a term now often associated with the underground work of Spiegelman and others beginning in the 1970s, and the more recent term "autographics," coined by life-writing scholar Gillian Whitlock.[1] The touchstone text of the form is *Maus*, Spiegelman's graphic narrative of his parents' experience of the Holocaust and his own transgenerational trauma, parts of which were first serialized in *Raw* magazine between 1980 and 1991, before appearing in book form in 1986 (volume one) and 1991 (volume two). Since *Maus*, other key texts in the hybrid autographics genre include Marjane Satrapi's *Persepolis: The Story of a Childhood* (2003) and *Persepolis 2: The Story of a Return* (2004), and Alison Bechdel's *Fun Home: A Family Tragicomic* (2006) and *Are You My Mother? A Comic Drama* (2012), all of which have reached a wide readership and garnered popular and critical acclaim, as well as scholarly attention. These texts share a preoccupation with exploring how subjects come into being in relation to experiences and events that are both ordinary and extraordinary, such as childhood, war, illness, trauma, shame, stigma, love, and hope. I argue here that this new, hybrid form is particularly well suited for treating the "posthuman condition."

According to feminist philosopher Rosi Braidotti, the "posthuman condition urges us to think critically and creatively about who and what we are actually in the process of becoming."[2] Many graphic narratives render this condition through various formal practices, including radical juxtaposition and assemblage as method, as well as through the articulation of a concept of the subject as always in the process of becoming in relation to both human and nonhuman others. I will discuss these graphic treatments of the posthuman condition using some examples from a sub-field of comics and graphic narratives – graphic medicine, a fascinating conjuncture between graphic narratives and clinical medicine. Focusing on graphic medicine allows me to think about some of the ways in which comics and graphic narratives have become important resources for communicating and discussing a range of ethical and aesthetic issues within particular contexts – in this case, within the discourses, practices, and institutions of medicine and healthcare. For medical practitioners, patients, families, and caregivers dealing with the experience and event of illness, such graphic narratives in their hybrid verbal/visual form help to reimagine the boundaries of "health," "illness," "life," and "death" and to rethink the status of the human in its entanglement with the nonhuman in everyday life.

Graphic Medicine

The phrase "graphic medicine" was first coined by the general practitioner and graphic artist Ian Williams as the name for a website he created in 2007, and since then, many other discourses, genres, and practices of graphic medicine have arisen or have been identified as operating *avant la lettre*. For Williams, graphic medicine is a "handy term to denote the role comics can play in the study and delivery of healthcare,"[3] suggesting a link, historically and methodologically, between the emergence of graphic medicine and the emergence of the interdisciplinary field of the medical humanities and one of its key methods, narrative medicine.[4] Narrative medicine takes seriously the writing, reading, and telling of stories in medicine, by doctors, patients and their families, nurses, and other health care practitioners. Michael J. Green and Kimberly R. Myers also point to the role that graphic narratives can play for narrative medicine. In these accounts, graphic narratives are instrumentalized as the means by which something – say, "compassion" or the "patient's experience" – is delivered into medicine. In this scenario, what is delivered is conceived of as always already other and external to medicine, warranting a call to bring in that which is other. Graphic narratives are most commonly understood, I argue, to provide a kind of "delivery system" of otherness into medicine under the auspices of a more expansive medical education.[5] Such a genealogy works to connect graphic medicine directly with the humanistic project of the so-called Medical Humanities, so much so that we might even describe graphic medicine as a subfield of the Medical Humanities. Without denying that this is one of the more obvious genealogies of graphic medicine, however, in my work I am more interested in tracing other, more indirect genealogies, what we might call graphic medicine's posthumanist genealogies; or, put another way, how graphic medicine articulates some of the key concepts and practices of posthumanism, including assemblage as method and becoming in relation.

Assemblage as Method

Graphic medicine can formally render illness as an assemblage, a complex interplay between and among bodies, minds, diagnoses, treatments, and clinical, critical, political, and narrative discourses and practices. Gilles Deleuze and Félix Guattari delineate the concept and practice of assemblage in *Kafka: Toward a Minor Literature*, noting that the "functioning of the assemblage can be explained only if one takes it apart to examine both the elements that make it up and the nature of the linkages."[6] Thus, Deleuze and Guattari are interested in both the form and content of assemblages, as well as the mechanisms by which assemblages are formed and unformed in time and space. How might we put this abstract concept of assemblage into practice? And what might be the political and therapeutic effects of such practices?

Of course, comics are themselves a kind of assemblage. As Will Eisner explains in his now classic instructional book, *Comics and Sequential Art*, first published in 1985, through the varied mix of panels and frames, as well as the lines, borders, and gutters linking and separating panels and frames, comics encapsulate events through their form as much as their content: as Eisner puts it, the panel "is used by the artist to capture or 'freeze' one segment in what is in reality an uninterrupted flow of action."[7] In comics, time becomes spatialized. In Eisner's realist formulation, success "stems from the artist's ability (usually more visceral than intellectual) to gauge the commonality of the reader's experience," suggesting that comics present experience as self-evident rather than as always already an interpretation open to further interpretation. Yet, on a formal level, I would argue, contra Eisner, that many, if not most graphic narratives work to *re*present and interpret "experience" as a category of analysis, by demonstrating both the desire to encapsulate an individual's "experience" in history and the impossibility of doing so. Illness narratives often offer what I have called an ethics of failure; this ethics emerges out of the situation of being at a loss, yet exploring various routes – the creative combination of failure and further exploration.[8] The experience of illness is multiple, and tracking that multiplicity demonstrates that even as diagnostic categories, treatments, and illness narratives seek to contain and reduce – or to frame in the language of graphic medicine – an illness experience, the experience always also falls outside the frame, overspills the container, gets messy. Similarly, in an early instantiation of posthumanist theory and practice, Margrit Shildrick argued that "leaks and flows across categories signal not so much the breakdown of security as the impossibility of fixed definition."[9] In their very form, comics thematize boundaries and their leakiness: panels are breached, borders dissolved, lines are drawn and undrawn, boundaries are played with, on, and beyond.

The practice of graphic medicine, then, materializes a means to think the multiplicity of illness as an assemblage. In thinking through how this happens on the page and beyond, we can explore the experience of drawing in general, and drawing the experience of illness, diagnosis, and treatment in particular, as central to the practice of graphic medicine. In *A Thousand Plateaus*, Deleuze and Guattari use the term "drawing" to help delineate their conceptual apparatus; in their collaborative work, they "draw" together the graphic, formal, and conceptual. As Brian Massumi explains, "to draw is an act of creation. What is drawn ... does not preexist the act of drawing. The French word *tracer* captures this better: It has all the graphic connotations of 'to draw' in English, but can also mean to blaze a trail or open a road."[10] In the graphic memoir *Epileptic*,[11] for example, I would argue that French cartoonist David B. attempts to draw his brother's epilepsy as a multiplicity and not a "pretraced destiny."[12] Through drawing in general and the creation of *Epileptic* in particular, David B. struggles to find a form to answer the question people ask him when they hear about his brother's condition: "So what's it like, a seizure?"[13] The graphic resolution that David B. arrives at over time is to draw his brother's epilepsy as a serpent that takes hold of and transforms his brother's body, emotional responses, and cognitive functions. The serpent also makes visible the way epilepsy insinuates itself into this otherwise mundane story of one French family; it slithers across and between panels, sometimes serving as that which connects and binds individuals and scenes or as that which borders and gives shape to panels and whole pages.

Epileptic shows epilepsy as serpent to be a slippery illness category – one that defies any easy delimitation as either a wholly mental or physical illness. Perhaps because of its ability to materialize an experience of illness, the graphic form is also effective in making visible – and giving form to – the varieties of experiences of mental illness, and the widely divergent diagnoses and treatments of mental illness across time and space.[14] To give just one example of how this might be done, Ellen Forney, in her graphic memoir *Marbles: Mania, Depression, Michelangelo, and Me*, visually contrasts graphic scenes of mania with graphic scenes of depression, which together provide a harrowing yet also life-affirming view of manic-depressive illness.[15]

FIGURE 8.1 A scene of mania from Ellen Forney's *Marbles: Mania, Depression, Michelangelo, and Me.*

In the scenes of mania, the thought and speech balloons become increasingly confused and difficult to follow. In one sequence of panels, Ellen's therapist asks, "How's work?" which generates images and texts that together appear to lose form, coherence, and sense (Figure 8.1). Forney creates an increasingly abstracted and vertiginous image of Ellen's manic face, with the mouth drawn as an ever-widening cavern and the eyes drawn as having become radiating black suns. In this scene, Ellen's abstract, manic face becomes unmoored from her body, eventually blasting off from the head of the Ellen who is shown to be still sitting in the chair talking to her therapist. This graphic experience of transcendence is short-lived as the mask-like manic face hits the top of the panel with a resounding "Konk!" surrounded by empty speech balloons, suggesting that the experience is both captured and contained by Forney's representation and, at the same time, uncapturable and uncontainable. Two manic double pages follow the page of Ellen's head blasting off: in the first, a larger-than-life Ellen strides forth across two pages to organize her 30th birthday party, and in the second, Ellen has become a strange human/nonhuman hybrid, with her head attached to several stretched nerve-like rope fibers connecting the many disparate friends and creative activities planned for the big party. These images suggest that a manic Ellen both is and isn't entirely herself and is and isn't entirely human, not unlike David B.'s depiction of epilepsy as human/serpent hybrid.

Graphic scenes of depression will replace these graphic scenes of mania, and the exuberant, full, and busy pages will become lethargic, empty, and still (Figure 8.2). On one page that serves as a chapter divider, Forney has assembled 14 small, simple line drawings that together tell a visually iconic story of depression. If Forney's graphic scenes of mania threaten to burst the boundaries of the panels and pages, these graphic scenes of depression take up as little space as possible and, although connected in a graphic narrative sequence contained on a single page, each drawing also seems to stand on its own in a little capsule of self-protection. The story begins and ends with a de-personalized lump on a surface. Through the graphic elements, even simpli-fied as they are, we come to realize that the lump is a person, but the person is empty of personhood and seems to be trapped in immanence. We first see the figure lying in bed under a blanket, though, like the drawing of the elephant eaten by a snake from *The Little Prince*, we don't know what we are seeing until the drawings that follow give us more information and context. The figure wakes up, slowly and seemingly unwillingly. A head appears and disappears, turtle-like, before the figure finally sits up on the bed. Yet, even when the figure sits up, the bed seems to pull it backward, the head appears too heavy to hold up. As if for protection, the figure wraps the blanket around itself, de-personalizing the figure again. Wrapped in its blanket, the figure passes through a door from one empty, formless room to another. The figure ends up on a couch, and the earlier sequence of the head slowly appearing is reversed as the head sinks back into the blanket and

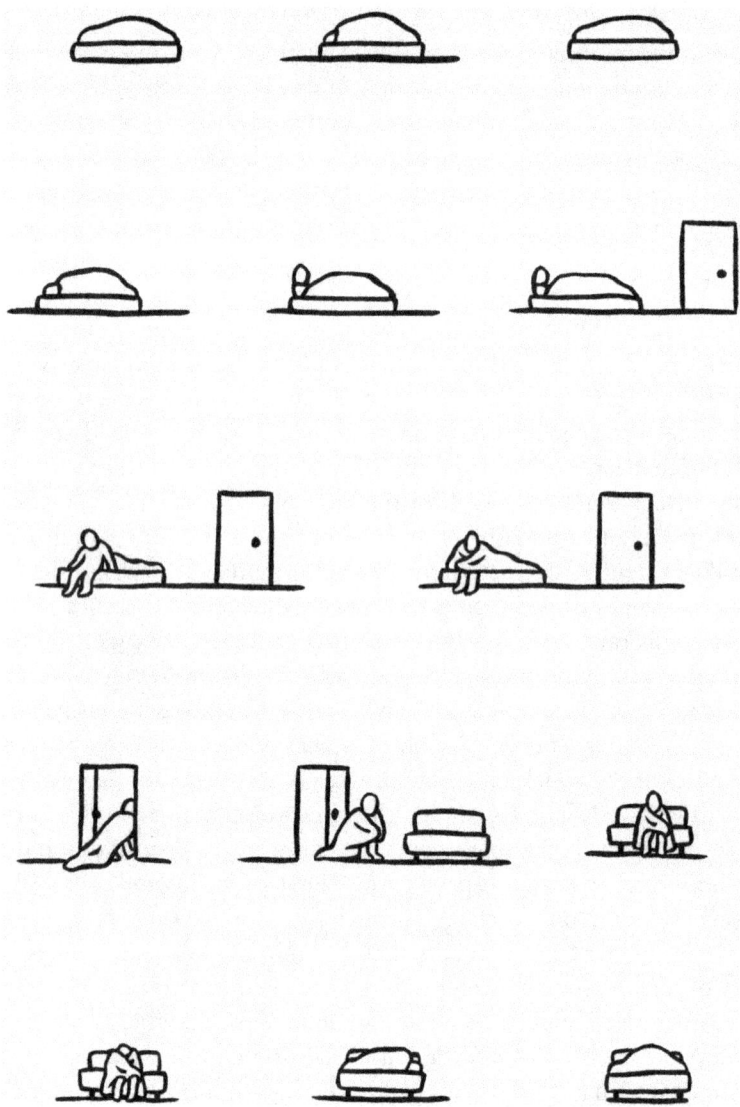

FIGURE 8.2 A scene of depression from Ellen Forney's *Marbles: Mania, Depression, Michelangelo, and Me.*

further into the body itself. The hieroglyphic sequence ends with the return of the immobile, slug-like lump, rendered impersonal, unrecognizable as human, and suggesting the recurrence of heavy and isolating feelings of depression.[16]

In Forney's simple yet eloquent graphic syntax of depression, the subject who experiences depression begins and ends in formlessness.[17] Through Forney's drawings of the divergent experiences of becoming manic and becoming depressive, the subject is de-subjectified, becoming an object for graphic analysis. We witness the experience and event of de-subjectification through drawing. The process of de-subjectification is not rendered as wholly pathological; in Forney's graphic interpretation, the process is experienced ambivalently. In *Marbles*, Forney includes a photographic image of the outside cover of one of her sketchbooks, as well as photographic images of several pages from inside showing a series of self-portraits she had drawn as a kind of therapeutic practice. She confesses that the "drawings both scared me and gave me comfort" (92). On the one hand, by tracing the "familiar lines of my face," she would "calm down and come back into [herself]. Inert on a piece of paper, the demons were more handleable" (98). On the other hand, some of her portraits serve as attempts to depict feelings of what Forney describes as mental images she "needed to get outside of me" (99). Images from the sketchbook – including a mental image of a contorted, barely human figure wrapped around itself, and snuggled in a bird's nest – are themselves now nested within Forney's graphic narrative. In this nested assemblage, the mental images are, paradoxically, both doubly contained and yet also further externalized by Forney through the practice of drawing. The process of containment and externalization is representational, and also potentially therapeutic, for Forney not just in the moment of drawing them but also in the many moments after, when readers encounter Forney's drawn mental image on the page in front of them. In this process, Forney puts spatial and temporal distance between herself and the mental images she needed to get out of herself.

Becoming in Relation

Graphic narratives work formally to deconstruct subjectivity in general and the experience of illness in particular. By emphasizing the subject as becoming through drawing, graphic narratives work to render the posthuman subject not as something one *is*, but rather as something one *does*, in relation to nonhuman objects and other human subjects.[18] In a graphic memoir about, say, cancer, the cancer can become visible and have agency outside of or beyond the human who has cancer. While this can also happen in text-only illness narratives, the graphic elements allow for a complex demonstration of movement across and between scales, from micro-cellular to macro-social environments and back again, as a way to demonstrate the ongoing and recursive processes of subjectification and de-subjectification through particular formal elements, including juxtaposition, nesting, and assemblage.

For example, in a two-page vignette entitled "Mom in Mathemagic Land" in the graphic memoir *Mom's Cancer*, Brian Fies demonstrates the problem of seeing a three-dimensional object – the tumor on his mother's lungs – in only two dimensions. On the left side of the page, in a panel without a border, Fies provides a simple geometry lesson, showing the difference between one, two, and three dimensions with drawings of lines, squares, and cubes. On the right, in a boxed panel, we see Fies, his mother, his mother's doctor, and Fies's two sisters looking at scans and trying to discern the effect of two months of chemotherapy on his mother's tumor. Fies draws the scans showing the tumor on the lung before and after chemotherapy, and he places them side by side. We look with the family looking at the difference, and we "see" that the tumor appears to have barely changed – the reduction of the tumor in the drawing of the second scan is hardly visible to the eye. In a caption at the bottom of the drawing of the two images and of the family and doctor looking at the images, Fies writes, "Your crushing disappointment only betrays your mathematical ignorance" (53). When we turn the page, the "mathemagics" of tumor volume is explained, and the doctor tells Fies's mother and her children, "I'd estimate it's fifty percent smaller! That's **great!**" (53, emphasis in original). The family's gloom turns to hope, even as the captions anchoring the three panels on this page can't help but add a hint of skepticism in the form of a dubious-sounding query, "See how understanding math helps?" (53).

Math becomes a discourse through which Fies's mother and her children experience her illness, and the tumor and its volume before and after chemotherapy is an object – both human and nonhuman – that suggests the complexity of posthuman subjectivity. In this scene, Fies draws the abstract language of math as a means by which the doctor communicates hope to her patient and her family. The notion that we cannot fully see or comprehend what is happening and has happened in the body is used here not to produce more fear, but less. Yet, even as his drawings attempt to picture the hopefulness in the possibility of a 50 percent reduction of the volume of the tumor, Fies's captions inject a note of doubt into the otherwise cheery scene. I would argue that it is precisely this tension – between the doctor's certainty that the math tells us something good, and the narrator's lingering uncertainty even as he learns to do the math on his mother's cancer – that characterizes the experience and event of illness. The point/counter-point of images and words in Fies's text captures this tension. As he demonstrates in his graphic analysis, Fies becomes subject not only in relation to his mom but also in relation to his mom's cancer *and* in relation to the math on his mom's cancer. As with Forney's desire to use the graphic form to both contain and externalize her own mental images of her depressed self, Fies invents "mathemagic land" in order to both contain and move between the biological event of the tumor inside his mother's body and the affective experience of his mom's cancer inside their family. The graphic helps us to "see" – and become in relation to – this double movement, between a biological event of cancer and an affective experience of cancer. Graphic narratives like Fies's provide a form for interdisciplinary encounters between the humanities and the natural sciences and medicine, as well as, in the more unusual case here, between literature and mathematics.

Such movements across and between biological events and affective experiences and across and between the human and the nonhuman can also be seen in Martina Schlünder, Pit Arens, and Axel Gerhardt's collaborative graphic narrative, "Becoming Bone Sheep," published in a special issue on Graphic Medicine for *Configurations*.[19] In her diagnosis of the posthuman condition, Braidotti is attentive to the ways in which "[a]dvanced capitalism and its bio-genetic technologies engender a perverse form of the posthuman. At its core there is a radical disruption of the human-animal interaction, but all living species are caught in the spinning machine of the global economy."[20] In her chapter on "Post-Anthropocentrism: Life Beyond Species," Braidotti explores not only the perverse forms of the posthuman predicament but also the possibility of "affirmative transformations," in particular of the interrelation between humans and animals as "a transformative or symbiotic relation that hybridizes and alters the 'nature' of each one and foregrounds the middle grounds of their interaction." For Braidotti, this "is the 'milieu' of the human/non-human continuum and it needs to be explored as an open experiment, not as a foregone moral conclusion about allegedly universal values or qualities."[21]

The graphic narrative "Becoming Bone Sheep" demonstrates both the perverse and affirmative transformations that Braidotti identifies as symptoms and signs of the posthuman condition. It also moves beyond the delivery of the patient's experience of illness into medicine as a function of the medical humanities by suggesting a new experimental form of graphic medicine, one that historicizes and makes visible spaces that help us "comprehend the structures of biomedicine."[22] What becomes visible in "Becoming Bone Sheep" is a real-life stable/veterinary hospital in the Swiss Alps in which "different sheep ontologies are produced" – that is, sheep produced not as meat to be eaten but as new knowledge for improving orthopedic surgery and bone fracture care for humans. The form for capturing this "odd mixture of farm, clinic and lab"[23] is itself an odd mixture – a collage of photographs, drawings, and words, intermingled together, sometimes bleeding into each other, sometimes cut up and rearranged.

At the center of this graphic narrative is a haunting close-up image of a sheep's head, split in half (Figure 8.3). On the right side, the sheep is drawn

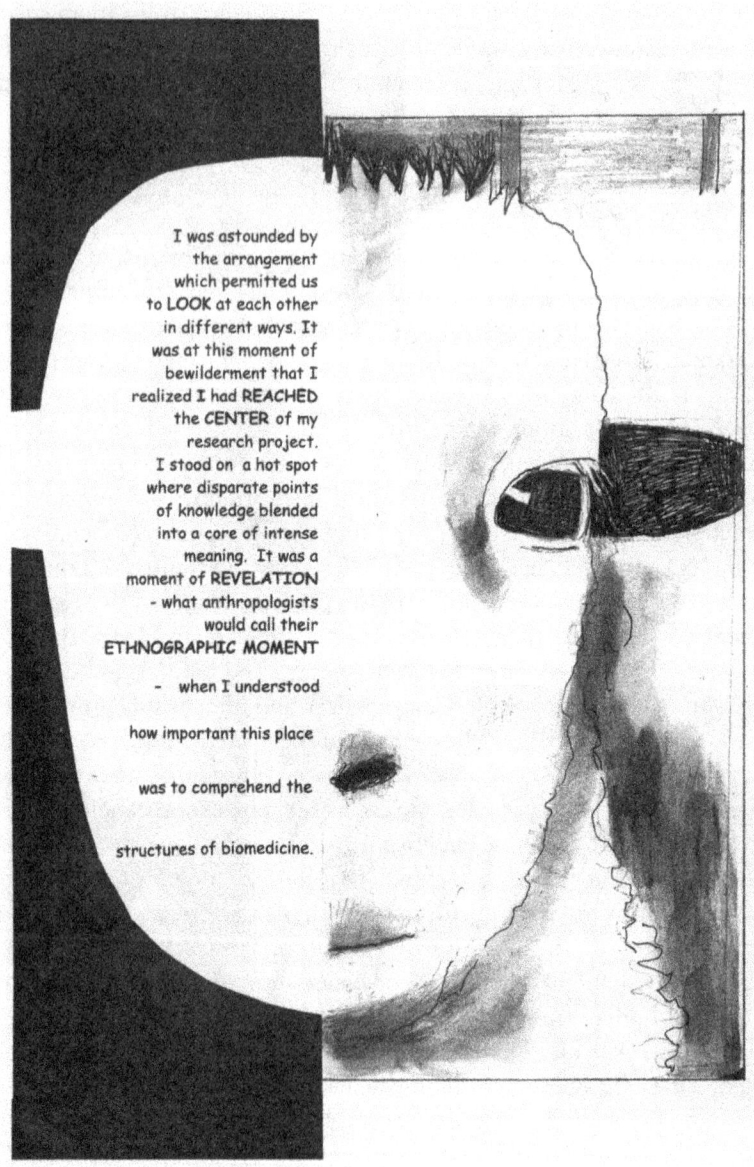

I was astounded by
the arrangement
which permitted us
to LOOK at each other
in different ways. It
was at this moment of
bewilderment that I
realized I had REACHED
the CENTER of my
research project.
I stood on a hot spot
where disparate points
of knowledge blended
into a core of intense
meaning. It was a
moment of REVELATION
- what anthropologists
would call their
ETHNOGRAPHIC MOMENT

- when I understood

how important this place

was to comprehend the

structures of biomedicine.

FIGURE 8.3 "Becoming Bone Sheep" by Martina Schlünder, Pit Arens, and Axel Gerhardt. (Copyright © 2014 Martina Schlünder, Pit Arens, and Axel Gerhardt. All rights reserved, reproduced with permission.)

looking at the human viewer/reader; the sheep's eye acts as the image's punctum, pulling the viewer into a relationship with the image/sheep. On the left, the outline of the shape of the sheep's head is continued, but in place of the left side of the sheep's face the graphic artists have included a contemplative text about the looks exchanged between the human narrator and sheep in the hybrid space of farm/lab/clinic; these exchanged looks, the narrator explains, create "bewilderment," "intense meaning," and "revelation" about the "structures of biomedicine."[24] The combination of words and image on this page enacts the human/nonhuman milieu Braidotti describes as "an open experiment, not as a foregone moral conclusion about allegedly universal values or qualities."[25] The experimental milieu is not only the farm/lab/clinic but also the graphic narrative "Becoming Bone Sheep" becoming another kind of experimental milieu for understanding the posthuman condition. Through their form as well as content, the graphic narratives I have explored here render the creative possibilities of posthuman/ist spaces, practices, and subjects.

NOTES

1. See Art Spiegelman, *Co-Mix: A Retrospective of Comics, Graphics, and Scraps* (Montreal: Drawn and Quarterly, 2013), and Gillian Whitlock, "Autographics: The Seeing 'I' of Comics," *MFS: Modern Fiction Studies* 52.4 (Winter 2006): 965–79.
2. Rosi Braidotti, *The Posthuman* (Cambridge, UK: Polity Press, 2013), 12.
3. See Ian Williams, "Why Graphic Medicine?," accessed January 22, 2015, www .graphicmedicine.org/why-graphic-medicine/. Williams notes that Michael Green and Kimberly R. Myers also give him credit for the term in their essay, "Graphic Medicine: Use of Comics in Medical Education and Patient Care," *BMJ* 340 (March 3, 2010), accessed January 22, 2015, www.bmj.com/theBMJ. Green and Myers's use of the term "graphic pathographies" adapts Ann Hunsaker Hawkins's term for illness narratives in her classic work, *Reconstructing Illness: Studies in Pathography* (West Lafayette: Purdue University Press, 1993).
4. For more on the practices of narrative medicine and bioethics, see *Stories Matter: The Role of Narrative in Medicine*, ed. Rita Charon and Martha Montello (New York: Routledge, 2002).
5. See David Palumbo-Liu, *The Deliverance of Others: Reading Literature in a Global Age* (Durham: Duke University Press, 2012), and Lisa Diedrich, "Against Compassion: Attending to Histories and Methods in Medical Humanities; Or, Doing Critical Medical Studies," in *Narrative Matters in Medical Contexts across Disciplines*, ed. Franziska Gygax and Miriam Locher (Amsterdam: John Benjamins, 2015), 167–82.
6. Gilles Deleuze and Félix Guattari, *Kafka: Toward a Minor Literature*, trans. Dana Polan (Minneapolis: University of Minnesota Press, 1986), 53.

7. Will Eisner, *Comics and Sequential Art: Principles and Practices from the Legendary Cartoonist* (New York: Norton, 2008), 39.

8. Lisa Diedrich, *Treatments: Language, Politics, and the Culture of Illness* (Minneapolis: University of Minnesota Press, 2007); see especially the conclusion, "Toward an Ethics of Failure," 148–66.

9. Margrit Shildrick, "Posthumanism and the Monstrous Body," *Body & Society* 2.1 (1996): 6.

10. Brian Massumi, "Notes on the Translation and Acknowledgments," in *A Thousand Plateaus: Capitalism and Schizophrenia*, ed. Gilles Deleuze and Félix Guattari, trans. Brian Massumi (Minneapolis: University of Minnesota Press, 1987), xvi.

11. B. David, *Epileptic* (New York: Pantheon Books, 2005).

12. Deleuze and Guattari, *A Thousand Plateaus*, 13.

13. David, *Epileptic*, 313.

14. Hillary Chute describes Lynda Barry's attempts to "map a process of memory – make it material on the page – through the spatializing form of comics," in "Materializing Memory: Lynda Barry's One Hundred Demons," in *Graphic Subjects: Critical Essays on Autobiography and Graphic Novels*, ed. Michael A. Chaney (Madison: University of Wisconsin Press, 2011), 293.

15. Ellen Forney, *Marbles: Mania, Depression, Michelangelo, and Me* (New York: Gotham Books, 2012).

16. See also Courtney Donovan, "Representations of Health, Embodiment, and Experience in Graphic Memoir," *Configurations: A Journal of Literature, Science, and Technology* 22.2 (Spring 2014): 237–53. Forney's drawings show "how the illness produces two distinct embodied experiences," mania and depression (253).

17. See Lisa Diedrich, "Graphic Analysis: Transitional Phenomena in Alison Bechdel's Are You My Mother?" *Configurations* 22.2 (Spring 2014): 183–203.

18. See Judith Butler, *Gender Trouble: Feminism and the Subversion of Identity* (New York and London: Routledge, 1990), and Annemarie Mol, *The Body Multiple: Ontology in Medical Practice* (Durham and London: Duke University Press, 2002).

19. Martina Schlünder, Pit Arens, and Axel Gerhardt, "Becoming Bone Sheep," *Configurations* 22.2 (Spring 2014): 263–94.

20. Braidotti, *The Posthuman*, 7.

21. *Ibid.*, 79–80.

22. Schlünder, Arens, and Gerhardt, "Becoming Bone Sheep," 278.

23. *Ibid.*, 277.

24. *Ibid.*, 278. See also John Berger's "Why Look at Animals?" in *About Looking* (New York: Vintage, 1980), 3–28: "In the accompanying ideology, animals are always the observed. The fact that they can observe us has lost all significance. They are the objects of our ever-extending knowledge. What we know about them is an index of our power, and thus an index of what separates us from them. The more we know, the further away they are" (16).

25. Braidotti, *The Posthuman*, 79–80.

9

ANNEKE SMELIK

Film

Contemporary visual culture often features love relations between humans and posthumans. To give some examples: in Björk's videoclip *All is Full of Love*, two female robots tenderly make love. In the television commercial "Robotskin" by Philips, a man is seduced by a female robot who helps him shave under the shower, leaving her yearning for him.[1] In the film *Her*, the throaty voice of Samantha, a computer operating system, both comforts and seduces Theodore Twombly after his separation. In *Ex Machina*, Caleb falls in love with a humanoid artificial intelligence named "Ava" and reprograms the security system so that she manages to escape, "cross-dressed" as a "real" woman to pass as human in the world outside her confines, but leaving him behind to face certain death. And in the Swedish television series *Real Humans*, "hubot" Mimi falls in love with Leo, half-human half-hubot, a love that survives in her memory after the forced recharging of her system when she is kidnapped.[2] These examples point to a rather intimate relation between humans and different figurations of the posthuman: robots, androids, replicants, cyborgs, hubots, avatars, AI systems, OS (operating systems), and so on. They show how the figure of the posthuman entices, fascinates, and seduces humans. This chapter sketches how the development of the posthuman image in science fiction (SF) cinema over the last few decades moves from anxiety over identity to mediated memories, and from the awareness of affect to actual love relations.[3] I will link these different figurations of the posthuman to specific cinematic techniques, thematic tropes, and narrative forms. At the end, I will return to the vexed question of love between humans and posthumans.

The Cinematic Cyborg

In cinema studies, the notion of the posthuman is primarily a speculative image rather than a philosophical concept; in that sense, I work in this chapter on a posthuman *imaginary*. I treat the posthuman here as a hybrid figure that transforms and deconstructs human subjectivity in a post-anthropocentric culture. As a cinematic figure, the posthuman is typically represented as a hybrid between a human being and something nonhuman, the latter ranging from machines or digital technologies to plants, animals, monsters, and aliens.[4] As the cyborg is one of the most prevalent posthuman images in cinema, I first focus on this figure in the hybrid genre of the cyborg film of the 1980s and 1990s with its roots in science fiction, horror, and action movies.[5]

The term "cyborg," a *cyb*ernetic *org*anism, originated in space studies.[6] As an updated version of the mechanical robot, the concept of the cyborg indicates a feedback system between human and machine. Donna Haraway introduced the notion into feminist scholarship as a posthumanist concept for "fractured" identity in her agenda-setting "Cyborg Manifesto."[7] In cultural studies, the cyborg has been hailed as a posthumanist configuration in its hybridity between human flesh and metal or digital material, its wavering between mind and matter, and its shifting boundaries between masculinity and femininity.[8] In philosophy, too, the cyborg is understood as a posthuman figure of the "in-between," in the words of Rosi Braidotti, "facilitating interrelations, multiple connections and assemblages."[9] However, this construction of the cyborg is not always the case in cinematic science fiction: here the figure of the cyborg conventionally projects a fantasy of a human who fuses with technology to become a superior, enhanced, and hence threatening being.[10] Hollywood cinema abounds in the celebration of the – quite masculine – superhuman, the overcoming of the perceived weaknesses of human flesh, emotion, and mind. This masculinized figuration could not be further removed from Haraway's utopian vision of the cyborg as "a hybrid of machine and organism, a creature from social reality as well as a creature of fiction."[11] It seems, then, that Hollywood favors a superhuman cyborg over a posthuman hybrid. Nonetheless, in all the display of superhuman power, many cyborg movies explore how the interaction between humans and machines affects them both, having them merge "through mutual simulation and modification."[12] Accordingly, I will trace some cinematic techniques of the 1990s for showing the hybridity of the cyborg – its simultaneously machine-like and human-like qualities. These techniques for depicting the cyborg – point of view shot, self-reparation, and mirror scenes – are still very much in place today.

A Cybernetic Point of View

A SF movie has to convince the spectator that the human figure on the screen is in fact a cyborg. Apart from obvious narrative clues in dialogue and plot, films use two *visual* strategies to make this ontological demarcation clear to the audience: the subjective camera shot and the self-repair scene. The cyborg is often introduced with a subjective point of view (POV) or an over-the-shoulder shot. Film scholars David Bordwell and Kristin Thompson describe the POV shot as a "shot taken with the camera placed approximately where the character's eyes would be, showing what that character would see; usually cut in before or after a shot of the character looking."[13] In the case of the cyborg, such a subjective POV shot generally contains computerized elements within the frame, representing the cyborg's eye as a video camera that can zoom in and out, process data, check a target, and rewind or repeat the image. For example, in *Terminator 2* (1991), when the Terminator (Arnold Schwarzenegger) lands nude on Earth from outer space, he surveys his new surroundings with a piercing gaze shown with a red, digitalized image through a sustained POV shot. *RoboCop* (1987) has several scenes with long POV shots in which the camera films as if it were the eye of RoboCop (Peter Weller) even while it is being fabricated in the laboratory, giving the idea of a robot being imprisoned in a human body. In *Eve of Destruction* (1990), a female cyborg, Eve 8 (Renée Soutendijk), checks out the men in a café through a POV shot with red lights and bleeping sounds before beating them up when they harass her. The computerized elements within the frame emphasize the machine-like aspect of the cyborg, as its eye functions like a camera with superior vision enhanced by technology.

However, the machinic side is not all there is to a cyborg – it can also be surprisingly human in its emotions and powers of self-reflection. The depiction of such capacities is again connected to the POV technique. While the POV shot with its technological cues ascertains the "cyborg-ness" of the character, typical techniques of the POV shot, such as mobile framing, close-ups, and camera movement, are at the same time powerful cinematic cues for subjectivity. In film studies, the impact of a POV shot is taken to produce character subjectivity.[14] Thus, POV shots simultaneously establish both the mechanicity and the subjectivity of the cyborg. This doubleness of the cinematic form allows the audience empathy and perhaps even identification with the "human-ness" of the posthuman figure of the cyborg.

Self-Reparation in the Mirror

Another visual *topos* in cyborg films is to systematically destroy the cyborg so as to repair it. Presumed invincibility may be one characteristic of the cyborg proving the superiority of technology over the human body, but the cinematic cyborg is remarkably vulnerable to assault and injury. After the cyborg is reduced to just a heap of shrapnel, it can be put together again, either by itself or in the lab.

Such self-repair scenes excel in ambiguity, as the once-unbeatable machine has become defenceless flesh. To give a few examples: in *The Terminator* (1984), the cyborg repairs his wounded eye in a typical horror scene that shows the wet flesh inside the mechanized body. When he takes out his eye and drops it into the washbasin, the socket not only shows a bloody wound but also a camera that still functions by zooming in and out. In *RoboCop*, the cyborg drills into his head with a screwdriver, taking off the metal prosthesis that reveals his human flesh. In *Eve of Destruction*, Eve 8 undresses and exposes a gaping gash in her chest, into which she enters with her own hand, apparently restoring something there and then gluing it over with red tape. While these horrific scenes disclose injured flesh, they show once again the superiority of the cyborg that can penetrate and repair its own wounds and continue as if nothing happened.

Self-reparation scenes are another cinematic way of visualizing the hybrid character of the cyborg, because they typically involve mirrors: the Terminator, RoboCop, and Eve 8 all look into a mirror while they are tending their wounds. The mirror is a well-known visual theme in cinema, where it functions for the character to provide a moment of self-reflection. Laura Mulvey and Christian Metz have connected the look into the mirror to the psychoanalytic concept of ego formation in the mirror stage as conceptualized by Jacques Lacan.[15] Mulvey and Metz argue that the child's pleasure in its identification with a perfect mirror image and the formation of its ego ideal on the basis of this idealized reflection is analogous to the film spectator's narcissistic pleasure in identifying with the perfected image of the hero on the screen. In other words, the silver screen of cinema altogether functions as a mirror for its audience, which unconsciously constructs ego ideals on the basis of idealized self-reflections or identifications.

Whereas self-repair suggests that the machine is sufficiently alive to have an instinct for self-preservation, self-reflection additionally presupposes a degree of subjective consciousness. A cyborg in front of a mirror looks like it is actually thinking about itself. In an older example, RoboCop becomes emotional as he checks out the mirror for signs of his former, human, self. In the more recent movie *Ex Machina*, Ava watches herself pensively in the mirror after she has taken her fully human form. The cyborg is often surrounded not only by mirrors but by reflective surfaces such as video monitors or computer screens.[16] In contemporary films such surfaces have become transparent plastic, glass, or liquid, as in *Minority Report* (2002), *Her* (2013), *Oblivion* (2013), *Transcendence* (2014), and *Ex Machina* (2015). Alison Landsberg argues that the mirroring surface allows for a moment of uncanny self-recognition in scenes that are reminiscent of the Lacanian mirror stage. On the one hand, the cyborg characters see a perfected image of the human figure reflected in the mirror, because as hybrids of human and machine, they are literally enhanced and thus perfected human beings. On the other hand, they see a distorted image in the mirror because they are injured and disfigured. These mirror scenes suggest that cyborgs are confused about their hybrid identity: What or who are they? Why do they experience pain or feelings? Do they have memories?

Mediated Memories

If the cinematic cyborg is uncertain about its own status, then its superhuman figure is after all quite posthuman in its in-between-ness. In fact, the hybridity of the posthuman figure in the movies typically produces its identity crisis. Is it a mere machine, or is it also a human, or both? Is artificial intelligence endowed with (or without) a body or consciousness? The crossing and blurring of binary oppositions confuses the cyborg character and, by extension, its spectator. Sometimes such confusion leads to comic relief: in *Total Recall* (1990), when the character who thinks he is Douglas Quaid (Arnold Schwarzenegger) finds out that he is not Quaid, but that his memory has been implanted and that his whole life, including his marriage and his wife, is a fake, he calls out in desperation: "But if I am not me, who the bloody hell am I?" In a sadder example from the cult classic *Blade Runner* (1982), the posthuman Rachael (Sean Young) was really convinced that she was a human being with her own personal memories and feelings, and bursts into tears when she finds out she is a "replicant." The paradoxical point here is that while replicants are not supposed to have emotions, this one cries, manifesting grief over the loss of its presumed human identity.

Whether comic or tragic, such identity crises are a stock theme in the SF films of the late twentieth century. The hybrid figures are confused about their own status, asking themselves questions that echo the Daoist question, "Am I a human dreaming that I am a butterfly, or am I a butterfly dreaming that I am human?" Moreover, the identity crisis is often *not* brought to closure, which is a rare ending for Hollywood cinema. *Blade Runner* suggests at the very end that even Deckard (Harrison Ford), the blade runner whose job is to terminate replicants, actually *is* a replicant. And in *Total Recall*, when the Quaid character has created a new Earth and a new heaven on Mars, his last words are: "And what if I have dreamt it all?" The films thus maintain the cyborg's hybridity until the very end. Taking hybridity as its most important characteristic, the cinematic cyborg is the posthuman figure *par excellence*.

Early cyborg movies, such as *Blade Runner, RoboCop, Total Recall* and the first two *Terminator* films, tell stories about the crisis of identity often induced or increased by prosthetic memory.[17] Such films focus on anxieties aroused by the paradoxical experience of remembering events that the character has not lived through.[18] The identity crisis is focused mostly on issues of memory, because personal memories index subjectivity. Prosthetic memory is thus typical of the cyborg movies of the 1980s and 1990s, where implantations complicate the relations among memory, experience, and identity. Typically, the visual clues for subjective memories are photographs, supposed to "prove" the personal past of the cyborgs. Kaja Silverman has argued that photography is thus used to expose the fragility of posthuman identity.[19] But where photos usually function as documents of truth, in cyborg films they acquire an ambiguous and much darker status as wilful manipulations of the past, suggesting that just as fake photos can be planted, so too seemingly personal memories can be implanted.

Digitizing Memory

In contemporary SF cinema, there has been a significant change in the treatment of the cyborg's identity crisis, because the technologies of memory have shifted away from implanted or prosthetic memory to other, now digital media. In the imaginary of cinema, this transition involves a transition from the "hardware" cyborg to the "software" cyborg, introducing new human–nonhuman interactions that are more connected to the brain than the body altogether. Earlier cyborg figurations still feature in Hollywood movies, but have been relegated to the realm of sequels or prequels and have lost much of their ambivalence in predictable tales of superhuman glory. The post-apocalyptic landscapes of disaster and destruction of the 1980s and 1990s have given way to translucent plastic, glass, liquid, or virtual settings in which humans happily – or sometimes not so happily – interact with the often invisible machines that surround them. In SF films of the twenty-first century, the new frontier of posthuman hybridity explores the relation between the superior memory of the computer and the failing memory of the human being. SF films, such as *Minority Report* (2002), *Final Cut* (2004), *The Butterfly Effect* (2004, and its sequel in 2006), the mangafilm *The Ghost in the Shell* (1995), *Inception* (2010), *Source Code* (2011), and the British television series *Life on Mars* (2006–07) and its sequel *Ashes to Ashes* (2008–09), feature fantasies about the (im)possibilities of digital technologies to register, manipulate, or delete individual memories.

In these films and television series, the issues center on manipulations – and confusions – of the mind. Cyberpunk writer William Gibson has claimed that for him computers are no more than a metaphor for human memory.[20] Digital media have created new ways of saving, retrieving, and archiving personal and collective memories.[21] Therefore, with current digital technology, the concern is no longer with the implantation of false memories. Typically, these more recent characters remember lived experiences. However, the *utopian* fantasy now focuses on the total recall that is enabled by the continuous enhancement of computer memory, feeding the desire to retain and save all memories throughout life, while the *dystopian* fantasy focuses on the deletion and distortion of digitalized memories, feeding the anxiety of possible manipulations of memory and the danger of losing data irretrievably.

I will give the example here of one of the first films in its genre, *Johnny Mnemonic* (1995), loosely based on an early short story by William Gibson. The hero uploads certified but stolen data into his brain in order to bring them to people on the other side of the world. To make space for the data, Johnny (Keanu Reeves) has to temporarily offload his personal memories of his deceased mother.[22] If he is unable to download the computer data within 24 hours, he will die of "information overload." Only when he can discharge the data is he able to reload the personal memories. Of course, Johnny is saved just in time to retrieve the early memories of his mother. Here we see how this sort of posthuman identity gets fully shot through with technology, as individual memory can be digitally retrieved, represented, remediated, transformed, or deleted.

Complex Narratives

In the first decade of this millennium, many SF films and television series pursue a disjointed time line in which past, present, and future get inextricably entangled, for example, in *Eternal Sunshine of the Spotless Mind*, *2046*, and the aforementioned movies. In these SF films and TV series, narrative fragmentation allows for the affect of the past to be processed; in other words, memory affects the experience of time.[23] Where Hollywood SF movies used to smooth over uncertainty by narrative closure, more recent films explore complexity and ambiguity. Not only do these films have no clear beginning, middle, or end, but they also collapse space and time in such a way that renders the spectator's orientation almost impossible. For example, *Inception* sets forward a complex puzzle with different layers of space as a – quite Freudian – visualization of deeper layers of consciousness, even descending into the unconscious. In *Source Code*, too, there is a deliberate blurring between different time lines, spaces, and realities. The complexity of the narratives becomes part of visual pleasure: can the spectator solve the narrative riddle of such convoluted time and space?[24]

I will focus on two independent films to show the posthuman effects of such complex narratives. In both 2046 and *Eternal Sunshine*, the memories of the main characters are enacted in a fragmented narrative that intensifies the spectator's affective experience for he or she is similarly enwrapped in a story almost impossible to unwrap. It is indeed not easy to follow the story line in those two films, because present, past, and future are continually confounded. The title 2046 refers both to the future, the year 2046, and to a specific location, a hotel room. In 2046, Chow Mo Wan (Tony Leung) relives an unhappy love affair with every other woman that he meets and whom he tries (but fails) to love, because each new relation reawakens the memories of the lost woman. The characters move in and out of the hotel room, which functions as a time portal. Without a conventional narrative structure, time and space collapse, bringing the vicissitudes of desires, memories, and affects to the fore.

Eternal Sunshine also tells the story of a failed love relationship, after which the former lovers proceed to delete one another from their memory. The film focuses on the moment when the male character seeks to erase his memories. In the process of deleting them, Joel Barish (Jim Carrey) finds himself transported back to the time of those same memories. Realizing that he is quite attached to them, he struggles to stop the process of erasure. The middle part of the film becomes a complicated, mental journey in which past, present, and future get thoroughly scrambled, confusing not only the characters but also the spectators. As in 2046, the dense narrative structure gets quite intricate because of the reorganization of linear time. This is digitally visualized as follows: while Joel and his girlfriend, Clementine (Kate Winslet), run through the sets of their own past, the setting around them is literally deleted; it disappears. The film thus shows the disconcerting affect of a past that is being undone while one is still in it.[25]

Both films portray feelings of loss and longing. Memory is a source of suffering, as the past loss of a loved one is still poignantly experienced in the present. In 2046, Chow Mo Wan revolves endlessly in a perplexing carousel of present, past, and future, thus never escaping from the emotions that he passively and passionately endures. In *Eternal Sunshine*, the characters hope to be delivered from their emotional pain by deleting the agonizing memories. Yet, the desired loss of memory also blocks any possibility of learning from failures and of preventing them in the future. In focusing on the affective register, both films show the intricacies of memory and the impossibility of disentangling reminiscence from desire and affect, even though technology can erase memories (in *Eternal Sunshine*) or project them into the future (in *2046*).

What is significant for posthuman culture is how the ambiguities of human–nonhuman interaction allow for a different way of storytelling. Cinematic and digital aesthetics have taken SF films and television series beyond the confines of classic structures of representation and narrative. When time turns inside out and outside in, the same can happen to space: real and virtual space can no longer be distinguished. The most spectacular visualization of such confused space is the staircase that leads to nowhere in *Inception*, looking much like a drawing by Giovanni Battista Piranesi or a print by M.C. Escher. It is in the first place the affect of the character's memories that provokes a nonlinear, dynamic vision of time and space. Rather than a humanistic emotion that is short-lived and object-oriented, the films portray affect as an overall state of the posthuman subject who lives through emotional disintegration, reflected in the breakdown of the narrative structure. As Mark B.N. Hansen reminds us, affect is "that modality ... through which we open ourselves to the experience of the new."[26] As the films disengage from the linear sequence of the story or fabula, their ambiguous stories invite the spectator to open up to corresponding affects. The spectator can thus change classical patterns of identification and establish an experiential relation to the posthumanist film, embracing the narrative as a loop that intricately connects present, past, and future.

The Affect of Love

"Affect arises in the midst of *in-between-ness*."[27] SF films explore different kinds of relations between humans and the "multiple others most of which, in the age of anthropocene, are quite simply not anthropomorphic."[28] Indeed, in times where we constantly stroke our mobile phones, tablets, or laptops, and welcome care robots for the elderly into our homes, humans are intimately involved with machines. As I mentioned in the opening of the chapter, recent SF films also feature explicit – and complicated – love relations between the human and the posthuman.

Science-fictional love relations conventionally involve a human (typically a shy, nerdy, lonely, or depressed man) who falls in love with a posthuman figure (typically a highly attractive and idealized woman), dithering on the ambiguous question whether the posthuman entity is at all capable of love.[29] In *Ex Machina*, Caleb may be fascinated with Ava, but he also distrusts – quite rightly, as it turns out – the way she looks. Her rather exaggerated female form is indeed a ruse to seduce and trap him. Ava is not only incapable of such banal human emotions as love but turns out to be a destructive force in the age-old tradition of the *femme fatale*. Similarly, at the end of the film *Her*, when the OS Samantha tells Theodore that she is retreating with other operating systems into another realm, he sadly asks her if she had other intimate relations while she was with him. She promptly answers: 641. Both Theodore and the spectator gasp for breath at this huge number, because even though Samantha only manifested herself as a sexy voice without a body, the suggestion of a unique relationship was indeed very strong and completely misleading.

According to Neil Badmington, a defining characteristic of the human is "to desire, to possess emotions, but to desire is to trouble the sacred distinction between the human and the inhuman."[30] The relationships depicted in these SF love stories fail because the gap between the human and the posthuman cannot be breached; to fall in love with an algorithm is an emotional "beyond" that the genre of the film does not dare to explore yet. Recent films seem to be haunted by a humanist impulse: humans are ruled by the desire to love the machines they live with, but with strict boundaries between them reinstated. Scott Loren argues that "the filmic narratives of posthuman cinema tend to position themselves anxiously in relation to logics of posthumanism and nostalgically, even desperately, in relation to tenets of humanism."[31] Indeed, the films revert to earlier configurations of humanist narratives: they regress to straight and linear storytelling while the melancholy mood captures the failure to successfully relate to the "multiple others" of posthumanity today.

In SF cinema, then, posthuman love relations turn out to be rather ambivalent. Yet, the ambiguity of affect may also point to some new shifts in-between the human and posthuman. For example, at the end of *Her*, Theodore joins his all-too-human neighbour Amy (Amy Adams) and together they stare out at the transparent surfaces and flickering screens of the city. The film suggests that Theodore and the other humans in the story have been taught by the Operating Systems to love one another, while giving up on the – disembodied – affair with their "private" OS. The posthuman entity thus proves more human than a human being in its capacity for love, or at least, for transmitting lessons on how to love. Something new has then emerged from the human–posthuman interaction: it is within the virtual realm of post-humanity that humans find solace in the enfleshed embrace of one another.

NOTES

1. www.youtube.com/watch?v=cfCh7KvoxJ4.
2. *All is Full of Love*, video by Chris Cunningham, lyrics by Björk, 1997; Robotskin, commercial for Philips by Bruno Aveillan, 2007; *Her*, Spike Jonze, 2013, with Scarlett Johansson (Samantha's voice) and Joaquin Phoenix (Theodore Twombly); *Ex Machina*, Alex Garland, 2015, with Domhnall Gleeson (Caleb) and Alicia Vikander (Ava); *Real Humans*, Swedish television series started in 2012, written by Lars Lundström, directed by Harald Hamrell and Levan Akin, with Lisette Pagler (Mimi, aka Anita).
3. This chapter draws on parts from two earlier publications: Anneke Smelik, "The Virtuality of Time: Memory in Science Fiction Films," in *Technologies of Memory in the Arts*, ed. Liedeke Plate and Anneke Smelik (Basingstoke: Palgrave Macmillan, 2009), 52–68; and Anneke Smelik, "Cinematic Fantasies of Becoming-Cyborg," in *The Scientific Imaginary in Visual Culture*, ed. Anneke Smelik (Göttingen: V&R Unipress, 2010), 86–100.
4. See Annette Kuhn, ed., *Alien Zone: Cultural Theory and Contemporary Science Fiction Cinema* (London: Verso, 1990), and *Alien Zone II: The Spaces of Science Fiction Cinema* (London: Verso, 1999); and Elaine Graham, *Representations of the Post-human: Monsters, Aliens, and Others in Popular Culture* (New Brunswick, NJ: Rutgers University Press, 2002).
5. Sidney Perkowitz, *Hollywood Science. Movies, Science, and the End of the World* (New York: Columbia University Press, 2007); Adam Roberts, *Science Fiction* (London and New York: Routledge, 2000).
6. Manfred Clynes and Nathan Kline, "Cyborgs and Space" (1960), reprinted and supplemented with an unpublished article by Clynes, "Cyborg II," and an interview with Clynes, in *The Cyborg Handbook*, ed. Chris Hables Gray (London: Routledge, 1995).
7. Donna Haraway, "A Manifesto for Cyborgs: Science, Technology, and Socialist Feminism in the 1980s," in *Simians, Cyborgs, and Women: The Reinvention of Nature*, Donna Haraway (London: Free Association Books, 1991), 149–81.
8. Chris Hables Gray, ed., *The Cyborg Handbook* (London: Routledge, 1995).
9. Rosi Braidotti, *The Posthuman* (Cambridge: Polity Press, 2013), 92.
10. Vivian Sobchack, *Screening Space. The American Science Fiction Film* (New Brunswick: Rutgers University Press, 1997).
11. Haraway, "Manifesto for Cyborgs," 149.
12. Braidotti, *The Posthuman*, 90.
13. David Bordwell and Kristin Thompson, *Film Art: An Introduction*, 10th edn. (New York: McGraw Hill, 2013), 504.
14. *Ibid.*, 92.
15. Christian Metz, *Psychoanalysis and Cinema. The Imaginary Signifier* (London: MacMillan, 1982; orig. 1977); Laura Mulvey, "Visual Pleasure and Narrative Cinema," (1975) reprinted in Laura Mulvey, *Visual and Other Pleasures* (London: Macmillan 1989), 14–26. Lacan, J., 1966, "The mirror stage as formative of the function of the I", in *Écrits. A Selection*. Norton, New York, London, pp 1–7.

16. See Alison Landsberg, *Prosthetic Memory: The Transformation of American Remembrance in the Age of Mass Culture* (New York: Columbia University Press, 2004).
17. Constance Penley, Elisabeth Lyon, Lynn Spiegel, and Jaanet Bergstrom, eds., *Close Encounters: Film, Feminism, and Science Fiction* (Minneapolis: University of Minnesota Press, 1991).
18. Susannah Radstone, ed., *Memory and Methodology* (Oxford: Berg, 2000).
19. Kaja Silverman, "Back to the Future," *Camera Obscura* 27 (1991): 109–32.
20. Dani Cavallaro, *Cyberpunk and Cyberculture: Science Fiction and the Work of William Gibson* (London: Athlone Press, 2000).
21. José van Dijck, *Mediated Memories in the Digital Age* (Stanford: Stanford University Press, 2007).
22. The memory of the mother figures more often as an oedipal motif for human identity and memory; e.g. in *Blade Runner* where Rachel is "humanized" by her prosthetic memories of her mother (see Silverman 1991). Compare also the scene in *Ex Machina* where Ava asks Caleb about his earliest memory. He answers, after first giving the "wrong" answer, that it is his mother's voice; in other words, he is "of woman born" as opposed to man-made Ava.
23. I follow Brian Massumi here in his distinction between affect as unassimilable intensity and emotion as a subjective feeling. Massumi, "The Autonomy of Affect," *Cultural Critique* 31 (1995): 83–109, 88. See also Patricia Clough, "The Affective Turn: Political Economy, Biomedia, and Bodies," *Theory, Culture, and Society* 25.1 (2008): 1–22.
24. The SF films are part of a wider trend in cinema to tell complex stories; see Warren Buckland, ed., *Puzzle Films: Complex Storytelling in Contemporary Cinema* (Oxford: Wiley-Blackwell, 2009).
25. For a related, further unfolding of this complex narrative, see Bruce Clarke, *Neocybernetics and Narrative* (Minneapolis: University of Minnesota Press, 2014), 100–4.
26. Mark B. N. Hansen, *New Philosophy for New Media* (Cambridge: MIT Press, 2004), 132.
27. Gregory Seigworth and Melissa Gregg, "An Inventory of Shimmers," in *The Affect Theory Reader*, ed. Melissa Gregg and Gregory Seigworth (Durham: Duke University Press, 2010), 1–25, 1 (original emphasis).
28. Braidotti, *The Posthuman*, 101.
29. For example, the earlier mentioned *Her* (2013) and *Ex Machina* (2015), and also *Under the Skin*, Jonathan Glazier, 2014, with Scarlett Johansson as the nameless woman.
30. Neil Badmington, "Pod Almighty! or, Humanism, Posthumanism, and the Strange Case of *Invasion of the Body Snatchers*," *Textual Practice* 15.1 (2001): 9.
31. Scott Loren, "Posthumanist Panic Cinema. Defining a Genre," in *Paradoxes of Authenticity: Studies on a Critical Concept*, ed. Julia Straub (New Brunswick and London: Transaction Publishers, 2012), 164.

10

IVAN CALLUS
AND
MARIO AQUILINA

E-Literature

Introduction: Paradoxes and Definitions

It reflects the nature of E-Literature (E-Lit) – electronic literature, or literature that is often defined as "born digital" – that some of the most helpful guides to it and its most comprehensive archives are to be found online. There may always be something slightly paradoxical in approaching born-digital (or, indeed, digital-only) literary practice through a different medium, but this chapter is set up not in lieu of the ampler digital resources devoted to E-Lit, which the reader is encouraged to explore (the links at the website of the Electronic Literature Organization, eliterature.org, provide some excellent prompts), but to offer some reflections on E-Lit's affinities with the posthuman. With this in mind, the next two sections briefly survey some broader relations between literature and (post)humanism, ahead of the more focused discussion on E-Lit and its posthuman affinities, developed in the final two sections. The preliminary considerations provide some depth of field to views on how the "tradition" (in T. S. Eliot's sense) can find itself realigned at interfaces between E-Lit and the posthuman. At those interfaces, the point is not so much "individual talent,"[1] but rather such conceptions as text generators and distributed cognition,[2] as well as "expressive processing,"[3] "recombinant poetics,"[4] "the polyphonic nature of digital identity,"[5] and dynamic heterarchies determined by multi-tiered feedback and feedforward loops, where "continuing interactions ... continuously inform and mutually determine each other."[6] In the forefront, therefore, is the question of the nature and extent of E-Lit's arguably post-literary space.

One further point, in preamble: the definition of E-Lit for the reader to keep in mind might be that reported in N. Katherine Hayles's *Electronic Literature: New Horizons for the Literary*. It tells of "work with an important literary aspect that takes advantage of the capabilities and contexts provided by the stand-alone or networked computer."[7] Strikingly, the Organization's foundation and Hayles's landmark study, *How We Became Posthuman*, both came about in the same year, 1999, the definition occurring when the Organization "convened a committee headed by Noah Wardrip-Fruin, himself a creator and critic of electronic literature, to come up with a definition appropriate to this new field."[8] E-Lit is in fact a creative context where group-based composition represents both an appropriate ethic and a productive procedure, though the question of authorship, as we shall see, is more complex still.

Lit (no "E") and Humanism (no "Post")

The view that literature and the posthuman might be mutually exclusive is not without some foundation. Literature might appear necessarily precarious within posthuman*ism*, especially when this is understood, in tendentious and not too nuanced perspectives, as that which supplants humanism and its constitutive investments in the cultures of the letter as distinct from increasingly dominant cultures of code and the digital, which are presumed to be more coextensive with the posthuman and to facilitate it. Certainly, there appears to be a ready affinity between humanism and *letters* (as far as the histories of these things go, this usage of the word has grown quaint only comparatively recently).[9] In that case, is the posthuman, logically, post-letteral, post-literary? Is it because literature is not as electrifying as formerly that E-Lit – the letter electric – might be cast as both deliverance and horizon? Is electronic literature, with its investments in digital affordances, code, and the algorithmic, just the kind of writing for today? Or is it the case that E-Lit is merely one of those avant-gardes that literature, in its own good time and without any particular need for revanchism, will co-opt, overtaking what was to exceed it?

This chapter cannot provide comprehensive responses to all these questions. It can, however, offer leads to ways in which they might be broached, as well as indicate some important considerations when considering the posthuman affinities of E-Lit. A good way to start might be as follows. It would be possible to string out reflections from Terence's *Homo sum, humani nihil a me alienum puto* on to Hamlet's "What a piece of work is man!" alongside familiar positions on the same theme in, for instance, Erasmus, Montaigne, or Pascal, all of which exemplify *lettered* humanism abetting *liberal* humanism: the paradigm affirming an exceptionalism of the human as this becomes manifest in art and culture. This is the exceptionalism that most posthumanist perspectives baulk from taking as a given. Dispositions have changed since Alexander Pope's cautionary lines about reconciliation to the human sphere:

> But of this frame the bearings, and the ties,
> The strong connections, nice dependencies,
> Gradations just, has thy pervading soul

Looked thro'? or can a part contain the whole?
  Is the great chain, that draws all to agree,
  And drawn supports, upheld by God, or thee?[10]

Ambivalent outlooks about the (post)human from literary tradition can be cited even up to Robert Musil's Ulrich and the prospect he offers of humanity's deliberated self-divesting of distinction, for here is an anti-hero who across *The Man without Qualities* grows akin to Agamben's "man without content" (on which more will be said toward this chapter's conclusion). The idea of the intrinsic nobility of the human dies hard notwithstanding the sense of originary abjection in the human condition, the projected overcoming of which opens one space for the posthuman. If poignancy endures in Samuel Beckett, it is because the idea of human exceptionalism does not quite recede, even in absurdist abjection. Indeed, it is possible to read literary tradition as accumulated evidence that literary cultures nurture anthropocentrism even when they ironize or decentre the human. As Stefan Herbrechter notes, "Literature – this humanist invention – might be seen as a privileged cultural practice that engages in this representational negotiation between the human and the inhuman. Where else therefore should one seek out the human/inhuman nexus than at the heart of the literary canon?"[11] Parallel to the survival of this reflex of the literary, the human(ist) survives likewise. It is therefore not fanciful to think that posthuman transformation requires change in the conception of the literary as, practically, a precondition.

E-Lit – where digital affordances are intrinsic, all(o)ying writing with code – consequently finds the stakes for its posthuman bearings loaded. It could not be otherwise. Words such as "art," "inspiration," "imagination," "originality," "creativity," "genius," "the beautiful," "the sublime," and "style," all of which are integral to "the biography of the idea of 'literature,'"[12] seem to have necessary and self-evident human reference, or presuppose human-referenced perception. Modernism, absurdism, diverse avant-gardes, and various "post-*x*" constructions of the twentieth century and since may have problematized each and every one of those words and its extensions, but it would be idle to think that the terms do not continue to operate in unreconstructed ways in their broader usage outside and even within the academy. As a discourse, posthumanism therefore needs the literary as a foil, if nothing else. For posthumanism, literature becomes something to push back against in its testing of how supposedly human-specific valences might be questioned or even exceeded.

That point made, the next section reviews four reasons (among thinkable others) for the posthuman's necessarily uneasy relationship with literature.

They prepare the ground for this chapter's closer look at E-Lit, its promise, and its discontents.

Some Thoughts on Literature, the Posthuman, and Their Mutual Suspicion

The points below exemplify motivations for mutual suspicion between literature and the posthuman (which is not to say that stronger affinities between E-Lit and the posthuman will necessarily mitigate them).

(1) Within literature there tends to be a valorization of the *individual*. To rapidly skim past various literary and critical histories and take the implications of this further: the prospect of a solitary cell, a point holding itself off from being a node in a system – psychopathologically, as Lukács might have said – was always going to run counter to contrary energies affirming broader predilections for the rhizomatic.[13] Affirmation of the integrity of the individual before prospects involving the mining of the human also subvert transhumanist scenarios where it might become possible to, as it were, *transcribe* the human, *remediating* it as information and code, opening it to technology's most radical and potentially subsuming affordances, so that *body* becomes prosthetically modular and open to being re-formed, while mind becomes tele-archivic and, no doubt, rewritable (now *that* streaming of consciousness would be a literary achievement of another kind).[14] In the posthuman, *autopoiesis* – self-creation, self-maintenance, self-readaptation – is in the end about the self-(re)constitution of *system*, not individuality. Posthumanists might argue that they uphold no individuality-obliterating dynamic, but literary (and other) cautionary prefigurations of posthuman worlds – as in Kazuo Ishiguro's *Never Let Me Go*, to mention just one example – remain motivated (un)consciously by apprehensiveness over an instrumental logic that risks seeming blind to personhood and hive-minded in its actions. The wariness of machinic, system-atic protocols extended to propensities and activities that might be thought of as irreducibly human – like the capacity for production *and* reception of the literary – will therefore be stronger still. It will be powerfully in the background for some readers, even as electronic literature seeks to potentiate and embody the counter-possibility of singularity conceived entirely differently, as the second point below illustrates, and as is further shown by work in E-Lit that "avoids the personalized, ego-centered position of the romantic, realist, or modernist 'I'" in order "to explore material dimensions of the text" instead, where "writing can be seen not as an individual personalized achievement, but as a series of strands in a larger social-spatial textual fabric (the network)."[15]

(2) Poststructuralism – arguably a paradigm that comes before posthumanism (at least some strands of it) quite counteringly – lays heavy

investments in the singularity of literature. This may be understood in the context of Derrida's idea of literature as the only discourse in which it is possible to "say anything, accept anything, receive anything, suffer anything, and simulate everything."[16] Also influential are Blanchot's perspectives on "the space of literature," or "writing begin[ning] only when it is the approach to that point where nothing reveals itself, ... a language which is still only in its image, an imaginary language and a language of the imaginary, the one nobody speaks, the murmur of the incessant and the interminable which one has to *silence* if one wants, at last, to be heard."[17] Commensurate with, if not equatable to, classical ideas on the sublime, from Longinus to Kant, such positions are relatable also to the idea of perspectives on the "Literary Absolute," where ideas on autopoiesis develop rather differently to their trajectory in, say, Niklas Luhmann's systems theory.[18] Here, in illustration, are Philippe Lacoue-Labarthe and Jean-Luc Nancy, who in their analysis of "the modern concept of literature in German romanticism" explain that "the literary Genre is Literature itself, the *Literary Absolute* – 'true literature,' as Schlegel will say ..., which is not 'this or that genre, content to attain some formation [*Bildung*] or other by chance, but rather literature itself that would be a great, thoroughly connected and organized Whole, comprehending many worlds of art in its unity, and being at the same time a unitary work of art.'"[19] This Whole allows "Literature (or Poetry)" to be "envisaged as a sort of beyond of literature itself," so that "[t]he process of absolutization or infinitization ... *exceeds* ... the general theoretical (or philosophical) power of which it is nonetheless the completion" (92). Consequently, "[t]he 'auto' movement, so to speak – auto-formation, auto-organization, auto-dissolution, and so on – is perpetually in excess in relation to itself," as Lacoue-Labarthe and Nancy put it, in their exploration of the reflection in *Athenaeum* Fragment 116 that "No theory can exhaust it [poetry], and only a divinatory criticism would dare to criticize its ideal" (92).

These words are important here because the idiom of "divinatory criticism" and of a "beyond" of literature itself institutes the kind of discourse that some posthumanist critique might wish to counter. E-Lit too may be expected to conceive of sublimity, or the absolute, differently, indicating the potential for an intriguing incongruity with certain well-established drifts in critical discourse.

(3) For some tastes, the preceding two points might have overindulged theory's mystiques of literature. Here is a rawer point. Literature is a fertile source for originary narratives telling the tale of how hopes of reengineering the human condition will find their comeuppance. Its instincts on this point are not markedly different to creation narratives punishing desires for

knowledges not allotted to human range. Faustus's predicament, in Marlowe and thereafter in explorations of the tale in Goethe, Mann, and beyond, is readable as a parable on why moving beyond what it seems maximally given to the human to be, do, and know will end unhappily. Indeed the posthuman, literature tends to suggest, could not possibly make for a very happy paradigm. It dares to dream of too much, setting itself up for a fall. It is born from restlessness: existential dissatisfaction, an impatience with human limitation, and a willingness to see if this can be extended and enhanced by artifactual means if necessary. This rarely ends well in literature, as narratives from Mary Shelley to Philip K. Dick demonstrate. To be sure, many posthuman tropes find their source in literature, but the tendency there is toward reminding the human that it ought to be cautious about what transformations and enhancements to wish for. The metamorphosis of the human, as Ovid indicated long ago, tends to make the transformed human repine.[20]

(4) Literature is inherently about language used "peculiarly."[21] But language "is not what it used to be," announces N. Katherine Hayles, which, if true, has evident implications for the literary and its resonances.[22] Hayles is of course sophisticatedly responsive to literary discourse, but statements like these arguably remain symptomatic of a default suspicion of the letter, the word, language in various posthumanist instincts, and, conversely, of a greater excitement about the bit, the digital, code, and their potentialities – about which literature might stand uncertain. Unless, that is, it's E-Lit we're talking about.

So What Is E-Lit? Is It Posthuman?

Indeed. What *is* E-Lit? As the Electronic Literature Organization's definition (see above) intimates, it goes far beyond the mere transposition of print literature onto searchable digital archives and platforms or the transmediatic publication of literature. Not so much digital-borne, then, as digital-born literature: conceived for and executed on digital media. *Executed* is an apt word here. The "writing" of an E-Lit "text" *can* be poetic, it *can* be poetry, but it may be of a different order and come about off structuring or compositional principles born from *encoding*, rather than being *set to* an electronic platform. Generative poetry or fiction, for example, may be *executed* by the reader interacting with it, instantiating in every reading one narrative or performance of the e-textual among the potentially infinite – at least for human purposes – permutations it enables. Or it may be "deterministic" and "non-interactive," as in several computational poems by Nick Montfort, but still profoundly determined by the algorithms which generate it, possibly for lengths of time that exceed the human.[23] This is why E-Lit is often as much about the loop of the algorithmic as the leap of inspiration.[24] Imagination is not, however, thereby diminished, nor invention restricted. Both are necessary and preeminent within E-Lit.

Admittedly, the first reaction of those unaccustomed to E-Lit is that it is not, so to speak, literature as they know it. Adaptive responses are required. E-Lit may be acknowledged to be ingenious, but this can key a backhanded compliment. Readers of this chapter will want to make their own open mind up, noting that E-Lit will go beyond what is envisaged, for instance, in Richard Powers's novel *Galatea 2.2*, where an Artificial Intelligence called Helen is devised capable of analysing literary texts.[25] E-Lit goes beyond hypothetical or real scenarios where a different kind of Turing test might be run, where the test subject must decide whether a text reaching them from behind a screen would have been written by a human or not, cueing, say, puzzlement over whether a text conjecturally bordering on the *sublime* is to be credited to algorithm, software, or Artificial Intelligence. However – and this is crucial – it would scarcely be very posthumanist to get *nonhuman literature* to merely simulate literature's familiarities (the provocations of this phrase, "nonhuman literature," are suddenly not incongruous, at least in certain contexts and before all the qualifications that will foreseeably be insisted upon). This cannot be "merely" an extension of humanity-trumped-by-AI scenarios – as in Deep Blue defeating a chess Grandmaster – where the form and modularity of the activity is not radically transformed by an other-than-human agency. If all that E-Lit does is to prompt marvelling disbelief that human and "nonhuman literature" can occasionally seem to become indistinguishable, then it cannot be said that conceptions of the literary have changed. Rather, E-Lit is at its most striking when it forces a recasting of presuppositions of what literature is. It forces the "reader" (if this word still applies) to contemplate forms of being-literary, of literary being, that may have needed (though not necessarily) nonhuman agency, albeit possibly in tandem with human co-design or human pre-coding. Again, familiar critical terms become a little anamorphic here, where their meaning shifts in E-Lit's contexts. It might well be wondered, for instance, what *metaphor* – that staple of literature's pre-electronic instantiations – might need to suggest in digital contexts: or, indeed, *how* it now suggests. The rhetoric of electronic literature, it will be intuited, is going to be different again.

Before we go there, inevitably, some history. Christopher Funkhouser's scholarship in this area, on "prehistoric digital poetry," is key, as is the work done on Pathfinders, a digital preservation project intent on ensuring that early e-texts survive despite the devices for which they were written becoming obsolete.[26] In any case, literary texts written to an austere combinatoric, generative, or algorithmic principle predate the digital age. Indeed, electronic literature's routines can find themselves prefigured in various earlier texts: in Jonathan Swift, for instance, or Roald Dahl, to cite two quite contrasting sources.[27] This raises interesting questions on whether E-Lit is necessarily consequent on digital premises presupposing the availability of electronics *and* electricity and on whether older combinatoric or generative works can quite be said to prefigure E-Lit simply on the strength of surface similarities. The more expected precursors can be found, for instance, in Surrealism. The game Exquisite Corpses (in which sentences are constructed in which a group of players provide words and phrases to a set syntactical routine, one at a time and in an agreed sequence) is one rudimentary example, while the generative principles underlying a number of the productions of the OuLiPo are well known.[28] More curious still is the method of Raymond Roussel in a novel like *Impressions d'Afrique*, composed on the basis of paronomasic association.[29] This leads to an important point. What is common to a number of the textual productions emerging from such contrivances is the surprise that meaningful (even if weirdly so) utterances can emerge in such situations, and that the meaningfulness can seem to lay some claim, however tenuous, on the literary. "Literary aspects" – to echo the definition of E-Lit quoted at the start – can emerge from quite random or rigidified agency. Language, it seems, sometimes just happens to fall literarily (or we perceive it to do so), whereupon it may not do to go looking for explanations of how this happens. There is a parable that warns against reading literature back to see whether such effects are the result of coded intention or of "the inductive word," in the comparatively unknown side of de Saussure (or "deux Saussures," to cite the pun induced in the commentaries) wherein he was seeking evidence for his hypothesis that the literature of antiquity was written to an arcane, hermetic, anagrammatic (or anaphonic) principle encrypting the names of gods, heroes, and other characters in the verse.[30] This is the same propensity that more recently induced Quentin Meillassoux, no less, to undertake not dissimilar speculations on the work of Mallarmé.[31] Proportion and perspective are best maintained in analysing how "literary aspects" happen. It is noteworthy, therefore, that studies of E-Lit highlighting different aspects and affordances of the "electronic" and the "literary" when these coincide have been typified by measured excitement, not excitable manifestos.

What have those studies been picking up? In the 1980s and 1990s, for instance, even before the advent of the Internet for public use, canonical work in the form of hypertext fiction can be located in Michael Joyce's *Afternoon*, Stuart Moulthrop's *Victory Garden*, and Shelley Jackson's *Patchwork Girl*.[32] "Hypertext," as theorized by George Landow but crucially, before that, by Ted Nelson, exploits linking as a structural property.[33]

It creates the possibility of the same texts or units of text being accessed in different ways and in different temporal sequences by readers. At stake here is disruption of narrative linearity as well as the ergodic element of "non-trivial" effort by the readers in navigation of the work's output.[34] There is a sense, however, that what hypertext fiction does is to merely enhance what is always already to be found in print literature. Borges's "The Garden of Forking Paths," for instance, provides one ready print analogy, or allegory, to hypertext fiction.[35]

A related genre of electronic literature which adds further layers of complexity is interactive fiction, which combines the narrative non-linearity of hypertext with the requirement of reader interaction through text commands. Nick Montfort's criticism provides a good window onto this and its distinction from chatterbots, conversation-generating computer programs.[36] Operating on the interface of literature and games, Michael Mateas and Andrew Stern's *Facade*, for instance, asks readers, who become players, to take on the role of a friend who has been invited to visit a couple as they are in the middle of an argument.[37] Players have to input text and move their character in ways which, through the AI running the software, determine the eventual outcome of the storyline. Earlier celebrated examples of this genre are Will Crowther's *Colossal Cave Adventure* and Tim Anderson, Marc Blank, Bruce Daniels, and Dave Lebling's *Zork*.[38]

The reader's participation is also central in interactive installations or interactive works that bring not only the reader's mouse clicks or text as input into the work but also the reader's body. Works such as Romy Achituv and Camille Utterback's *Text Rain* and Bruno Nadeau and Jason Lewis's *Still Standing* bring the poetic text (or letter) to the reader through the reader's own bodily interaction with the installation.[39] Noah Wardrip-Fruin et al's *Screen* combines interactive and playful elements with Virtual Reality technology to create a literary experience about memory and loss.[40] Kate Pullinger's "The Breathing Wall" depends on the reader's breathing patterns for the narrative to develop. Such interactive works clearly problematize what is meant by "reading." Hermeneutics and reader-reception theory have scant purchase here, where what is "of greatest interest are the convergences and irritations that occur on the boundaries of code and text: it is not interactive fiction but interactive friction that warms the text."[41] What changes is the experientiality of literature in the midst of this frictional interactivity. The impression, perhaps, might take root that the work must be *busied* – so that one must respond with appropriate initiative, in the process forcing critical orthodoxies on writerly as distinct from readerly texts, on authorship, or on the (non)play with closure across classic realist to metafictional works to be rethought.

As anticipated above, another direction in E-Lit has been the computational development of a literary tradition of constrained generative poetry in the mould of OuLiPo.[42] More recently, Nick Montfort's #! uses short computer programs to create poetic output on the basis of several constraints.[43] In the case of "Round," for example, the computation of pi, which is potentially infinite, is used to produce equally infinite poetic sequences. Montfort's collaboration with Stephanie Strickland in "Sea and Spar Between," on the other hand, uses words from the poetry of Emily Dickinson and Herman Melville's *Moby Dick* to generate around 225 trillion stanzas of poetry.[44] Any reading of a work like this may be a unique reading, lending weight to the idea that E-Lit is always an event (see below). More significantly, no reading of "Sea and Spar Between" can ever be a complete or exhaustive reading as the text generated far exceeds what may be humanly readable. The privileging of the "whole," or organic unity, that marks certain schools of literary criticism is incommensurable with such works.

The affordances of the digital have also marked E-Lit through multimodality and kineticism. Brian Kim Stefans's *The Dreamlife of Letters* is a well-known example of words and letters set to movement.[45] The letters dance around the screen in this non-interactive piece, and they convey meaning through more than semantics. Video, sound, image, and interactivity come together in works like Stephanie Strickland's "slippingglimpse" and David Jhave Johnston's "Sooth."[46] Here, the letter – as that which is at least etymologically defining of literature – becomes only a part of art works that require a multi-sensory engagement and that achieve poetic effects also through non-linguistic means often associated with other art forms.

Across these examples, art where agency is human-engendered but not human-dependent, where there is a machinic and stochastic automatism driving what proffers itself to interaction, unsettles assumptions on the necessary anthropocentrism to literature or its print-dominant platform existence. What emerges, indeed, in E-Lit as a modality that seems to be particularly worth exploring, though there is not quite the space for it here, is *dimension*. The manners in which E-Lit is received, experienced, interacted with, and recast thoroughly in each iteration beg questions on *where* it is that all this happens. It is all very well to pose the question of the space of literature in the terms of Blanchot, but the space of E-Lit – the dimensions where it is encountered, and the manner in which the instigation of the encounter *is* the creation of dimension – prompts questions that are equally imponderable, stretching the suppleness of literary criticism's discourse when moving beyond "codexspace."[47] E-Lit's affinities with the posthuman exist also in the palpability yet indefiniteness of this space and its dimensions, extending across the layers and levels born from the potentiation by code of emergent experientiality. "A poetic language literally made of light in space-time," to quote Edouardo Kac, does rather change things (155). If the post-literary opens in dimensions such as these, the interest lies in the way in which the repertoires of the literary and the operations of critique as conventionally pitched can only be stretched by it. Everybody will know that E-Lit and digital games make *character*, for instance, a category that can seem a touch flat if *avatars* could only be rounder.[48] But make a list of the other ready protocols for literary analysis – *theme, plot, form, ambiguity*, and then the big one underlying them all, *close reading* – and it will all look a little strained when applied to E-Lit. It is not clear, either, that the protocols of computational criticism and *distant reading*, as carried forward by figures like Franco Moretti and Matthew Jockers or institutions like the Stanford Literary Lab, are not themselves stretched by E-Lit's non-collapsibility to familiar routines in critique.[49]

Does the rhetoric of E-Lit, transcending "figures of speech," open onto "figures of code"? What code brings to figuration, the (post)human will find it can(not) (only) (mis)read, in activity and agency where execution and performance unsettle interpretation and hermeneutics. Understanding the poetics of E-Lit and the ways in which it reflects or exceeds (or finds itself exceeded by) rhetoric as it has hitherto been envisaged is a fascinating challenge for criticism. A lot has already been done, not least in establishing E-Lit's distinctness within studies of new media and remediation.[50] Beyond works referenced already, it is good to recall Michael Heim's pioneering work on "electric language" and Jerome J. McGann's on "radiant textuality,"[51] together with Mark B. N. Hansen's reflections on embodiment, technesis, the nonrepresentational nature of E-Lit, and, more recently, on feed-forward dynamics.[52] Recent work by Roberto Simanowski has given the lie to the idea that E-Lit is opaque to close reading protocols,[53] while the political propensities of E-Lit are addressed in Rita Raley's *Tactical Media*.[54] But it is perhaps in the coextensiveness of E-Lit with event and emergence that the affinities with both posthumanist *and* poststructuralist ideas on literariness cohere. "Singularity," as Derek Attridge writes, is "not a property but an event, the event of singularizing which takes place in reception: it does not occur outside the responses of those who encounter and thereby constitute it."[55] This accords with E-Lit's celebration of "emerging from the study with wires tangled in our hair, pixels in our spirit, happy to find that physical interaction with the intangible that makes it *making*,"[56] and with its openness to the idea of "constantly shifting *eventfulness*" [emphasis added] born from "huge datasets that are sublimely overwhelming," where "stratigraphic time" and "real-time performative events" participated in by "communicative peers" occur.[57] Posthumanism could do worse than to study its investments in emergence and the virtual in the light of these perceptions.[58]

Conclusion: The Posthumanist Affinities of Electronic Literature

E-Lit, in theory and practice, holds itself separate from (though not necessarily unsympathetic to) affirmation of literary culture, as we know it, in an age of "disappearing ink," where questions like *Can Poetry Matter?* appear urgent.[59] E-Lit's instincts are not to fight literature's rearguard action before digital cultures, not when "digitality has become the textual condition of twenty-first-century literature."[60] The practitioners and theorists of E-Lit are instead driven by the curiosity, opportunities, and inventiveness opened by what is, in effect, an entirely new *aesthetic*. E-Lit *matters*, because it potentiates the literary differently: not discontinuously (otherwise one could really speak of "veering,"[61] where nothing of the literary remains valued except the expediency of invoking the term), but in a manner that has resonance because it creatively undoes the stabilities that settle around understandings of literariness. Nothing within literary cultures is proofed against consequent transformation, not when the (post-)literary necessarily co-mutates with the (post)human. The reader is here invited, in fact, to go back to the four points reviewed in this chapter's second section and reflect on how the natures of E-Lit might recode the affinities between the (post-)literary and the (post)human. While doing so, a glance at a work like Jessica Pressman, Mark C. Marino, and Jeremy Douglass's *Reading Project: A Collaborative Analysis of William Poundstone's* Project for Tachitoscope (Bottomless Pit) will suggest just how multifaceted and eclectic critical discourse in this area already is, and how there are in fact richer resonances with tradition (again, in Eliot's sense) than can superficially appear to be the case.[62]

One thing can punningly be said: E-Lit does not entirely execute the literary. Only three reasons need be mentioned in evidence. Firstly, there is a sense that, despite the potential for widespread accessibility afforded by platforms like mobile devices, E-Lit evolves in quite niche environments within both the academy and the public sphere. It enjoys some very special spaces indeed, in institutions, across online fora, and beyond. But it carries on as one quite particular district of literary studies: a space where a "geek sublime" (the term is Vikram Chandra's[63]) can proceed happily but with debatable impact on the manner in which the business of literature is more generally prosecuted, its meaning understood, its outcomes received in the academy and mainstream literary circuits. E-Lit requires receptivities and an "electracy" and "transliteracies" whose pervasiveness is not yet as secure as that of the platforms through which it can be mediated.[64] Secondly, theorists of contemporary affordances of literature are themselves not disposed to let go of literature as it is more conventionally understood: witness, for instance, moves in the work of Hansen or Jessica Pressman to discuss print literature's remarkable modalities even when they discuss "bodies in code" or "digital modernism."[65] Thirdly, it is not always bad for art or critique to wait a little for and upon the world's dispositions. Various settlements await. For instance: the phrase "electronic literature" will continue to seem a contradiction in terms to some observers; the continuities and coextensiveness across digital games, textual art, and E-Lit make for intriguing (in)distinctions demanding further exploration; additionally, time is needed for E-Lit to be more broadly perceived as self-evidently literary.

Yet, it cannot be doubted that it is in E-Lit's capacity to execute literature differently that its value *and* its posthuman affinities lie. Two differently toned visions of posthuman(ist) art might, in conclusion and in illustration of the stakes of E-Lit, be flagged here. They are taken neither from the theory of E-Lit nor of posthumanism, but from continental philosophy and the comparative arts.

In *The Man without Content*, Giorgio Agamben asks whether art "has completed the circle of its metaphysical destiny and . . . reentered the dawn of an origin in which not only its destiny but the very destiny of man could be put in question in an initial manner."[66] In that posthumanist, post-literary situation, the artist "discovers that no content is now immediately identified with his innermost consciousness" (54). What occurs is "the general decline of all contents," where "the pure creative-formal principle, split from any content, is the absolute abstract inessence, which annihilates and dissolves every content in its continuous effort to transcend and actualize itself" (54). E-Lit, to which this becoming is far from alien, is one space where content is overridden by a practice of in-experience, by the dis-content of art and literature manifest in the (ir)relevance of (post)humanist desire felt by "the artist [as] the man without content": the posthuman "who has no other identity than a perpetual emerging out of the nothingness of expression and no other ground than this incomprehensible station on this side of himself" (55).

The late Daniel Albright's vision of the arts stresses not dis-content but panaesthetics, arguably a more powerful vision in the "postprint era" than that opening onto "comparative textual media."[67] "Every medium is intimate with every other," writes Albright, "because the senses themselves are only weakly segregated."[68] The human remains at the core in this vision – "there is something peculiarly seductive, warmly human, in the sidestep across media" (280) – but "[t]o some extent the aesthetic phenomenon is a mode of understanding how the human body winds and unwinds, sleeks itself, through the artwork. The artwork's surface is always, in a sense, skin." Consequently – and things turn unwittingly posthumanist here – "[t]he human race and its art is always co-evolving. Maybe art is helping us sprout new sense organs ... " (284). Albright notes intimations of this unusual prosthesis in Ezra Pound, who spoke of "hyper-aesthesia," and concludes that "[t]o learn to see with the epigastrium and to hear with the elbows is part of the mission of the artwork: to read with the skin and all that is beneath the skin" (286). E-Lit has the affordances and dimensions to organ-ize this newly, and perhaps it does not matter in the end if the experience is more human(ist) or posthuman(ist), advanced in intermediatic space or in the silence of "no medium" where art's platforms are blank.[69] For the overriding question of poetics in E-Lit is not quite the one bound up with understanding its different rhetoric or figures in play – or at rest. It is, rather, that of realizing that E-Lit is itself as complex and diverse a metaphor of posthuman desire and its discontentment as any that could be encountered. (Mis)reading it, we (mis) read the posthuman.

NOTES

1. T. S. Eliot, "Tradition and the Individual Talent," in *Selected Prose*, ed. John Hayward (Harmondsworth: Penguin, 1953), 21–30.
2. See, for instance, N. Katherine Hayles, "Distributed Cognition at/in Work: Strickland, Lawson Jaramillo, and Ryan's *slippingglimpse*," *Frame* 21.1 (2008): 15–29.
3. Noah Wardrip-Fruin, *Expressive Processing: Digital Fictions, Computer Games, and Software Studies* (Cambridge, MA: MIT Press, 2009).
4. Bill Seaman, "Recombinant Poetics," in *Media Poetry: An International Anthology*, ed. Eduardo Kac (Bristol: Intellect Books, 2007), 157–74.
5. Milad Douehi, *Digital Cultures* (Cambridge, MA: Harvard University Press, 2011), 51.
6. N. Katherine Hayles, *Electronic Literature: New Horizons for the Literary* (Notre Dame: University of Notre Dame Press, 2008), 45.
7. Hayles, *Electronic Literature*, 3.
8. Hayles, *Electronic Literature*, 3. Curiously, this volume never mentions posthumanism.
9. For a sense of how things used to be, see John Gross, *The Rise and Fall of the Man of Letters: English Literary Life since 1800* (London: Weidenfeld and Nicolson, 1969).
10. Alexander Pope, "An Essay on Man," in *The Poems of Alexander Pope*, ed. John Butt (London: Routledge, 1989), 505.
11. Stefan Herbrechter, *Posthumanism: A Critical Analysis* (London: Bloomsbury, 2013), 57.

12. Adrian Marino, *The Biography of the Idea of "Literature": From Antiquity to the Baroque*, trans. Virgil Stanciu and Charles M. Carlton (Albany, NY: State University of New York Press, 1996).

13. See Georg Lukács, *The Meaning of Contemporary Realism*, trans. John Mander and Necka Mander (London: Merlin Press, 1963); on the rhizome, see Gilles Deleuze and Félix Guattari, *A Thousand Plateaus*, trans. Brian Massumi (London: The Athlone Press, 1988).

14. For examples of contrary views on scenarios glimpsed in this sentence, see Jacques Derrida, *Archive Fever: A Freudian Impression*, trans. Eric Prenowitz (Chicago: University of Chicago Press, 1995); Patricia Ticineto Clough, *Autoaffection: Unconscious Thought in an Age of Teletechnology* (Minneapolis: University of Minnesota Press, 2000); Marquard Smith and Joanne Morra, eds., *The Prosthetic Impulse: From a Posthuman Present to a Biocultural Future* (Cambridge, MA: MIT Press, 2006); Julian Savulescu and Nick Bostrom, eds., *Human Enhancement* (Oxford: Oxford University Press, 2009); and Ray Kurzweil, *The Singularity Is Near: When Humans Transcend Biology* (London: Viking, 2005).

15. Loss Pequeño Glazier, *Digital Poetics: The Making of E-Poetries* (Tuscaloosa: University of Alabama Press, 2002), 174–75.

16. Jacques Derrida, "Demeure," in Maurice Blanchot / Jacques Derrida, *The Instant of My Death / Demeure*, trans. Elizabeth Rottenberg (Stanford, CA: Stanford University Press, 2000), 29.

17. Maurice Blanchot, *The Space of Literature*, trans. Ann Smock (Lincoln: University of Nebraska Press, 1982), 48.

18. Niklas Luhmann, *Social Systems*, trans. John Bednarz, Jr. with Dirk Baecker (Stanford, CA: Stanford University Press, 1995).

19. Philippe Lacoue-Labarthe and Jean-Luc Nancy, *The Literary Absolute: The Theory of Literature in German Romanticism*, trans. Philip Barnard and Cheryl Lester (Albany, NY: State University of New York Press, 1988), 91. The first phrase quoted is taken from the book's blurb. Further page references to this work are given in parentheses in the main text.

20. For a more searching study of ideas of metamorphosis in posthumanism and second-order systems theory, see Bruce Clarke, *Posthuman Metamorphosis: Narrative and Systems* (New York: Fordham University Press, 2008).

21. Derek Attridge, *Peculiar Language* (London: Routledge, 2011).

22. N. Katherine Hayles, "Traumas of Code," *Critical Inquiry* 33.1 (2006): 136.

23. Nick Montfort, "Round: Author Description," *elmcip* (*elmcip*, 2014), accessed August 8, 2015, http://elmcip01.norstore.uio.no/node/10077. See also Brian Kim Stefans, "Generative Poetry," *Electronic Literature Collection*, Vol. 1 (Electronic Literature Organization, 2006), accessed August 8, 2015, http://collection.eliterature.org/1/works/geniwate_generative_poetry.html.

24. See the tenth "dimension" in Stephanie Strickland, "Writing the Virtual: Eleven Dimensions of E-Poetry," *Leonardo On-Line* 14.5 (2006) www.leoalmanac.org/wp-content/uploads/2012/09/06Writing-the-Virtual-Eleven-Dimensions-of-E-Poetry-by-Stephanie-Strickland-Vol-14-No-5-6-September-2006-Leonardo-Electronic-Almanac.pdf [accessed May 10, 2016].

25. Richard Powers, *Galatea 2.2* (New York: Farrar, Straus and Giroux, 1995).

26. C. T. Funkhouser, *Prehistoric Digital Poetry: An Archaeology of Forms, 1959–1995* (Tuscaloosa: University of Alabama Press, 2007). See Pathfinders: Documenting the Experience of Early Digital Literature, accessed August 8, 2015, http://dtc-wsuv.org/wp/pathfinders.

27. See Jonathan Swift, *Gulliver's Travels* (Oxford: Oxford University Press, 2008), for the description in Book III, chapter 7 of a text-generating "Engine," and also Roald Dahl, "The Great Automatic Grammatizator," in *The Great Automatic Grammatizator and Other Stories* (London: Penguin, 2001).

28. For an introduction to the OuLiPo see Warren F. Motte Jr., *Oulipo: A Primer of Potential Literature* (Lincoln: University of Nebraska Press, 1996).

29. Michel Foucault provided a landmark study of Roussel's way with literature: see *Death and the Labyrinth*, trans. Charles Ruas, postscript by John Ashbery, rev. edn (London: Bloomsbury, 2007).

30. See Jean Starobinski, *Words upon Words: The Anagrams of Ferdinand de Saussure*, trans. Olivia Emmet (New Haven, CT: Yale University Press, 1979).

31. Quentin Meillassoux, *The Number and the Siren: A Decipherment of Mallarmé's Coup de dés*, trans. Robin Mackay (Falmouth: Urbanomic / New York: Sequence Press, 2012).

32. See Michael Joyce, *Afternoon, a Story*, Environment: Storyspace (Watertown, MA: Eastgate Systems, 1990); Stuart Moulthrop, *Victory Garden*, Environment: Storyspace (Watertown, MA: Eastgate Systems, 1991); John McDaid, *Uncle Buddy's Phantom Funhouse* (Watertown, MA: Eastgate Systems, 1993); Shelley Jackson, *Patchwork Girl*, Environment: Storyspace (Watertown, MA: Eastgate Systems, 1995).

33. See George P. Landow, *HyperText: The Convergence of Contemporary Critical Theory and Technology* (Baltimore, MD: Johns Hopkins University Press, 1997); *Hypertext 2.0* (Baltimore, MD: Johns Hopkins University Press, 1997); and *Hypertext 3.0: Critical Theory and New Media in an Era of Globalization* (Baltimore, MD: Johns Hopkins University Press, 2006), but also Ted Nelson, *Literary Machines: The Report on, and of, Project Xanadu Concerning Word Processing, Electronic Publishing, Hypertext, Thinkertoys, Tomorrow's Intellectual Revolution, and Certain Other Topics including Knowledge, Education and Freedom* (Sausalito, CA: Mindful Press, 1980).

34. See Espen J. Aarseth, *Cybertext: Perspectives on Ergodic Literature* (Baltimore, MD: Johns Hopkins University Press, 1996).

35. Jorge Luis Borges, "The Garden of Forking Paths," in *Collected Fictions*, ed. Andrew Hurley (New York: Penguin, 1998), 119–28.

36. Nick Montfort, *Twisty Little Passages: An Approach to Interactive Fiction* (Cambridge: MIT Press, 2004).

37. Michael Mateas and Andrew Stern, *Façade* (Procedural Arts, 2005), accessed July 20, 2015, www.interactivestory.net.

38. Will Crowther and Don Woods, *Colossal Cave Adventure*. FORTRAN (1977). Tim Anderson, Marc Blank, Bruce Daniels and David Lebling, *Zork* (Personal Software, 1979).

39. See Romy Achituv and Camille Utterback, *Text Rain* (1999), accessed August 20, 2015, http://camilleutterback.com/projects/text-rain, and Bruno Nadeau and Jason Edward Lewis, *Still Standing*, in *Electronic*

E-Literature

Literature Collection, Vol. 2, ed. Laura Borràs Castanyer, Talan Memmott, Rita Raley, and Brian Kim Stefans (Electronic Literature Organization, 2011).

40. Kate Pullinger, Chris Joseph, and Stefan Schemat, *The Breathing Wall* (De Montfort: University Open Research Archive, 2004).
41. Glazier, 174.
42. See Motte, *Oulipo, passim.*
43. Nick Montfort, *#!* (Denver, CO: Counterpath Press, 2014).
44. Nick Montfort and Stephanie Strickland, *"Sea and Spar Between"* (Chicago: Dear Navigator, 2012), accessed July 30, 2015, http://nickm.com/montfort_strickland/sea_and_spar_between/.
45. Brian Kim Stefans, *The Dreamlife of Letters, in Electronic Literature Collection*, Vol. 1, ed. N. Katherine Hayles, Nick Montfort, Scott Rettberg, and Stephanie Strickland (Electronic Literature Organization, 2006), accessed July 30, 2015, http://collection.eliterature.org/1/works/stefans_the_dreamlife_of_letters.html.
46. David Jhave Johnston, "Sooth," in *Electronic Literature Collection*, Vol. 2, ed. Laura Borràs Castanyer, Talan Memmott, Rita Raley, and Brian Kim Stefans (Electronic Literature Organization, 2011), accessed July 30, 2015, http://collection.eliterature.org/2/works/johnston_sooth.html.
47. John Cayley, "Beyond Codexspace: Potentialities of Literary Cybertext," in *Media Poetry: An International Anthology*, ed. Eduardo Kac (Bristol: Intellect Books, 2007), 105–25.
48. See Ann Weinstone, *Avatar Bodies: A Tantra for Posthumanism* (Minneapolis: University of Minnesota Press, 2003).
49. See Franco Moretti, *Distant Reading* (London: Verso, 2013); Matthew Jockers, *Macroanalysis: Digital Methods and Literary History* (Chicago: University of Illinois Press, 2013); and the "Pamphlets" issued by the Stanford Literary Lab, accessed July 31, 2015, http://litlab.stanford.edu/pamphlets.
50. E-Lit is now more distinct as a field than it may have been at the time of studies like Jay David Bolter and Richard Grusin, *Remediation: Understanding New Media* (Cambridge, MA: MIT Press, 1998); Lev Manovich, *The Language of New Media* (Cambridge, MA: MIT Press, 2001); and Noah Wardrip-Fruin and Nick Montfort, eds., *The New Media Reader* (Cambridge, MA: MIT Press, 2003).
51. See Michael Heim, *Electric Language: A Philosophical Study of Word Processing* (New Haven, CT: Yale University Press, 1987), a second edition of which was published in 1999; Jerome McGann, *Radiant Textuality: Literature after the World Wide Web* (Houndmills: Palgrave Macmillan, 2001).
52. Mark B. N. Hansen, *Embodying Technesis: Technology Beyond Writing* (Ann Arbor: University of Michigan Press, 2000); *New Philosophy for New Media* (Cambridge, MA: MIT Press, 2004); *Feed-Forward: On the Future of Twenty-First Century Media* (Chicago: University of Chicago Press, 2015); see Hayles, Electronic Literature, 102ff., on Hansen's work in these areas.
53. Roberto Simanowski, *Digital Art and Meaning: Reading Kinetic Poetry, Text Machines, Mapping Art, and Interactive Installations* (Minneapolis: Minnesota University Press, 2011). See also Francisco J. Ricardo, *Literary Art in Digital Performance: Case Studies in New Media Art and Criticism* (London: Continuum, 2009).

54. Rita Raley, *Tactical Media* (Minneapolis: University of Minnesota Press, 2009).

55. Derek Attridge, *The Singularity of Literature* (London: Routledge, 2004), 64.

56. Glazier, *Digital Poetics*, 179.

57. See the first section of Strickland's "Writing the Virtual."

58. See Rosi Braidotti, *The Posthuman* (London: Polity, 2013) and Gilles Deleuze, *Desert Islands and Other Texts 1953–1974*, ed. David Lapoujade, trans. Michael Taormina (Los Angeles: Semiotext(e), 2004), 101ff.

59. Dana Gioia, *Disappearing Ink: Poetry at the End of Print Culture* (St Paul, MN: Graywolf Press, 2004) and *Can Poetry Matter?: Essays on Poetry and American Culture* (St Paul, MN: Graywolf Press, 2002).

60. Hayles, *Electronic Literature*, 186.

61. Nicholas Royle, *Veering: A Theory of Literature* (Edinburgh: Edinburgh University Press, 2011).

62. Jessica Pressman, Mark C. Marino, and Jeremy Douglass, *Reading Project: A Collaborative Analysis of William Poundstone's Project for Tachitoscope {Bottomless Pit}* (Iowa City: University of Iowa Press, 2015).

63. Vikram Chandra, *Geek Sublime: Writing Fiction, Coding Software* (London: Faber and Faber, 2014).

64. Gregory Ulmer, *Internet Invention: From Literacy to Electracy* (New York: Longman, 2002) and the Transliteracies Project, accessed June 8, 2015, http://transliteracies.english.ucsb.edu/category/research-project.

65. Mark B. N. Hansen, *Bodies in Code: Interfaces with Digital Media* (New York: Routledge, 2006) and Jessica Pressman, *Digital Modernism: Making It New in New Media* (Oxford: Oxford University Press, 2004).

66. Giorgio Agamben, *The Man without Content* (Stanford, CA: Stanford University Press, 1999), 54. Other page references to this work occur in parentheses in the main text.

67. See Daniel Albright, *Panaesthetics: On the Unity and Diversity of the Arts* (New Haven, CT: Yale University Press, 2014), and N. Katherine Hayles and Jessica Pressman, eds., *Comparative Textual Media: Transforming the Humanities in the Postprint Era* (Minneapolis: University of Minnesota Press, 2013).

68. Albright, 280. Further page references to this work are given within parentheses in the main text.

69. Craig Dworkin, *No Medium* (Cambridge, MA: MIT Press, 2013).

PART III

Posthuman Themes

11

BRUCE CLARKE

The Nonhuman

The posthuman imaginary starts from some transformation of the human image. The historical moment of this event is unfixed. For the duration of their transformations, Bottom and Mr. Hyde are as posthuman as Molly the razorgirl. Tales about human metamorphs intimate that the form of the human has neither somatic nor psychic fixity.[1] Granted this longer view of the topic, a posthuman event names some transformative outcome that once followed, is now following, or will at some point follow from the human. The posthuman per se is a mythopoetic production: this is its power and its glamor for literary and other creative genres. Thus, the ostensible fictionality of these events is also a side issue. Posthumanism is something else, a discursive practice typically but not necessarily attending to posthuman images to develop larger philosophical and speculative ends of critical observation and theoretical conjecture. Posthumanism's discursive projects aim to decenter the human by terminally disrupting the scripts of humanism.

Humanism deconstructs itself whenever "the human" is observed not as a unity but as an assemblage. In the parlance of earlier literary, philosophical, and theological texts, the human frays into gradations of subhuman, inhuman, and superhuman – the bestial, the daemonic, or the divine. Evolutionary modernity supplements the human with the prehuman and the posthuman. Systems theory then constructs a posthumanist technic of consciousness and communication that subtends the unity of the humanist subject, separating its psychic and social components by operational differentiations bound together by ahuman mediatic structures.[2] For instance, in the face of the logocentric privilege that prioritizes mind over society, consciousness over communication, Niklas Luhmann's contention that "humans cannot communicate" is a deliberate provocation disarming high-humanist presumptions of subjective prerogative with the posthumanist dictum that "communication constructs itself."[3] In other words, once social systems are observed as constituted by the recursive re-production of communicative events, human beings (along with their streams of consciousness) properly reside in the environments of communication systems.

What then of "the nonhuman," as that distinction has come forward in recent philosophical and cultural discussion? Systems theory's posthumanist discourse of the nonhuman moment in communication systems indicates the conceptual proximity here. We read in a recent anthology on the topic: "the nonhuman turn ... is engaged in decentering the human in favor of a turn toward and concern for the nonhuman, understood variously in terms of animals, affectivity, bodies, organic and geophysical systems, materiality, or technologies."[4] However, to distinguish the nonhuman by negation of the human does not absolve it of the semantic vagaries and ultimate attachments of these other prefixal terms. The category of the nonhuman is necessarily as incoherent as the category of the human itself. In like manner, there is a surplus of play in the concept of the posthuman. The notion of the posthuman that centers this volume is itself too equivocal, too volatile to underwrite a reliable decentering of the human. As we have noted, the posthuman event does not issue directly in a discourse but in an aesthetic production, an image or narrative that may then become the theme of a discourse that can start to make that call. Unlike the posthuman, the nonhuman per se does not immediately yield an image, although it may well clear space for an image to occur. The nonhuman operates not by pos(i)ting but by negating. The distinction of the nonhuman may free a conceptual space for varieties of "nonhumanism," potentially potent variant dialects of posthumanism.

The Nonhuman and the Nonmodern

In its recent theoretical development in the critical humanities, the notion of the nonhuman is a back-formation from Bruno Latour's concept of "the nonmodern." As Richard Grusin notes, "The nonhuman turn insists (to paraphrase Latour) that 'we have never been human' but that the human has always coevolved, coexisted, or collaborated with the nonhuman – and that the human is characterized precisely by this indistinction from the nonhuman" (*NT* ix–x). Grusin refers to the famous declaration of Latour's theoretical manifesto from the early 1990s, *We Have Never Been Modern*. In brief, despite modernity's self-description as having outgrown premodern idolatries and purified its knowledge of natural things from non-natural social and ideological artifacts, nonetheless, it has never actually left the "ancient anthropological matrix" that jumbled together human societies and nonhuman natures: "we have never stopped building our collectives with raw materials made of poor humans and humble nonhumans."[5] Just as, according to Grusin, to be human is to be bound up in an indistinction between the human and the nonhuman, so too, following Latour, to recover our nonmodernity is to reconstitute an effective awareness of our own hybridity, of the actual composition of the human, be it ever so modern or postmodern, out of inexorably impure mixtures of human and nonhuman.

In its original moment, Latour's thinking of the nonmodern was a strategic departure from the discourse of the postmodern. Poised against postmodernist discourses of disorientation and lack – the loss of stable reference in authors such as Jean Baudrillard, and most famously, the lapse of grand narratives (*metarécits*) as formulated in Francois Lyotard's *The Postmodern Condition* – Latour's evocation of the nonmodern as the creative unconscious of modernity was the heady rediscovery of a forgotten inheritance.[6] In a parallel move, Grusin presents the current discourse of the nonhuman as a departure from the discourse of the posthuman. The parallel premise appears to be that the posthuman lingers in an all-too-human mode of (post)modernity, relative to the inexhaustible reserves of the nonmodern nonhuman.

> Unlike the posthuman turn with which it is often confused, the nonhuman turn does not make a claim about teleology or progress in which we begin with the human and see a transformation from the human to the posthuman, after or beyond the human. Although the best work on the posthuman seeks to avoid such teleology, even these works oscillate between seeing the posthuman as a new stage in human development and seeing it as calling attention to the inseparability of human and nonhuman. Nonetheless, the very idea of the posthuman entails a historical development from human to something after the human, even as it invokes the imbrication of human and nonhuman in making up the posthuman turn. (*NT* xix)

The idea of the posthuman, however, may be parsed more finely than as the promotion of a "posthuman turn." Temporality is bound up in the *post-* of the posthuman, but the time of the posthuman does not have to revert to a grand or grotesque narrative of human overcoming.[7]

Let us follow Grusin's lead and look briefly into a work of Latour that predates his formulation of the nonmodern but still has important things to say about the nonhuman. Latour reflects at the end of part one of *The Pasteurization of France*, "War and Peace of Microbes," on how, in his account, "Microbes play ... a more personal role than in so-called scientific histories and a more central role than in the so-called social histories. Indeed, as soon as we stop reducing the sciences to a few authorities that stand in place of them, what reappears is not only the crowds of human beings, as in Tolstoy, but also the 'nonhuman,'" indeed, the "emancipation of the nonhumans from the double domination of society and science."[8] The conceptual destination of

Latour's project has always been *posthumanist*, in that it aims to displace the reigning humanist biases of both natural science and sociology in favor of symmetrical relations between human and nonhuman – in this instance, microbial – actors. As we will see, microbes can also be key actors in literary narratives of the nonhuman.

The Nonhuman and the Sublime

The literary nonhuman often appears as a territory we can survey or imagine or respond to, aesthetically or otherwise, but not precisely occupy. It is a state into which we may be momentarily transported:

> Oh! when I have hung
> Above the raven's nest, by knots of grass
> And half-inch fissures in the slippery rock
> But ill sustained, and almost (so it seemed)
> Suspended by the blast that blew amain,
> Shouldering the naked crag, oh, at that time
> While on the perilous ridge I hung alone,
> With what strange utterance did the loud dry wind
> Blow through my ear! the sky seemed not a sky
> Of earth – and with what motion moved the clouds![9]

The impetuous youthful self later remembered by the poet clings to the granite face of Nature in its nonhuman materialities of grass, rock, blowing wind, and moving cloud. He confronts these natural manifestations as possessing an unearthly power to produce "strange utterance." Thomas Weiskel's magisterial reading posits the Romantic sublime between the poles of the human and the superhuman. This passage from William Wordsworth's *Prelude* intimates that the youth has encountered a daemonic feeling that took him out of himself, which he did not possess in any manner other than feeling, but which, on the contrary, for those moments, possessed him:

> The essential claim of the sublime is that man can, in feeling and in speech, transcend the human. What, if anything, lies beyond the human – God or the gods, the daemon or Nature – is matter for great disagreement. What, if anything, defines the range of the human is scarcely less sure ... Without some notion of the beyond, some credible discourse of the superhuman, the sublime founders; or it becomes a "problem." This is as true in Romanticism as in antiquity. "The beautiful," says Schiller, "is valuable only with reference to the

human being, but the sublime with reference to the *pure daemon*" in man, "the statutes of pure spirit." A humanistic sublime is an oxymoron.[10]

A humanistic sublime *is* an oxymoron because, for one, humanism is ostensibly a secular stance in opposition to "God or the gods," that is, to transcendentalisms in general, and for another, the sublime itself is not a doctrine but a feeling – a mode of aesthetic affect. In a word, as an aesthetic experience of the force of the nonhuman, the natural sublime is a prefiguration of the posthuman. In like manner, the encounter with the nonhuman may be fashioned as a sort of desublimated transcendentalism.

From Natural Selection to the Alien

The Romantic crest of the natural sublime is followed in short order by the epochal transformation of Nature wrought by Charles Darwin's *Origin of Species* (1859). Backed up by the deep fossil record as expounded in Charles Lyell's *Principles of Geology* (1830–33), a new vista of prehuman life and nonhuman time comes into view. Although a nascent discipline of archaeology lengthened the period of human presence, the existence of the human is no longer coextensive with the genesis of the world itself, no longer a metonymy of *its* existence. Darwin's discourse joins with the concurrent rise of thermodynamics to usher the concept of nature into the realm of irreversible time.[11] Through the unfolding of geological time in the register of biological evolution, natural history emerges as a partial but conclusive, almost entirely nonhuman, chronicle of evanescence and extinction. Natural selection covers its tracks by exterminating the losers. The extant world before the human gaze metamorphoses into an eons-long outcome of variations and deletions that send forward an infinitesimal number of the total possibilities: "of the species living at any one period, extremely few will transmit descendants to a remote futurity."[12] The human now mingles with a motley nonhuman crew of fellow survivors. If the posthuman image has a discernible point of modern origin, it is here in the *Origin*, where evolutionary futures are always visions of extinction and transformation.

The terrestrial nonhuman of the *Origin of Species* echoes related speculative discourses of the cosmic nonhuman.[13] By the time of its appearance, what Peter Sloterdijk terms "terrestrial globalization" has completely foreclosed prior human convictions in the divine protection of cosmic spheres:

> In a dawn that took centuries, the earth rose as the only and true orb, the basis of all contexts of life, while almost everything that had previously been considered the partnered, meaning-filled sky was emptied. This fatalization of the earth, brought about by human practices and taking place at the same time as

the loss of reality among the once-vital numinous spheres, does not merely provide the background to these events; it is itself the drama of globalization. Its core lies in the observation that the conditions of human immunity fundamentally change on the discovered, interconnected and singularized earth.[14]

The nonhuman now takes possession of the outside world. Today, only faint cosmic signatures of the human remain upon and radiating out from Earth, the deposition into the planetary environs of the unique by-products of human life and mind – space junk, radio and television emissions, and such. This nonhumanization of the outside is the obverse of the process Sloterdijk calls "crystallization," the creation of a "world interior" as a "protective shell" (WIC 171). Modern humanity places itself within an artificial sphere, epitomized by the 1851 construction of the Crystal Palace in London, immunizing itself against the nonhuman.[15] The universe sheds, along with the human form of life and sentience, the vestiges of human meanings. It is rendered fully alien. Hereafter the extraterrestrial beyond can send us emissaries only of the cosmic nonhuman. The literary imaginary obliges by conjuring up our new alien visitors:

> No one would have believed in the last years of the nineteenth century that human affairs were being watched keenly and closely by intelligences greater than man's and yet as mortal as his own; that as men busied themselves about their affairs they were scrutinized and studied, perhaps almost as narrowly as a man with a microscope might scrutinize the transient creatures that swarm and multiply in a drop of water.[16]

So begins H. G. Wells's *The War of the Worlds* in 1898, in a work that contributes to the consolidation of the image of the alien nonhuman, the extraterrestrial nonhuman, in literary narratives now too numberless to enumerate.[17] But the utter nonhumanity of the Martians is mitigated by their shared "intelligence," and indeed by their all-too-human presumption of superiority and impunity toward living beings deemed of lesser intellect: "Yet across the gulf of space, minds that are to our minds as ours are to those of the beasts that perish, intellects vast and cool and unsympathetic, regarded this earth with envious eyes, and slowly and surely drew their plans against us" (WW 41). Tellingly, in this tale the greater burden of the nonhuman will be carried instead by "the transient creatures that swarm," and it is to these alien forms of *terrestrial* life that humanity will owe its rescue from the Martian invasion.

Continuing the "war and peace of microbes" limned by Latour, the microbes in *The War of the Worlds* provide bioimmunitary defenses to the very species that in the wake of Pasteur has marshalled new intelligence about them to forge antibiotic armaments against them. Whereas the Martians rudely breach the defenses of the Crystal Palace, the Earthly microbes offer an implicit rebuke to imperial humanity's auto-immunitary project. We thought to build a fortress of (human) self only to have its impossibility thrust upon us by the sheer ecological contingency of our existence as a species. While Wells's novel locates terrestrial bacteria in relation to human evolution largely as aggressive arch-Darwinian competitors, intransigent enemies, their immunitary benefit provides the ironic twist to the denouement of the narrative. The microbes make themselves known when a Martian plant imported to Earth, the Red Weed, at first enjoys invasive success but suddenly collapses, signaling the Martians' lack of immunity to Earth life:

> In the end the Red Weed succumbed almost as quickly as it had spread. A cankering disease, due, it is believed, to the action of certain bacteria, presently seized upon it. Now by the action of natural selection, all terrestrial plants have acquired a resisting power against bacterial diseases – they never succumb without a severe struggle, but the red weed rotted like a thing already dead. (WW 161)

Considered the lowest form of nonhuman life and largely as agents of putrefaction and disease, bacteria present a natural evil from which humanity culled through natural selection has received the terrestrial benefits of immunity. The tale recruits bacteria to be our indigenous nonhuman "allies" in the war to defend human dominion over the Earth from the cosmic nonhuman:

> These germs of disease have taken toll of humanity since the beginning of things – taken toll of our pre-human ancestors since life began here. But by virtue of this natural selection of our kind we have developed resisting power; to no germs do we succumb without a struggle, and to many – those that cause putrefaction in dead matter, for instance – our living frames are altogether immune. But there are no bacteria in Mars, and directly these invaders arrived, directly they drank and fed, our microscopic allies began to work their overthrow. (WW 181)

The Nonhuman Posthuman

The nonhuman is explicitly posthuman when what comes after the human involves the elimination or replacement of the human. A particularly strident vision of a nonhuman posthuman world makes a memorable appearance in

D. H. Lawrence's *Women in Love*. Lawrence stated that this novel, published in 1920, channeled without explicit internal dating "the bitterness of the war" recently ended.[18] The narrative's resident misanthrope, Rupert Birkin, voices an image of desire for a posthuman world rendered "nonhuman" and thus emptied of human futility: "If only man were swept off the face of the earth, creation would go on so marvelously, with a new start, nonhuman. Man is one of the mistakes of creation – like the ichthyosauri. – If only he were gone again, think what lovely things would come out of the liberated days; – things straight out of the fire" (*WL* 128). The distinctly modernist dissemination and deformation of evolutionary tropes in this statement frame the posthuman through a vitalist imaginary in which the origin and extinction of species signify cosmic and hence nonhuman judgments upon the works of the Life Force, upon certain missteps or culde-sacs of the *élan vital*. At the end of the novel, as Birkin grieves over the frozen corpse of his friend Gerald Crich, whose suicide is emblematic of modern humanity's entropic dead end, he contemplates the nonhuman in and of itself. This conceptual vignette is ostensibly antihumanistic, but arguably, read back into Birkin's earlier statement, a prolepsis of posthumanism as a critique of triumphalist humanism: "Whatever the mystery which has brought forth man and the universe, it is a non-human mystery, it has its own great ends, man is not the criterion ... The eternal creative mystery could dispose of man, and replace him with a finer created being" (*WL* 478).

Measured against more recent images of the death of the human, however, Birkin's vision of the Earth that remains once humanity has been eliminated by a transcendental telos appears relatively sanguine, like the mere discarding of a rough draft. Compare the scenario of Ronald Wright's dark satire *A Scientific Romance*, published in 1997.[19] On Millennium Eve, a Cambridge-educated archaeologist working as a curator for a London museum of Victorian machines stumbles upon an actual time machine inspired by the 1895 publication of H. G. Wells's *The Time Machine*, its technical challenges solved by a protégée of Nikola Tesla. In November, 2000, David Lambert sets off for the future, but has only enough juice to get to 2500 AD. When he pops the lid off the device in a Thames estuary, he finds himself in a tropical world denuded of human beings. The story is now driven along by the mystery of this depopulated England: in what manner is this near-future world also now a nonhuman world?

Lambert keeps a journal on a solar-powered laptop: "Warming, obviously, as many foresaw" (*SR* 104). He considers with studied understatement: "A sudden bonfire of the planet's coal and oil and timber can hardly have been a good idea" (*SR* 105). Finding the environs of London to be devoid of fellow humans, he questions his sanity: "Have I been driven mad by the wrong books ... by the 'deserted and utterly extinct' London of Richard Jefferies," author of the apocalyptic back-to-nature fantasy *After London* of 1885. Recalling those quaint readings from his uncanny future vantage, Lambert affirms the speculative prophecies of "All those tall tales that bloomed like a cold sweat in the midnight terrors of the Steam Age, when civilization first began to guess that it had found the means to suicide" (*SR* 106). The nonhuman is particularly posthuman when the state of non-humanity follows after humanity's own self-destruction.

At the same time, for all he can see of the face of the Earth in the year 2500, it is flourishing. Human depopulation has made room once again for nonhuman diversity. Add global warming and one gets at the 51st parallel north the species richness of a rain forest. Among the new fauna, Lambert encounters a manta ray, sergeant-majors, a lobster, a great sea turtle, pelicans, sea lions, flying foxes, scarlet macaws, fiddler crabs, and a puma. Amidst the mangroves and palmettos, he puzzles out the new profusion of plant life:

> I saw tropical cedars, locusts, and a good-sized mahogany. Suddenly I understood: these trees hadn't crept north from Africa; they'd escaped from Kew! And the smaller plants on the forest floor, spiraling trunks, crowding ledges and sills – these too were runaways from botanical gardens, conservatories, and a million living-rooms. Ficus and avocados, oleander and epiphytes, orchids and plumerias, brought from Belize to Belsize, had outlived their owners and inherited this corner of the earth. (*SR* 117)

Lambert eventually pieces together the holocaust of humanity: it comes in the 2030s complete with assisted-suicide facilities to handle a mass die-off due to some combination of CJD (Creutzfeldt–Jakob disease, the human form of mad cow disease) and AIDS, yielding a syndrome labeled "RISC" for rapid immune-system collapse. In this scientific romance, the Crystal Palace of human immunity shatters from within. As global heating builds up the temporary shelter of a new outdoor greenhouse, the outside that had been behind walls or under glass in "botanical gardens, conservatories, and a million living-rooms" runs wild once more. Lambert is under no Romantic illusions about this verdant landscape: it "is no virgin, but old and used, riddled with man-made hazards and abominations" (*SR* 111). But for the moment it exudes a rush of vitality as it returns to geological time to sort out this latest roll of the evolutionary dice.

Situated, in the text's own proleptic phrasing, on "the fraying border between humanity and artefact" (*SR* 18), this future landscape is no untouched wilderness but a wild hybrid of human and nonhuman productions – the Anthropocene in overdrive, minus the Anthropos. In the collaborative formulation of Michel Serres and Bruno Latour capturing the potential agency of nonhuman objects, of *things* under posthumanist observation, in *A Scientific Romance* the entire face of the posthuman Earth has become a *quasi-object*.[20] Seeking a highway north, Lambert finds thriving upon the M25 a "last functioning artefact, living beyond its time like a zombie, defying a nature that has taken her revenge on its creators" (*SR* 200). Careless of human hand is a razor-sharp turf bio-engineered back in the day by combining "genetic material from nitrogen-fixing plants" with "the self-limiting properties of human pubic hair" (*SR* 164). Lambert's archaeological eye turns from this post-biotic quasi-object to the dead detritus of an expired modernity, evoking a contemporary world awash in a hybrid ecology of nonhuman objects:

> Zamfir recordings, yo-yos, xylophones, weedkillers, video games, train sets, televisions, stereos, snuff films, rocket silos, railways, pinball tables, one-armed bandits, oil refineries, nuclear piles, motorhomes, milk cartons, lipsticks, lawnmowers, lava lamps, Kleenex holders, Jacuzzis, hula-hoops, houseboats, gravy boats, golf carts, footballs, fondue sets, drinks trolleys, cameras, bottles, beds, airliners – all those splendid Things that made up the sum of the world, which we had to keep on making and buying to keep ourselves diverted and employed – were just garbage-to-be.   (*SR* 185)

Here is another face of the posthuman sublime, a scene of endless obsolescence in a distinctly human vista of commodity ruination. And yet, even as the random junk of a general human ruination, all these commodities are recoverable as objects returning to the nonhuman side of their hybrid natures, the fossilized quasi-biota of techno-nature.[21]

Nonhumanism

The present theoretical moment demands a positive concept of the nonhuman, a stable signifier under which to place all the multifarious ontological positivity currently imputed to the other-than-human. In "Cultivating Humanity: Towards a Non-Humanist Ethics of Technology," Peter-Paul Verbeek consolidates the emergent consensus that the human, ontologically speaking, can no longer proceed under the mistaken presumption that, rising above the nonhuman, it goes it alone. That was the grand dream and narrative of high humanism. Rather, the human needs the nonhuman to come into the mode of its own becoming. Following Heidegger and Latour, Verbeek remarks: "'Things' can be seen as entities that gather human and non-human entities around themselves, as the focus of new practices and interpretations. From this approach, technological 'things' not only mediate our existence, but also are places where these mediations are made explicit ... The posthumanism I defend here ... simply gives a central place to the idea that the human can only exist in its relations to the nonhuman."[22] Even if the very positivity of the nonhuman rests upon the negativity of its distinction from the human, the nonhuman apart from and as a part of the human is to be valued for that very intimate alterity. Nonhumanism is an alter-ego of posthumanism.

NOTES

1. See Bruce Clarke, *Posthuman Metamorphosis: Narrative and Systems* (New York: Fordham University Press, 2008), hereafter *PM*; and *Allegories of Writing: The Subject of Metamorphosis* (Albany: State University of New York Press, 1995).
2. See Niklas Luhmann, "Identity – What or How?," in *Theories of Distinction: Redescribing the Descriptions of Modernity*, ed. William Rasch (Stanford: Stanford University Press, 2002), 113–27; Cary Wolfe, "Meaning and Event, or Systems Theory and 'The Reconstruction of Deconstruction,'" in *What is Posthumanism?* (Minneapolis: University of Minnesota Press, 2010), 3–29; and Bruce Clarke, *Neocybernetics and Narrative* (Minneapolis: University of Minnesota Press, 2014).
3. Niklas Luhmann, "How Can the Mind Participate in Communication," in *Theories of Distinction*, 176–77.
4. Richard Grusin, "Introduction," in *The Nonhuman Turn*, ed. Richard Grusin (Minneapolis: University of Minnesota Press, 2015), vii; hereafter *NT*.
5. Bruno Latour, *We Have Never Been Modern*, trans. Catherine Porter (Cambridge: Harvard University Press, 1993), 115.
6. Jean Baudrillard, *Simulation and Simulacra*, trans. Sheila Faria Glaser (Ann Arbor: University of Michigan Press, 1984); and Jean-François Lyotard, *The Postmodern Condition: A Report on Knowledge*, trans. Geoff Bennington and Brian Massumi (Minneapolis: University of Minnesota Press, 1984).
7. On these issues of the posthuman vis-à-vis the postmodern, and on the logic of the prefix post-altogether, see Herbrechter, "Postmodern," in this volume.
8. Bruno Latour, *The Pasteurization of France*, trans. Alan Sheridan and John Law (Cambridge: Harvard University Press, 1988), 149–50.
9. William Wordsworth, *The Prelude: A Parallel Text*, ed. J. C. Maxwell (New Haven: Yale University Press, 1981), 53. The passage given is Book One, ll. 330–39 of the 1850 text.
10. Thomas Weiskel, *The Romantic Sublime: Studies in the Structure and Psychology of Transcendence* (1976; Baltimore: Johns Hopkins University Press, 1986), 3.
11. See Bruce Clarke, *Energy Forms: Allegory and Science in the Era of Classical Thermodynamics* (Ann Arbor: University of Michigan Press, 2001), esp. "Benjamin's Dialectical Image," 36–42.

12. Charles Darwin, *On the Origin of Species by Means of Natural Selection, in Evolutionary Writings*, ed. James A. Secord (New York: Oxford University Press, 2008), 170.

13. For a prime example of the popular cosmology into which Darwin's *Origin* was received, see James A. Secord, *Victorian Sensation: The Extraordinary Publication, Reception, and Secret Authorship of Vestiges of the Natural History of Creation* (Chicago: University of Chicago Press, 2001).

14. Peter Sloterdijk, *In the World Interior of Capital: For a Philosophical Theory of Globalization*, trans. Wieland Hoban (Malden, MA: Polity, 2013), 5; hereafter, *WIC*.

15. The intellectual hype surrounding "the Anthropocene" is a contemporary manifestation of this collective-hysterical process of crystallization, foisted now upon the nonhuman environment. See Bruce Clarke, "'The Anthropocene,' or, Gaia Shrugs," *Journal of Contemporary Archaeology* 1.1 (2014): 101–4.

16. H. G. Wells, *The War of the Worlds*, ed. Martin A. Danahay (1898; Orchard Park, NY: Broadview, 2003), 41; hereafter *WW*.

17. See Neil Badmington, *Alien Chic: Posthumanism and the Other Within* (New York: Routledge, 2004).

18. D. H. Lawrence, "Foreword to *Women in Love*," in *Women in Love*, ed. David Farmer, Lindeth Vasey, and John Worthen (New York: Cambridge University Press, 1995), 485; hereafter *WL*.

19. Ronald Wright, *A Scientific Romance* (New York: Picador, 1997); hereafter *SR*.

20. To discuss "the interdefinition of the actors" in the "variable-ontology world" of technological projects, Latour's *Aramis* introduces the related formulation of "*(x)-morphism*" to handle the subtle and sliding distinctions called forth by the symmetrical treatment of humans and nonhumans: "it is better to speak of *(x)-morphism* instead of becoming indignant when humans are treated as nonhumans or vice versa. The human form is as unknown to us as the nonhuman." Bruno Latour, *Aramis, or the Love of Technology*, trans. Catherine Porter (Cambridge: Harvard University Press, 1996), 173, 227. On the quasi-object, see Bruce Clarke, "Nonmodern Metamorphosis," in *PM*, 43–60; and "Observing *Aramis, or the Love of Technology*: Objects and Projects in Gilbert Simondon and Bruno Latour," in *Neocybernetics and Narrative*, 111–38.

21. *Neuromancer* glimpses a comparable posthuman vision when the hero Case sizes up the warehouse of his fence, the Finn: "The junk looked like something that had grown there, a fungus of twisted metal and plastic ... It seemed that is was changing subtly, cooking itself down under the pressure of time, silent invisible flakes settling to form a mulch, a crystalline essence of discarded technology, flowering secretly in the Sprawl's waste places." William Gibson, *Neuromancer* (New York: Ace, 1984), 48, 72.

22. Peter-Paul Verbeek, "Cultivating Humanity: Towards a Non-Humanist Ethics of Technology," in *New Waves in Philosophy of Technology*, ed. Jan Kyrre, Berg Olsen Friis, Evan Selinger, and Søren Riis (New York: Palgrave Macmillan, 2009), 261.

12

MANUELA ROSSINI

Bodies

When Ihab Hassan "helplessly" observed the advent of posthumanism in academe (see the opening of the Preface to this *Companion*), he was primarily concerned with alterations in the psychic and symbolic fabric of the human: "the human form – including human desire and all its external representations – may be changing radically, and thus must be re-visioned."[1] In the wake of the "linguistic turn," such revisions have indeed taken place in posthumanist cultural production for several decades now and, even more "radically" perhaps, in critical theory. Meanwhile, I would like to argue, current transformations of what it means to be human are the result not only of epistemological and ontological shifts brought about by anti-humanist and poststructuralist thought but, much more effectively, of the rapidly accelerating potential for technological modifications of the human body, from its largest outer parts down to its smallest inner components. In addition to the imminent possibility of superintelligent and sentient robots, the latest research into animal cognition challenges the humanist assumption that "we" are special. Moreover, tissue and organ transfers between human beings and across species barriers destabilize apparently secure boundaries between self and other, making it more and more difficult to identify a core essence that constitutes "true" humanness – if ever there was such a thing. In late capitalist countries, technoscience is turning more and more people into posthuman bodies, eroding the putatively bounded, self-determined, and supreme category "Man" and offering humanity in-stead a prosthetic existence, a "cyborg subjectivity"[2] which is perpetually under (de)construction.

In fact, current theoretical, cultural, and technoscientific trajectories for the future of the human seem to go hand in hand. In the dominant imaginary and increasingly in reality, bodies become infinitely malleable, plastic and liquid, to be performed and invented anew. The humanities are now expected to reenchant disenchanted "knowledge societies" worldwide and to "soften" the damage done to the planet by the "hard" sciences. Whether happily entered into or (more often) not, then, this alliance between what used to be diametrically opposed value systems is now seen both to fuel and to be fueled by neoliberal flexibility and consumer attitudes. However, the belief in the capacity of discursive interventions to change the order of things as well as the faith in technological solutions to social problems are both marked by an indifference to the nonhuman environment, from which wider milieu human bodies seem to be separated somehow – the label "Anthropocene" is evidence of such a distancing that posits humanity as the driving force acting on a passive, abstracted nature. Writers in various academic fields – not least in literary studies – have tried to queer such accounts and counterbalance overemphasis on either the discursive or the material side of things. They have reminded us that "co-habitation" and "co-evolution" have always shaped organic and nonorganic life on earth. Indeed, for some time now analytical attention has shifted from "the body" in its normative singularity to bodies in their plurality and entanglement with nonhuman actors.

The Corporeal and Material Turns

Simone de Beauvoir's famous statement that "One is not born, but rather becomes, woman,"[3] meanwhile turned into a feminist slogan, and Michel Foucault's work on sexuality in the late 1970s and early 1980s,[4] can be seen as starting points for innumerable writings on changes in social attitude toward the human body and bodily functions in different cultural and historical contexts. To put it schematically, the body has a history and comes in diverse shapes and colors. Such studies dismantle the ideal human form – represented perhaps most famously by Leonardo da Vinci's Vitruvian Man – not only as androcentric and Eurocentric but also as ableist – that is, as prejudicial against people with disabilities – in the ostensible demonstration of certain elite human bodies as the measure for all humanity and for what counts as a healthy and perfect body, with all the privileges such a normative shape implies. In particular, I would like to argue, Foucault's question regarding the power/knowledge nexus – "I wonder whether, before one poses the question of ideology, it wouldn't be more materialist to study the body and the effects of power on it"[5] – was highly influential in centering discussions around the discursive construction of bodies, addressing not only the histories and practices of the disciplining of unruly bodily behavior but also the potential for resisting and undoing negative images as well as for the making of more positive and (self-)empowering constructions of diverse forms of the body.

Such a critique of hierarchical "bodybuilding" has been vital for emancipatory movements. At least since the Renaissance, to be "human" has meant not only *not* to be a "beast"[6] but also to subscribe to a specific code of humanity, a code that has essentialized differences of ethnicity and race, class, gender, and sexuality.[7] These "natural" differences – putatively biological and innate to specific bodies – helped to build hierarchical systems of domination as well as taxonomies of the human/inhuman/nonhuman that for centuries have legitimated (and continue today to legitimate) the oppression, torturing, eating, and killing of beings not falling into the category "human." While it is totally understandable that colored, disabled, or transsexual people, for example, claim universal human rights, too, to do so in the name of "our shared humanity" can be predicated as much on exclusion from the collective "we" as on inclusion in it. For this demand occurs with the concomitant coding of what cannot but remain thought of as nonhuman, as not representing the extended but still distinct "standard" version of humanity.

Moreover, the discourse of humanism is supported by a speciesist logic of domination that allows for the treatment of gendered or racialized others as "animals" who are then, ultimately, exploitable or killable by human beings designated to that purpose without liability of punishment for such violent acts.[8] Precisely because humanist and anthropocentric ideologies are detrimental not only to nonhuman animals but also to many human animals as well, Cary Wolfe insists that speciesism needs to be countered by a posthumanist theory of the subject that *"has nothing to do with whether you like animals"* and strives to end "violence against the social other of *whatever* species – or gender, or race, or class, or sexual difference."[9] Such a theory, it must be hoped, will contribute to a future in which the experience of embodiment in all its richness and variety marks post/humanity and in which the lived body remains the ground not only of individual subjectivity but also of interaction and connection with the world and with others. N. Katherine Hayles's statement on her nightmare and dream outlook on a posthuman world is one to rally around:

> If my nightmare is a culture inhabited by posthumans who regard their bodies as fashion accessories [...], my dream is a version of the posthuman that embraces the possibilities of information technologies without being seduced by fantasies of unlimited power and disembodied immortality, that recognizes and celebrates finitude as a condition of human being, and that understands human life is embedded in a material world of great complexity, one on which we depend for our continued survival.[10]

Stacy Alaimo's reflections on "trans-corporeality" provide a further useful paradigm underlining such embeddedness and dependence in the forging of an ethics based on "interacting biological, climatic, economic, and political forces."[11] Alaimo is one of the strongest voices within literary scholarship to offer alternatives to the abiological circumscription of the human body that has dominated the humanities. In addition, from within the sciences and critical science studies, Donna Haraway's paradigm of "companion species"[12] and Karen Barad's concept of "intra-action"[13] provide truly interdisciplinary frames for studying the interminglings of nature and culture and of the human and the nonhuman, as well as for questioning the foundations of related hierarchical dualisms (self–other, mind–body, men–women, inside–outside, etc.).

The turn to the "nonhuman" in posthumanist discourse and posthuman figurations, addressed in Chapter 11 of this *Companion*, along with the turn to inter- or trans-corporeal multiplicities, is part of a broader shift in analytical attention to the material substrate underlying cultural and social forms. Under the label "new materialism," researchers – above all feminists working in diverse disciplines and across them[14] – have demonstrated that bodies matter not only in the way proposed by Judith Butler, with social and cultural norms regulating "the materialization and signification of those material effects"[15] on natural bodies (including "sex" and sexual behavior), but also in a much "deeper," interactive, and integral sense. Molecular biologist Anne Fausto-Sterling is a pioneer in showing convincingly that categories of difference inscribe themselves beyond the surface of bodies by going literally beneath the skin: "[E]vents outside the body become incorporated into our very flesh."[16]

At every moment, socioculturally shaped behavioral patterns as well as reactions of the neural system to external signals affect one's muscles, bones, nerves, and even the architecture of one's cells. As psychologist Susan Oyama has spelled out, all animal bodies (and minds – if one still wants to make such a distinction), including developments and behaviors that seem to be culturally transmitted, are in fact biologically and physically constructed. Disassociating the concept of "construction" from "program," Oyama writes that organisms (including people) "are, at every moment, products of, and participants in, their own and others' developmental processes. They are not self-determining in any simple sense but they affect and 'select' influences on themselves by attending to and interpreting stimuli, by seeking environments and companions, by being susceptible to various factors, by evoking reactions from others."[17] Such "response-ability" of developmental systems is also emphasized by Haraway when she insists that "em-bodiment ... is not about fixed location in a reified body ... but about nodes in fields, inflections in orientations, and responsibility for difference in material-semiotic fields of meaning."[18] In other words, the human body is knotted into interdependent networks that are both corporeal and discursive, natural and cultural, forming what Ira Livingston and Judith Halberstam aptly call "a zoo of posthumanities."[19] Not only is there a pluralization and queering of Humanity (with a capital H as in "The Family of Man") but an inter-disciplinary interrogation that de-privileges the human (body, culture, subject) as the object of the humanities, opening it up for what I call an "imagineering"[20] by various disciplines as well as by "bodybuilders" outside academia.

The theoretical work introduced thus far participates in the forging of what French philosopher Jean-Luc Nancy calls "co-ontology" or "plural ontology." The life of any mortal creature writes itself in the singular plural; there is no human or nonhuman being that is not, at the same time, an embodied "being-with" or co-existence of self and other: "*Being singular plural* means the essence of Being is only as coessence. In turn, coessence, or *being-with* (being-with-many), designates the essence of the *co-...* Coessentiality signifies the essential sharing of essentiality, sharing as assembling."[21] In the next section, an analysis of Nancy's essay "The Intruder" frames my subsequent, decidedly critical-posthumanist and new-materialist feminist reading of posthuman bodies in selected writings by contemporary American author Shelley Jackson. Her well-known and widely discussed hypertext *Patchwork Girl* already flaunts in its title identity as a singular plurality.

Ergo cum: Transcorporeality in Jean-Luc Nancy's "The Intruder"

Ten years after he had to undergo a life-saving heart transplant around the age of 50, Jean-Luc Nancy published *L'Intrus*[22] as a philosophical reflection of that "intrusive" corporeal experience and suffering. Partly autobiographical, the essay could be grouped with other so-called pathographies. Through the act of writing, such texts usually attempt to restabilize a sense of corporeal integrity, wholeness, and/or identity, an identity that severe, often terminal illness has rendered shaky. The majority of such narratives follow the pattern of a quest and rebirth. Nancy's memoir subscribes to that tradition but also departs from it, insofar as it does not pursue something like a stable and bounded self or "whole-some" body.

Describing the donor heart with the metaphor of "the intruder," Nancy counters Susan Sontag's argument that a "truthful" account of illness needs to use a metaphor-free language.[23] Instead, he would follow Paul de Man's understanding that the "authentic" self established in autobiographies is in reality a fiction based on metaphors, because any writing can only ever represent likenesses in language and not reality itself.[24] More significantly for the purpose of this chapter, the metaphor of the intruder allows Nancy not only to make sense of his own experience but also to link his thinking to larger political issues such as migration and border regimes. Thus, his ruminations exceed the level of narcissistic self-observation that mark most pathographies and, instead, connect the individual body to the collective. The very first paragraphs of *L'intrus* already establish the figure of the intruder to advocate a "politically correct" attitude toward the coming of strangers:

> The intruder enters by force, through surprise or ruse, in any case without the right and without having first been admitted. There must be something of the *intrus* in the stranger; otherwise, the stranger would lose its strangeness: if he already has the right to enter and remain, if he is awaited and received without any part of him being unexpected or unwelcome, he is no longer the *intrus*, nor is he any longer the stranger. It is thus neither logically acceptable, nor ethically admissible, to exclude all intrusion in the coming of the stranger, the foreign.
>
> (*L'Intrus* 1)

Central to this endeavor is his breaking with Judeo-Christian uses of the heart. In the Hebrew Bible, for example, the heart is the sheet on which God writes his laws that are then transformed into deeds. In Augustine's *Confessions* the heart is clearly the location of the kind of interiority commonly associated with the liberal-humanist subject at the onset of modernity: "My heart is where I am, such as I am."[25] It is also within this European tradition that, around the twelfth century, the trope of the heart as text develops to the point where the written text itself is seen as a kind of body – hence the term *corpus* to denote both.

The invasive yet welcome advent of the donor heart in Nancy's *corpus* – in his body and in his text (as metaphor) – as "foreign/strange" (*étrange*) is also opposed to a surgeon's view of the heart as a machine pumping blood around the body. Whereas for the medical profession a heart transplant becomes primarily a technical question, for patients such an event raises all kinds of metaphysical questions. Yet, the precondition of extended life is exactly the exclusion of the prior symbolic meanings of the heart in favor of admitting a strange, demystified heart. In the process, for Nancy not only the donor heart but now also his own heart becomes a foreigner, one whose strangeness (as sick and calling attention to itself) comes *before* the other foreigner: "My heart was becoming my own foreigner – a stranger precisely because it was inside. Yet this strangeness could only come from outside for having first emerged inside" (*L'Intrus* 4). And he continues: "We are armed with cautionary recommendations vis-à-vis the outside world (crowds, stores, swimming pools, small children, those who are sick). But the most vigorous enemies are inside: the old viruses that have always been lurking in the shadow of my immune system – life-long intrus, as they have always been there (*L'Intrus* 9). What Nancy refers to here is the necessity, after the implant is received, for the immune system to give up its primary role of defending the self against the other. This is done with the help of immuno-suppressive drugs. Such intensive medicalization inevitably leads to the paradoxical situation that the "proper" body must let in substances that are healing and life-sustaining and, at the same time, poisonous because bad viruses *within* the body then turn against it, causing cells to develop cancer, as happened with Nancy. This means that, all of a sudden, through the awareness of material agents within his body, for Nancy "life" becomes more than just the functioning of the heart; yet, at the same time, it is fully co-terminous with it: "What is this life 'proper' that it is a matter of 'saving'? At the very least, it turns out that it in no way resides in 'my' body; it is not situated anywhere, not even in this organ whose symbolic renown has long been established … A life 'proper' that resides in no one organ but that without them is nothing" (*L'Intrus* 7, 8).

This new subjectivity becomes distributed and prosthetic. The posthuman subject has no property in the body but is both open and closed, receptive of outsiders as well as dependent on a continuous self-exteriorization: "I am closed open. There is in fact an opening through which passes a stream of unremitting strangeness: the immuno-depressive medication . . .; the repeated monitoring and observation; an entire existence set on a new register, swept from top to bottom" ("L'Intrus" 10). Indeed, the experience is one of becoming posthuman, a human–robot hybrid, or a zombie character known to him from a science-fiction or horror movie:

> I am the illness and the medical intervention, I am the cancerous cell and the grafted organ, I am the immuno-depressive agents and their palliatives, I am the bits of wire that hold together my sternum, and I am this injection site perma-nently stitched in below my clavicle, just as I was already these screws in my hip and this plate in my groin. I am becoming like a science-fiction android, or the living-dead. (*L'Intrus* 13)

As these last two quotations signal, Nancy does not uncritically embrace "cyborgification" and the proliferation of the "I." While the donor heart saved his life – which life, we might want to ask? – the post-transplant experience is also utterly alienating. He is not really undergoing a *restitutio ad integrum* – the medical term for the restitution of one's integrity – but is, in effect, subjected to technologies that measure, scan, control, and hence disintegrate him and his writing. These breaks are expressed materially, in the typography: many words are put in quotation marks, there are empty lines (sometimes almost a full empty page) and several passages are put between brackets. The layout thus parallels the tension between linearity/ continuity (life) and discontinuity (death) of the heart transplant and its aftermath. Receiving the heart of a 30-year-old woman of unknown nationality added age, gender, and possibly also ethnic discontinuities.

Like "The Intruder," the three works by American writer Shelley Jackson I am going to discuss next point to the limits of language or writing to present such a life-saving yet alienating experience of being "singular plural." They trouble corporeal boundaries not only between humans but also between human and nonhuman species. Whereas Nancy's awareness, as Gernot Böhme rightly observes, that "his identity as a self has a bodily sub-stratum"[26] is created only *after* the operation or "invasive technification" of his body, Jackson seems to have a much more essential and thoroughly posthumanist view of a shared corporeality, even if the intended monstrosity of the "patchworked" body might be a troubling eyesore to the liberal-humanist vision.

Monstrous Bodies: Shelley Jackson's Corporeal Experiments

Shelley Jackson's decision to call her website "INERADICABLE STAIN" already signals the kind of "self-pollution" (as she subtitles the biographical note "WHO IS WHO") that marks anybody – *any* body – with foreign traces and signs unavoidably intruding on the home(page). Having a talent for narrating origin stories across the human–animal divide, it also comes as no surprise when she tells us that she was "extracted from the bum leg of a water buffalo in 1963 in the Philippines";[27] nor that, with the eye and hand of a pathologist, she engages in a virtual dissecting act with *my body – a Wunderkammer*, "a semi-autobiographical hypertext combining text and image in an exploration of the body" (as the author herself describes it).[28] Here and in the stories of body parts composing *The Melancholy of Anatomy*,[29] as the playful but significant reversal of the title of Robert Burton's seventeenth-century medical treatise indicates, matter is seen to be endowed with agency and consciousness. Like the heart in Nancy's corpus, the heart whose story opens that collection acquires a life of its own that is wonderfully strange and familiar at the same time. Both works are noteworthy bodily experiments, yet Jackson is probably best known for her ground-breaking hypertext from 1995, *Patchwork Girl*. This text will be the central literary text I will discuss in this chapter, intersected by very brief references to her ongoing Skin project and her first novel *Half Life*.

While Jackson's literary dialogue with the electronic medium is, arguably, the best way to present a view of identity as intercorporeal and meaning as intertextual, all of her works articulate the same basic understanding of the physical and material conditions that produce (textual/sexual) bodies. Moreover, Jackson did not immediately start to compose *Patchwork Girl* digitally, but with a drawing on a page of her notebook – the drawing of a naked woman with dotted-line scars.[30] There are two models for the creation of this figure: the proto-feminist heroine of Frank Baum's *The Patchwork Girl of Oz* (1913) and, more directly also for the whole plot, Mary Shelley's *Frankenstein*, both the novel of 1818 and the film adaptation of 1994[31] in which Dr. Frankenstein – unlike the outcome in the original novel – did succeed in creating a female companion for his male monster. The female "monster" (as the character refers to herself) is "resurrected," put together again by Mary Shelley, and the suggestion is that the whole work is co-authored by Mary Shelley, Shelley Jackson, and the monster herself. (It is of course fortuitous that Jackson's first name is Shelley.) Acknowledged already in the title page, written "BY MARY/SHELLEY, AND HERSELF," Jackson's corporeal co-existence is expressed as the co-authorship of the textual body not only by these three authors but also by the software and, not least at all, by the reader. As the Patchwork Girl herself describes our material practice: "I am buried here. You can resurrect me, but only piecemeal. If you want to see the whole, you will have to sew me together yourself (a graveyard)."[32]

Like the female monster's body, the body of this hypertext is also seamed and ruptured, composed of five distinct narrative parts with extensive links between them: a graveyard, a journal, a quilt; a story, broken accents. Especially in the graveyard and quilt parts, as Jackson lets us know, she wanted to "literally embody the fragmentation and multiplicity"[33] that she speaks about in the other sections of *Patchwork Girl*. Thus, in the graveyard lie the stories of the creatures some of whose body parts were used to form the monster, and each tale is endowed with a distinctive voice, narrating concerns that are not the protagonist's. The intercorporeality, and hence multivocality, finds an analogy in the intertextuality of the quilt section, with excerpts from Baum's *Patchwork Girl of Oz* as well as re-inscriptions from other parts of the whole hypertext. In addition, metareflections and passages from other sources on hypertextual and human bodies abound, especially when opening the lexia called "body of text."

The posthuman subject assembled here distinguishes itself from notions and representations of self or personhood that dominated the Enlightenment humanism of the late eighteenth and the early nineteenth centuries (when *Frankenstein* was written). To remind ourselves quickly: embedded within the political theory of what philosopher C. B. Macpherson labeled "possessive individualism," the liberal-humanist subject emerging during that proto-

modernity who can fashion themselves in their own image and are separate from other living entities.

As Hayles observes, a similar collaboration takes place between the hypertextual body and the body of the reader: "The user inscribes her subjectivity into this text by choosing which links to activate, which scars to trace . . . . The scars/links thus function to join the text with the corporeal body of the user."[42] At first glance, Jackson, too, seems to be happy with the text/body conflation when she claims that "all bodies are written bodies, all lives pieces of writing" (all written). But then, this lexia is linked to the following one:

> our infinitely various forms are composed from a limited number of similar elements, a kind of alphabet, and we have guidelines as to which arrangements are acceptable, are valid words, legible sentences, and which are typographical or grammatical errors: "monsters."
>
> We are inevitably annexed to other bodies: human bodies, and bodies of knowledge. We are coupled to constructions of meaning; we are legible, partially; we are cooperative with meanings, but irreducible to any one. The form is not absolutely malleable to the intentions of the author; what may be thought is contingent on the means of expression.
>
> (body of text/bodies too)

In the age of global capitalism and the seemingly endless plasticity and proliferation of just about everything, it is important to insist, as Jackson does, that neither physical nor textual bodies are neutral and passive sites for the inscription of meaning by writing technologies. It is precisely *not* the case that everyone can become the author of meaning and creator of other bodies or his or her own body. Still, in spite of all these constraints, writing and subjectivity are always patchworks of re-inscription.

Imagineering Bodies for the Posthuman Future

Literature, and Science fiction in particular, is an important cultural resource for dealing with advances in medicine, biotechnologies, and informatics. But literature does not merely react to technological development and offer ethical guidance. Rather, there is a double movement: the technological potential will affect the way the human body/subject is defined but these new meanings (produced in texts and images) will influence, if not our actual use and even development of them, our handling of technologies. Rather sooner than later, cyborgs and other hybrids, androids, and technologically enhanced humans will people the earth (and maybe other planets). Imagineered in "scientifictive" texts, I suggest, such embodied subjects can be seen as cultural prefigurations of future human beings in the 'real' world.

It can be speculated that writers of any genre interested in changing the symbolic order that maintains and reproduces hierarchies of class, race and ethnicity, gender and sexuality, age, dis/ability, religion, and other differences will continue their fictive engineering of new images of the human and offer them as models to be imitated by all those who feel that older representations do no longer correspond to their postmodern or posthumanist sensibility, their experience, or their desires as embodied beings.

The relation between the introductory paragraphs of this chapter and the succeeding sections on Jean-Luc Nancy and Shelley Jackson could be read in that light. Nancy with *L'Intrus* and Jackson with *Patchwork Girl* and her other writings describe the corporeal human as always already a composition of various bits and pieces: precisely, a patchwork. These texts do not present identity as a case of discrete individualism but, instead, subscribe to living (and dead) bodies' corporeal interconnectedness to the world and to other actors – whether these are humans, animals, machines, or texts that together perform a dance of becoming singular plural. As "science/fiction" of a quite distinct kind, posthumanist narratives – whether literary or scientific – offer accounts of life that insist on the co-constitutive entanglement across machinic, animal, human, and microbial textures that break down any notion of an individual organism's "self-defense." As Ed Cohen's study reminds us, "biological immunity" is a scientific invention of the late nineteenth century.[43] Within a posthumanist frame, the human body or subject is seen as just another knot in the web of interspecies or intersubjective dependencies. All organic and inorganic creatures are woven together into an instrumental economy in which "we" live in and through the use of one another's bodies, being reciprocally means and ends to each other. In short, total closure or perfect immunity is not possible. The scientific as well as fictive texts conceptualize bodies as open and closed at the same time: not so much in terms of closing off the intruding other but in not allowing the extruded self to come back in. Being is being-with, living-with strangers and foreigners, including the foreigners within – be it within a cell or a nation or, to end on a more cosmopolitical note – our planet. Last but not least, the works I have offered as paradigmatic examples of posthumanist science/fiction invite us to consider the long-term consequences of our own technological inventions with great care but without being technophobic, least of all in respect of the technology of writing as "bodybuilding."

NOTES

1. Ihab Hassan, "Prometheus as Performer: Toward a Posthumanist Culture?" *Georgia Review* 31.4 (Winter 1977): 843.
2. N. Katherine Hayles, "Flickering Connectivities in Shelley Jackson's *Patchwork Girl*: The Importance of Media-Specific Analysis," *Postmodern Culture* 10.2

(2000): 13. For a feminist discussion of cyborg subjectivities more broadly, see Chapter 4 in Rosi Bradotti, *Nomadic Subjects: Embodiment and Sexual Difference in Contemporary Feminist Theory* (New York: Columbia University Press, 1994; new and revised edition, 2011).

3. Simone de Beauvoir, *The Second Sex*, trans. Constance Borde and Sheila Malovany-Chevallier (New York: Vintage Books, 2011), 283.

4. See, for example, his three-volume study *The History of Sexuality*, published between 1976 and 1984.

5. Michel Foucault, "Body/Power," in *Power/Knowledge: Selected Interviews and Other Writings 1972–1977*, ed. Colin Gordon (New York: Pantheon Books, 1980), 58.

6. For efforts (and failures thereof) to construct boundaries between the human and its others (including female and native beings of the same species, animals and machines) in literary, cultural, and scientific writings from the mid-sixteenth century to the late-eighteenth century, see, for example, *At the Borders of the Human: Beasts, Bodies and Natural Philosophy in the Early Modern Period*, ed. Erica Fudge, Ruth Gilbert, and Susan Wiseman (Houndmills: Palgrave, 1999).

7. See, for example, Diana Fuss, "Introduction: Human All Too Human," in *Human All Too Human*, ed. Diana Fuss (London: Routledge, 1996), 1–7.

8. For the analogy between the edible body of animals and the sexualized body of women, see Carol Adams, *The Sexual Politics of Meat: A Feminist-Vegetarian Critical Theory* (New York: Continuum, 1999); for close interconnections between the discourse of species and race, see Marjorie Spiegel, *The Dreaded Comparison: Human and Animal Slavery* (New York: Mirror Books, 1996); and for further examples that intersect various categories of difference, see my own essay, "I Am Not an Animal! I Am a Human Being! I ... Am ... a ... Man!' Is Female to Male as animal to human?," in *Exploring the Animal Turn: Human-Animal Relations in Science, Society and Culture*, ed. Erika Andersson Cederholm, Amelie Björck, Kristina Jennbert, and Ann-Sofie Lönngren (Lund: MediaTryck, 2014), 111–23, accessed July 20, 2015, www.pi .lu.se/sites/pi.lu.se/files/exploring_the_animal_turn_hela.pdf.

9. Cary Wolfe, *Animal Rites: American Culture, the Discourse of Species, and Posthumanist Theory* (Chicago: University of Chicago Press, 2003), 7, 8; emphasis in the original.

10. N. Katherine Hayles, *How We Became Posthuman: Virtual Bodies in Cybernetics, Literature, and Informatics* (Chicago: University of Chicago Press, 1999), 5.

11. Stacy Alaimo, *Bodily Natures. Science, Environment, and the Material Self* (Bloomington: Indian a University Press, 2010), 2. For an ethics of posthumanism, see also Patricia MacCormack, *Posthuman Ethics: Embodiment and Cultural Theory* (Farnham: Ashgate, 2012).

12. Donna Haraway, *The Companion Species Manifesto. Dogs, People, and Significant Otherness* (Chicago: Prickly Paradigm Press, 2003). As her later work makes clear though, Haraway prefers to speak of "companion species" as an alternative to both her earlier figuration of "the cyborg" as well as to "the posthuman," Donna Haraway, *When Species Meet* (Minneapolis: Minnesota University Press, 2007), 17, yet I would nevertheless include her approach within

the canon of critical posthumanism, insofar as she participates in the working through of humanism.

13. As early as 2003, Barad drew on physicist Niels Boer's concept of "intra-action" as the grounding concept of what she then called "posthumanist performativity." Unlike "interaction" (which takes the existence of independent, pre-constituted entities for granted), "intra-action" or "intra-activity" insists that phenomena only exist as relations and are thus constantly in the process of becoming. See Karen Barad, "Posthumanist Performativity: Toward an Understanding of How Matter Comes to Matter," *Signs: Journal of Women in Culture and Society* 28.3 (2003): 801–31, accessed October 25, 2015, umweb.ucsc.edu/feministstudies/faculty/barad/barad-posthumanist.pdf.

14. See the following collection of essays: *New Materialisms: Ontology, Agency, and Politics*, ed. Diana Coole and Samantha Frost (Durham: Duke University Press, 2010) and *Material Feminisms*, ed. Stacy Alaimo and Susan Hekman (Bloomington: Indiana University Press, 2008); for an earlier programmatic text, including a bibliography of neomaterialist studies, see my own essay "To the Dogs: Companion Speciesism and the New Feminist Materialism," *Kritikos* 3 (2006), accessed on October 25, 2015, intertheory.org/Rossini; for current trends in new materialism, see the following European research project, accessed October 25, 2015, www.cost.eu/COST_Actions/isch/IS1307.

15. Judith Butler, *Bodies that Matter: On the Discursive Limits of "Sex"* (New York: Routledge, 1993), 2.

16. Anne Fausto-Sterling, *Sexing the Body: Gender Politics and the Construction of Sexuality* (New York: Basic Books, 2000), 238.

17. Susan Oyama, *Evolution's Eye: A Systems View of the Biology-Culture Divide* (Durham: Duke University Press, 2000), 180–81.

18. Donna Haraway, *Simians, Cyborgs, and Women: The Reinvention of Nature* (New York: Routledge, 1991), 195.

19. Judith Halberstam and Ira Livingston, "Introduction: Posthuman Bodies," in *Posthuman Bodies*, ed. Judith Halberstam and Ira Livingston (Bloomington and Indianapolis: Indiana University Press, 1995), 3.

20. Manuela Rossini, "Science/Fiction: Imagineering Posthuman Bodies," presented at the 5th European Feminist Research Conference in Lund in 2003, accessed July 20, 2015, www.iiav.nl/epublications/2003/gender_and_power/5thfeminist/paper_709.pdf.

21. Jean-Luc Nancy, *Being Singular Plural* (Stanford: Stanford University Press, 2000), 30.

22. The text first appeared in 1999 as a commissioned essay for the special issue "La venue de l'étranger" (in English: "the coming of the stranger or the foreigner") of the journal *Dédale*. It was then published in book form as *L'Intrus* (Paris: Éditions Galilée, 2000) and later translated by Richard A. Rand into English for the collection *Corpus* (Fordham University Press, 2008). Quotations are from the online translation by Susan Hanson, accessed August 29, 2015, www.maxvanmanen.com/files/2014/10/Nancy-LIntrus.pdf; hereafter, "L'Intrus."

23. Susan Sontag, *Illness as Metaphor* (New York: Farrar, Straus and Giroux, 1978), 3.

24. Paul de Man, *The Rhetoric of Romanticism* (New York: Columbia University Press, 1984). See Chapter 4, "Autobiography as De-Facement," especially 70–72.

25. As quoted in Martin L. Warren, "Hypertext: A Sacred (He)Art? Cor ad cor loquitur from Augustine to Shelley Jackson," *Medieval Forum* 2 (March 2003), accessed July 20, 2015, www.sfsu.edu/~medieval/Volume2/Warren2.html.

26. Gernot Böhme, *Invasive Technification: Critical Essays in the Philosophy of Technology* (London: Bloomsbury, 2012), 233.

27. See "WHO IS WHO self-pollution," accessed August 29, 2015, ineradicablestain .com.

28. Shelley Jackson, *my Body – a Wunderkammer* (1997), accessed September 12, 2015, http://collection.eliterature.org/1/works/jackson_my_body_a_wunder kammer.html.

29. Shelley Jackson, *The Melancholy of Anatomy* (New York: Anchor Books, 2002).

30. A good sense of how the reading of the text works comes from Jackson's navigating through her work for the Pathfinders project, led by Dene Grigar and Stuart Moulthrop, available on YouTube in four parts, accessed September 6, 2015, part 1: www.youtube.com/watch?v=ZHUR6phuOrc; part 2: www.youtube.com/watch?v=21YxTeVit1c; part 3: www.youtube.com/watch?v=tPnKbegzo50; part 4: www.youtube.com/watch?v=qihmuNBTX28.

31. *Mary Shelley's Frankenstein*. Directed by Kenneth Branagh, produced by Francis Ford Coppola. Culver City, CA: TriStar Pictures, 1994.

32. I follow the conventional reference system for hypertext: main text box/lexia, followed by subsections (if available).

33. Interview with Shelley Jackson by Dene Grigar, October 2013, accessed September 6, 2015, www.youtube.com/watch?v=1zkT97DzQUI.

34. John Locke, *Two Treatises of Government*, first published anonymously in 1670, Book II, chapter V, section 27, accessed September 11, 2015, www .johnlocke.net/two-treatises-of-government-book-ii/#CHAPTER_V.

35. René Descartes, *A Discourse on Method and the Meditations*, trans. F. E. Sutcliffe (London: Penguin Books, 1968), 154.

36. Mark Rose, *Authors and Owners: The Invention of Copyright* (Cambridge, MA: Harvard University Press, 1993).

37. Jackson on her project, "a mortal story": www.youtube.com/watch? v=bdujEfv9uO4; video of the project: www.youtube.com/watch?v=viF- xuLrGvA.

38. Shelley Jackson, *Half Life* (New York: HarperCollins, 2006).

39. To my best knowledge, the label "new biology" arose in the context of a number of conferences organized by William Irwin Thompson in the 1980s. See *Gaia –A Way of Knowing: Political Implications of the New Biology*, ed. William Irwin Thompson (Great Barrington, MA: Lindisfarne Press, 1987). It is used for work in theoretical biology that counters genocentric, neo-Darwinian biol- ogy where natural selection and competition alone explain the emergence of new life forms. By contrast, "new biologists" would look to molecular and intracel- lular levels where creative acts take place that, as Brian Goodwin writes, have "no purpose, no progress, no sense of direction," and thus no necessary connec- tion to Neo-Darwinism's adaptationist agendas. See Goodwin's 1995 essay,

"Biology is Just a Dance," accessed October 10, 2015, http://edge.org/conversa tion/brian_goodwin-chapter-4-biology-is-just-a-dance.

40. Dorion Sagan, "Metametazoa: Biology and Multiplicity," in *Zone 6: In corporations*, ed. Jonathan Crary and Sanford Kwinter (Cambridge: Zone Books, 1992), 362.

41. Lynn Margulis and Dorion Sagan, *Acquiring Genomes: A Theory of the Origins of Species* (New York: Basic Books, 2003).

42. N. Katherine Hayles, *My Mother Was a Computer: Digital Subjects and Literary Texts* (Chicago: The University of Chicago Press, 2005), 159.

43. Ed Cohen, *A Body Worth Defending: Immunity, Biopolitics and the Apotheosis of the Modern Body* (Durham: Duke University Press, 2009). See also Roberto Esposito, *Immunitas: The Protection and Negation of Life*, trans. Zakiya Hanafi (Malden, MA: Polity Press, 2011).

13

RIDVAN ASKIN

Objects

The Literary Object and the Object of Literature

Continental philosophy has recently seen a turn away from questions of subjectivity toward a renewed interest in things and objects in their own right. In this vein, thinkers have been theorizing thing-power, subjectless objects, and their fourfold constitution.[1] At the same time, discourse on objects has long been a staple of analytic philosophy, which presents us with a dizzying array of all kinds of objects: ordinary objects, abstract objects, fictional objects, possible objects, and even nonexistent objects.[2] All these approaches – continental and analytic – are concerned with what could be called the "objecthood of objects" (or the thingliness of things), whether general or particular. In contrast, while this chapter is dedicated to two particular kinds of objects, namely the literary object and the object of literature, it is concerned not so much with their objecthood as with their essential qualities. In other words, I will focus on the literary and the very aim of the literary. This constitutes another attempt at answering what seems to be a perennial question: What is literature? But in the context of this volume, a second question immediately arises: How is the question of literature, arguably the epitome of a *humanist* question, related to posthumanist concerns? I will thus tackle the relation between literature and the posthuman in the most direct of ways to suggest an answer that goes precisely *beyond* the human. Coupling Russian formalism with Gilles Deleuze's philosophy of difference and presenting two exemplary readings – of Margaret Fuller's *Summer on the Lakes, in 1843* and Charles Olson's "The Ring of" – I will go against the grain of much recent mainstream literary theory to demonstrate nothing less than the essentially posthuman status of literature per se.

For decades, the question of what literature is has been either side-lined as impossible to answer, due to its essentialist and therefore self-deconstructive thrust (as the well-known argument goes), or deliberately deflected onto a socio-historical level, thus yielding only temporary and provisional answers. In fact, since these two claims easily reinforce one another, they often appear conjointly in what could be called "the historico-deconstructionist two-step."

In this vein, literature is presented as something essentially elusive (that is, something essentially without essence) that can only ever be temporarily and provisionally determined, depending on the given social, cultural, and historical context and its concomitant ways of reading.[3]

But things have not always been this way. Indeed, whereas the second half of the twentieth century saw the gradual establishment of the explanatory framework sketched above, much of the first half was devoted precisely to attempts at pinpointing the essence of literature. Among the most notorious is Russian formalism. Thus, in his famous essay "Art as Device," Viktor Shklovsky introduces his concept of "enstrangement," coined to capture literature's defining quality and power to *re*-familiarize us (rather than *de*-familiarize, as the most well-known translation of Shklovsky's Russian neologism *ostranenie* has it) with both our own perceptual processes, which otherwise tend to go unnoticed, and the very essence of that which we perceive, which is otherwise lost in the process of cognition.[4] In other words, Shklovsky conceives of literature as a tool (the very "device" of his essay's title) that makes us aware of what we otherwise are not aware of: *that* and *how* we perceive and *what* we perceive. His account will lead us directly to the chapter's more explicitly posthuman concerns.

According to Shklovsky, the reason why we are not aware of perception and so need this tool called "literature" is grounded in the fact that our cognitive apparatus, our predisposition to conceptual thought, tends to override perception; rather than "simply" perceive things, we incessantly recognize them. While the economizing abstractions of conceptual thought – its subsumption of particulars under a general term – are a prerequisite for both human communication and abstract reasoning, they lose sight of the very particularity of the particular. In other words, conceptual thought gives us objects in general and in the abstract – as concepts – but misses out on the concrete object itself – the particular thing. In contrast, art in general and literature in particular (it is notable that Shklovsky, despite his essay's title, discusses only literary works) can give us the very thing in its particularity. Literature is a "tool" that makes us "feel objects," makes "a stone feel stony" as Shklovsky's famous expression has it ("AD" 6). Works of literature are thus quintessential *aesthetic objects*: the literary object, qua tool, pries open any object whatsoever by virtue of being a tool of *aisthesis* – of feeling, perception, sensation. In addition, the literary object also discloses the very process of *aisthesis* itself. The literary object is an aesthetic object constituting a preeminent site of *aisthesis* at work, while the twofold object of literature is both the very process of *aisthesis* itself and any object whatsoever that it is apt to disclose by means of *aisthesis*.

From a posthumanist perspective, what is interesting in this conception of literature is that Shklovsky presents literature as the very *human* means of going *beyond the human*. It gives us access to the essence of things, for example, the stoniness of stones, because it bypasses conceptual thought and operates directly on and via sensation. The literary work is an object of sensation created by humans for the purpose of getting out of themselves and into things. Viewed in this way, Shklovsky's theory of art undercuts Immanuel Kant's ban on speculation. In his *Critique of Pure Reason*, Kant famously distinguishes between *phenomena* and *noumena*, things as they appear to us and things as they are in themselves, restricting thought to the realm of phenomena and maintaining that things in themselves remain beyond the limits of thought and thus inaccessible. In contrast, Shklovsky maintains that while things in themselves might be inaccessible to conceptual thought, they are very much accessible to non-conceptual sensation. In this sense, literature per se is essentially posthumanist.

Literature as Speculative Experiment in Metaphysics

Despite all of the above, Shklovsky does not say much about the stoniness of the stone – the essence of the very things that literature is apt to disclose. This is consistent with his focus on aesthetic experience: he gives us an account of the kind of experience that literary texts provide, not of what is being experienced. His focus is on the function and essence of literature, not on the essence of the things that it is the essence of literature to disclose. Shklovsky thus remains within the sphere of lived experience. While he indeed highlights literature's anti-Kantian thrust beyond the limits of thought, he himself desists from following through on this trajectory. Put differently, while he emphasizes literature's speculative drive, he refrains from its genuine metaphysical implications. In yet other words, Shklovsky remains on the level of surface appearance but misses out on the depths of its essence. Everything Shklovsky lists as characteristic features of literature belongs to this level of surface: employment of rhetorical schemes and tropes, of narrative strategies, certain uses of syntax and linguistic devices in general; in short, employment of what he terms "poetic language." As they are the *form* in which the underlying essence of literature *appears*, these features are important, of course, but they constitute only half the story. If one wishes to explore the depths of literature, one needs to turn elsewhere. I want to suggest the philosophy of Gilles Deleuze (and, to a lesser extent, Félix Guattari) as an apposite resource here. Like Shklovsky, Deleuze sees literature (and art in general) as primarily engaged with sensations. He also thinks that literature is a device to get us out of ourselves, but unlike Shklovsky, he actually provides the metaphysical grounding to do so. While Shklovsky remains preoccupied with the very human realm of language even as he takes its poetic use to be disclosing the beyond of language, Deleuze zooms in on this beyond.

In accordance with Shklovsky, Deleuze and Guattari bluntly state that whether "through words, colors, sounds, or stone, art is the language of sensations."[5] It is precisely in their concept of sensation, however, that they markedly differ from Shklovsky's traditional take where sensation refers to the human sensorium and its attendant range of human perceptions and feelings. Their concept of sensation is genuinely metaphysical and nonhuman, as it denotes what they call percepts and affects, "*beings* whose validity lies in themselves and exceeds any lived" (*WIP* 164; original emphasis). Sensations qua autonomous beings are thus not necessarily correlated with humans, or only insofar as they make up the nonhuman aspect of this correlation: "*Affects are precisely these nonhuman becomings of man*, just as percepts ... are *nonhuman landscapes of nature*" (*WIP* 169; original emphasis).

Deleuze's earlier work *Difference and Repetition* helps to unpack this rather obscure-sounding remark. Here, Deleuze notes that "aesthetics" understood as the "science of the sensible" cannot be possibly founded on representation (that is, cognition).[6] In that case, there would simply be no proper science of the sensible as the sensible would remain subsumed within the intelligible – it would cease to be an autonomous realm of inquiry. But neither can it be determined by simply subtracting representation. In this case, it would be completely cut off from thought, something we could not possibly make any sense of, something that by definition could not ever enter our cognitive processes, not even in altered form, and thus would have to remain unnoticed and irrelevant. Deleuze's solution to this problem is what he terms "transcendental empiricism": in addition to our everyday empirical use of the senses, there has to be a genuine transcendental use, a use that goes beyond our familiar everyday empirical realm. "Empiricism truly becomes transcendental," Deleuze says,

> and aesthetics an apodictic discipline, only when we apprehend directly in the sensible that which can only be sensed, the very being *of* the sensible: difference, potential difference and difference in intensity as the reason behind qualitative diversity. It is in difference that movement is produced as an "effect," that phenomena flash their meaning like signs. (*DR* 68)

In short, Deleuze connects the realms of the intelligible and the sensible without subsuming the sensible under the intelligible. Whereas the empirical use of our senses is immediately taken up in processes of cognition and thus indeed tied to representation, the transcendental use bears directly on that which can *only* be sensed (that is, which cannot be thought). Sensibility thus preserves its autonomy *and* becomes our means to access the beyond of thought and representation. Aesthetics gets directly at the heart of things – Deleuze's realm of intensive difference. In Deleuze's philosophy, intensive difference is the underlying principle that generates extensive identities. In this way, Deleuze inverts the usual relation between identity and difference. With difference, the grounding principle is no longer a unity, as it is now fractured from the outset – it becomes a differential field rather than a unitary point. But what exactly are these differentials and what is this field? They are the very Deleuzian nonhuman landscape and nonhuman becomings of affects and percepts, that is, sensation. In other words, Deleuzian difference is essentially sensational and Deleuzian sensation is essentially differential. This is how sensation assumes general ontological weight. And it is in this way that literature, as the preeminent site of *aisthesis* at work, offers the very human means of accessing the nonhuman sensational fabric of things. Literary works thus become veritable speculative experiments in metaphysics.

Case Studies

I will now provide two brief case studies in order to trace literature's capacity both to access the very essence of things and at the same time to make the very procedure of this accessing explicit. Literature thus always also sheds light on its own essence. My tutor texts will be Margaret Fuller's *Summer on the Lakes, in 1843* and Charles Olson's poem "The Ring of." As befits my universalist claim, namely that my above account holds true for all literary works, these texts are marked by both a clear generic and a clear literary historical difference with a romantic travel narrative on the one hand and a late-modernist poem on the other.[7]

Romantic Travel Narrative
Summer on the Lakes, in 1843 records Margaret Fuller's experiences, impressions, and thoughts during her travel through the Great Lakes region. Clearly a travel narrative, the text presents a peculiarly disjointed, impressionistic, digressive, and fragmented account that is interwoven with illustrations, poems, dramatizations, a fictionalized autobiographical sketch, and a retelling and part-translation of a German esoteric novel that is itself the fictionalized retelling of the life and death of Friederike Hauffe, the so-called Seeress of Prevorst. These formal peculiarities go hand in hand with Fuller's

thematic interests. While the travelogue time and again touches on highly pertinent social and political issues, particularly with respect to the situation of Native Americans and that of women at the frontier, these considerations always rest on a genuine transcendentalist concern with the relation of the human to nature. A passage toward the very end of the text presenting Fuller's musings on the elevated character of Native Americans makes this quite explicit:

> There is a language of eye and motion which cannot be put into words, and which teaches what words never can. I feel acquainted with the soul of this race; I read its nobler thought in their defaced figures. There was a greatness, unique and precious, which he who does not feel will never duly appreciate the majesty of nature in this American continent.[8]

I do not wish to explore any further the political and ethical implications of Fuller's portrayal of Native Americans, whom she clearly aligns in these lines with nature rather than culture, just as she repeatedly evokes the noble-savage trope throughout her little book. Suffice it to say that, whatever the implications, she clearly positions herself on their side of the divide. Rather, I wish to emphasize that her political intervention on behalf of Native Americans (and women) rests on her philosophical valuation of nature and a certain non-conceptual epistemology, in that her transcendentalist philosophy of nature gives priority to *aisthesis* over *noesis*. The "majesty of nature" can be accessed only by means of the "nobler thought" – that is, the "language of eye and motion."

Summer on the Lakes introduces the importance of the aesthetic in its very first paragraph when it evokes the central romantic notion of the sublime: "Yet I, like others, have little to say where the spectacle is, for once, great enough to fill the whole life, and supersede thought, giving us only its own presence" (*SoL* 3). That Niagara Falls, the trip's first stage, does not turn out to unveil this spectacle is just the first in a series of failed encounters. But the stakes of the narrative are made unmistakably clear, namely to hunt down the fullness of life beyond the limits of thought. And, in due transcendentalist fashion, this fullness is to be found in nature, specifically American nature, which here means the American West. Accordingly, Fuller is interested not so much in accurate descriptions of the places she visits as in rendering "the poetic impression of the country at large," a country that, crucially, is "still all new, boundless, limitless" (*SoL* 42, 40). She immediately adds that "what is limitless is alone divine," clearly identifying the West as the site where the plenitude of life could potentially be unearthed.

However, the West's potential remains untapped as human culture relentlessly exploits nonhuman nature: Fuller decries "an age ... of *utility*," Americans' general lack of "tenderness of feeling" (*SoL* 25), the settlers' spirit of "calculation" and "accumulation" (*SoL* 12), and their "habit of imitating Europe" (*SoL* 40). These traits keep them from living up to the potential of what Fuller does not hesitate to call "Elysium" (*SoL* 29), "Eden" (*SoL* 75), and "the capital of nature's art" compared to which "Rome and Florence are" mere "suburbs" (*SoL* 33). For Fuller, only women and Native Americans seem to have the sensibility needed to reach beyond calculative thought and unearth divine being. But the former are locked up in the domestic sphere and the latter are driven away or killed. Women and Native Americans are thus emblematic of the missed opportunity, the untapped potential. This is why Fuller devotes long stretches of her narrative to the plight of Native Americans and gives us the rather curious accounts of Mariana – the fictionalized autobiography – and the Seeress of Prevorst in the book's two central chapters. Both these stories are symptomatic of how the West's true potential is not recognized and even impeded.

The former portrays the very short life of Mariana, a young woman with both the "power of excitement" (*SoL* 51) and a "very intellectual being" (*SoL* 59), but who, confined to the domestic sphere, withers away and dies. The latter is the fictionalized account of Friederike Hauffe, a young woman who is said to have prophetic powers and direct access to the world of spirits, as she herself seems to live in a permanent state "betwixt life and death" (*SoL* 91): "The spirit of things, about which we have no perception, was sensible to her" (*SoL* 90). Crucially, the story of the Seeress also stresses that her states of somnambulism compel her to compose poems, something she is otherwise not prone to do (*SoL* 85, 92–93). Fuller thus posits the realm of spirit as the creative source of both things and poems and in this way runs together the creative principles of nature and poetry into one great principle of *poiesis*. Nonhuman nature and human poetry are thus presented as expressions of one and the same principle. This is why poetry – and by proxy literature and art – is apt to disclose this very principle. Ultimately, Fuller casts literature as just as somnambulic as the Seeress. In a sense, for Fuller, literature *is* somnambulism.

These two accounts are at the book's center because they aptly capture what is wrong with settlement at the frontier as it closes down rather than opens up the very principle of life. They also highlight what it would take to open it up (again) and emphasize once more that this principle cannot be accessed rationally – rational thought in its calculations is precisely what impedes the access. Rather, one has to proceed aesthetically, by means of veritable visions. With these two central chapters, Fuller's narrative also lives up to its own professed aim to render "the poetic impression" of the West as these two accounts, rather than any accurate description of frontier wilderness, constitute the apposite rendering of the West's untapped potential.

And while the general tenor of the book might thus seem to be one of desperation and despair, formally, the account is a manifestation of joy as it performs a great counter-actualization, a re-opening and un-settling of the West, a speculative exploration of its potential, an investment in its untapped affects.[9] It is this constitutive tension between despair and joy that governs the whole book and that is expressed in its formal and thematic peculiarities. The very affects that circulate in the West and the calculative thought that overrides them can only be aptly captured by means of a disjointed, digressive, and fragmented narrative. Only such a narrative provides an adequate "vision," the very *aisthetic* means needed to tap the transcendental source of things.

Modernist Poetry

Similar to Fuller's narrative, Charles Olson's poem "The Ring of," published in 1953, plays out the themes of creation and beauty in the two registers of human art and nonhuman nature. The relation itself is manifested via recourse to myth, one of Olson's recurrent concerns.[10] This is particularly suitable as myth itself is precisely determined by its negotiation of the human and nonhuman realms. Still, most of the poem seems to be concerned with the nonhuman world of gods and nature. Accordingly, the birth of beauty (stanzas 1–2) is presented as the result of a coming together of natural and divine forces (in myth the distinction tends to be indistinguishable), as Aphrodite is born from the ocean's "genital/wave" and "delicate/foam" and subsequently brought "to her isle" by the "west wind" (Zephyros), where she is then clad and brought "to the face of the gods" by "the hours" (the Horai). She rejects all of her suitors only to accept "the ugliest/to bed with" (Hephaistos; stanza 3) though "the handsome/mars ha[s] her" later. The poem then evokes Eros, "the arrow of/as the flight of, the move of/his mother" (stanza 4), and ends with an invocation of the powers of Aphrodite (stanza 5).[11] As a hymn praising Aphrodite, the goddess of beauty, love, and procreation, the poem presents an allegory of the divine creation of beauty and, conversely, the beauty of divine creation.

Things become more complicated, however, when we turn to issues of form. First of all, the rendering of the poem's content happens by very *human* means – lyrical storytelling in the case of Olson and epic storytelling in the case of myth. This human factor is indeed already taken up within the poem's content when, just after the fourth stanza invokes the birth of Eros, his "mother" is said to "adorn[…]//with myrtle the dolphin and words." Having now transitioned into stanza five, the poem ends: "they rise, they

do who/are born of like/elements." The poem here self-reflexively acknowledges the role of words, that is, the role of distinctly *human* creation, of
poetry as human *poiesis*, as several meanings are run together and super-
imposed on one another in the poem's ending: depending on what one
believes to be the referent of the pronoun "they," the final stanza can say
that (1) anyone who is made of the same elements as Aphrodite rises just like
her, (2) Aphrodite and Eros, made of the same elements, are both rising, (3)
words are rising and they are made of the same elements that Aphrodite was
made of, (4) words are rising and they are made of the same elements that
Aphrodite *and* Eros were made of, (5) the dolphin and words are rising and
they are made of the same elements, or (6) some or all of the above.

This semantic multiplicity directly showcases the very creativity and
beauty of words, their procreative power. Poetry is thus posited as equally
beautiful, as equally passionate, and as equally creative as Beauty
(Aphrodite), Love (Eros), and Creation themselves. Art is explicitly projected, as Deleuze and Guattari have it, as an "enterprise of co-creation"
(*WIP* 173). Ultimately, this is already apparent in the poem's recourse to
myth, since *muthos* means nothing other than *narrative*, and it is no coincidence that the poem, though highly lyrical, is narrative in nature. The poem
thus interweaves from the get-go acts of creation with acts of storytelling.
Crucially, however, this does not mean that nonhuman creation is thus
always already correlated with human storytelling. Rather, as in Fuller's
Summer on the Lakes, both human and nonhuman creation are posited as
stemming from the same ground, as "born of like/elements."[12]

But then, what are these elements? On the surface, what the poem suggests
are the four primordial elements earth, water, air, and fire as they are evoked
repeatedly in the poem, an allusion consistent with the poem's elaboration on
myth. Just as the birth of Aphrodite stands for the creation of beauty and the
beauty of creation, the four elements stand for the principle of genesis per se.
In his poetological treatise "Projective Verse," Olson names this principle
"breath."[13] While this identification seems intuitive enough in the case of
poetry, the context of myth elicits wider connotations: breath is also *pneuma*,
the animating spirit, the very force that brings things into being. With its
recourse to myth and specifically to the myth of the creation of beauty, then,
"The Ring of" weaves together the specific and general senses of *poiesis* as
human artistic creation on the one hand and the general nonhuman process of
creation on the other. While on the level of content this superimposition plays
out in the poem's recourse to the myth of Aphrodite and the self-reflexive
acknowledgment of the importance of words in casting this myth, on the level
of form the poem is structured according to Olson's well-known "composition
by field," his championing of "open verse," for which breath determines

rhythm ("PV" 16, 15). The verses do not follow any specific meter, nor are they organized according to syntactical units. The rhythm is driven by enjambments, internal rhymes, alliterations, fragmented syntax, and a wealth of figures of repetition. But the most outstanding formal device is a curious bit of empty space, a caesura reinforced by means of layout, in line 4 of stanza 4. This little empty space coincides precisely with the birth of Eros:

> mars had her   And the child
> had that name, the arrow of

The poem thus formally redoubles "the ring of sea pink" that gave birth to Aphrodite (just as on the level of content the birth of Eros redoubles the birth of Aphrodite). This empty space amounts to the formal rendering of "the ring of" creation, the eternal return of the in-between where all and everything is generated, that is, difference itself. This spacing is the poem's manifestation of what Deleuze and Guattari call "a zone of indetermination" where "things, beasts, and persons" dissolve in the realm "that immediately precedes their natural differentiation" (*WIP* 173), the very realm of sensation, of affects and percepts. It is telling that Olson's poem evokes this realm precisely in the context of the birth of love. It is thus a hymn not only to the interplay of creation and beauty but to the very passions involved in this relation. It is a hymn to love and passion – in both their spiritual and carnal senses – and their power to create, that is, to the very power of affect as such. It is a celebration of a generalized eroticism: the grand creative passion of the elements, the fructifying circulation of sensations, of affects and percepts. And it is precisely through its expression in the poem's inextricable joining of form and content that this generalized eroticism becomes aesthetically tangible.

The Great Outdoors Within

Although from different literary periods and pertaining to different literary genres and thus in very different ways, both of my tutor texts stress the principle of creation and literature's aptitude to disclose this principle. What is more, both suggest that this principle grounds both human poetic creation and nonhuman natural (or divine) creation. But since the principle is itself clearly nonhuman, there is a fundamental asymmetry in the relation between the human and the nonhuman: the nonhuman turns out to comprise the human, and the human becomes just a variation of the nonhuman. I believe this to be what the two texts convey. But more importantly, they also convey that if the space of reason, that is, the space of representation, marks the level of the specifically human, then the space of sensibility, that is, the space of sensation, marks the level of convergence between the human and the nonhuman as it permeates both realms. Sensation turns out to be the very stuff of being as such. This is why literature (and art in general), as the very manifestation of the Deleuzian transcendental use of the senses, is the adequate tool to unveil the relation that holds between the human and the nonhuman. Moreover, if sensation is the very stuff of being in itself, this is tantamount to saying that the nonhuman is as much within as outside us. This is precisely what literature takes advantage of. Otherwise it would not be able to disclose anything at all, as an unsurpassable gap would separate the human from the nonhuman.

I will unpack this point by means of a contrast. In *After Finitude*, French philosopher Quentin Meillassoux calls the nonhuman realm as it is in-itself "the *great outdoors*."[14] Meillassoux is attacking the Kantian ban on speculation, which indeed expels things-in-themselves while at the same time erecting the unassailable realm of thought. Henceforth, everything is always already correlated to thought; nothing can be conceived in-itself, since the attempt to conceive something in-itself merely results in its conceiving, that is, thought. This is the position that Meillassoux terms "*correlationism*" (AF 5, original emphasis). Meillassoux's program subsequently consists in the attempt to implode correlationism from within. Without getting into his complex argument here, let me merely note that Meillassoux thinks the sheer formalism of mathematics can build the bridges needed *to get us out* into the great outdoors. In contrast, what I have traced in this chapter is the way that literature opens up fissures in the bulwark of representation in order to let the great outdoors *seep in*. In this sense, literature inundates us with the nonhuman. This is not a mere question of directionality. While Meillassoux's building of bridges essentially leaves intact the separation of the two realms, literature's inundation of the human with the nonhuman makes us aware that the human is just one specific entity among a multiplicity of others. And all are grounded by the same nonhuman forces: differential affects and percepts.

Where, then, does this leave the literary object? Quite simply, literature amounts to the manifestation of this underlying realm of nonhuman differential sensations as seen *from the human point of view*. Literary objects are the very human manifestation of difference in-itself, that is, of the general principle of creation.

NOTES

1. See, respectively, Jane Bennett, *Vibrant Matter: A Political Ecology of Things* (Durham: Duke University Press, 2010); Levi R. Bryant, *The Democracy of Objects* (Ann Arbor: Open Humanities Press, 2011); and Graham Harman, *The Quadruple Object* (Winchester: Zero, 2010).
2. See, for example, Amie L. Thomasson, *Ordinary Objects* (Oxford: Oxford University Press, 2007); Edward N. Zalta, *Abstract Objects: An Introduction to*

Axiomatic Metaphysics (Dordrecht: D. Reidel/Kluwer, 1983); Stuart Brock and Anthony Everett, eds., *Fictional Objects* (Oxford: Oxford University Press, 2015); and Graham Priest, *Towards Non-Being: The Logic and Metaphysics of Intentionality* (Oxford: Oxford University Press, 2005).

3. A canonical expression of this view is Terry Eagleton, *Literary Theory: An Introduction*, 2nd edn. (1983; Malden: Blackwell, 1996). See also J. Hillis Miller, *On Literature* (London: Routledge, 2002); Derek Attridge, *The Singularity of Literature* (London: Routledge, 2004); Derek Attridge, "Introduction: Derrida and the Questioning of Literature," in Jacques Derrida, *Acts of Literature* (New York: Routledge, 1992), 1–29; and most recently, Andrew Bennett and Nicholas Royle, *This Thing Called Literature: Reading, Thinking, Writing* (Abingdon: Routledge, 2015).

4. Viktor Shklovsky, "Art as Device," in *Theory of Prose*, trans. Benjamin Sher (Champaign: Dalkey Archive Press, 2009), 1–14; hereafter "AD."

5. Gilles Deleuze and Félix Guattari, *What Is Philosophy?*, trans. Hugh Tomlinson and Graham Burchill (London: Verso, 1994), 176; hereafter *WIP*.

6. Gilles Deleuze, *Difference and Repetition*, trans. Paul Patton (London: Continuum, 2004), 68, hereafter *DR*.

7. For a detailed account of literature's speculative thrust and genuine metaphysical connotations that is based on a reworked notion of narrativity and includes close readings of a range of contemporary North American fictions, see Ridvan Askin, *Narrative and Becoming* (Edinburgh: Edinburgh University Press, 2016). A shorter text that also includes analysis of a late nineteenth-century realist text is Ridvan Askin, "Prolegomenon to a Differential Theory of Narrative," *SubStance* 44.3 (2015): 155–70.

8. Margaret Fuller, *Summer on the Lakes, in 1843* (Urbana: University of Illinois Press, 1991), 153, hereafter *SoL*.

9. For an account of Fuller's "vision of an apprehensive creative energy" (117), see Bruce Mills, *Poe, Fuller, and the Mesmeric Arts: Transition States in the American Renaissance* (Columbia: University of Missouri Press, 2006), 115–36. See also Dorri Beam, "Fuller, Feminism, Pantheism," in *Margaret Fuller and Her Circles*, ed. Brigitte Bailey, Katheryne P. Viens, and Conrad Edick Wright (Durham: University of New Hampshire Press, 2013), 52–76; and, on romanticism's general speculative character, Greg Ellermann, "Speculative Romanticism," *SubStance* 44.1 (2015): 154–74.

10. See Miriam Nichols, "Myth and the Document in Charles Olson's *Maximus Poems*," in *Contemporary Olson*, ed. David Herd (Manchester: Manchester University Press, 2015), 25–37.

11. Charles Olson, "The Ring of," in *Collected Poems of Charles Olson: Excluding the Maximus Poems*, ed. George F. Butterick (Berkeley: University of California Press, 1987), 243; all subsequent references are to this page.

12. On Olson's anti-anthropocentrism, see Mark Byers, "Environmental Pedagogues: Charles Olson and R. Buckminster Fuller," *English* 62.238 (2013): 248–68.

13. Charles Olson, "Projective Verse," in *Selected Writings of Charles Olson*, ed. Robert Creeley (New York: New Directions, 1966), 15, 17; hereafter "PV."

14. Quentin Meillassoux, *After Finitude: An Essay on the Necessity of Contingency*, trans. Ray Brassier (London: Continuum, 2009), 7; hereafter *AF*.

14

R. L. RUTSKY

Technologies

The Dialectic of Technology

A common assumption of recent decades is that "our" world has become increasingly technological. Yet, arguably, perceptions of an ever-growing technologization and of technology's increasing domination over the natural world have existed since the Industrial Revolution or even earlier (in some views, it can be traced to the so-called Age of Enlightenment or even to the Renaissance). This sense of the increasing power, influence, and in some cases encroachment of technology was, not surprisingly, a prevalent feature in many literary portrayals during the Industrial Revolution, with industrialized cities, machines and factories, and railroads often providing both a milieu and a thematic for the work of writers such as Charles Dickens, Herman Melville, Elizabeth Barrett Browning, Elizabeth Gaskell, and Walt Whitman. Similarly, technological development has been a common theme – some would say the founding theme – of science fiction, in both literature and cinema, with particular emphasis on the relationship between human beings and new or developing technologies.

For convenience, we may divide these portrayals of the relationship between technology and humans into two main categories – the utopian and the dystopian – based on whether they present a positive or a negative representation of technology. Traditionally, of course, this dichotomy in attitudes toward technology has hinged on a rather simplistic proposition about the proper relation of technology to humanity: to the extent that technologies are seen as tools or instruments for human use, to the extent that they seem to remain under human control, directed toward human ends, they are seen in positive, utopian terms. To the extent, on the other hand, that technologies are viewed as escaping human control, no longer serving human ends and interests, or, in more extreme cases, as threatening to "take over" the role of the human master and enslave or robotize human beings, they are almost always portrayed as dystopian, monstrous forces.

The starkness of this opposition between "good" and "bad" technologies seems to affirm the idea that the dividing line between technology and humanity must always be upheld; technology must know its "proper" place, even when – or especially when – it comes to life, as can be seen in the long series of artificial beings, sentient machines, robots and androids, cyborgs, and artificial intelligences portrayed in literature, films, and other media that have threatened to destroy, enslave, or replace humanity. Alpha 60 in Godard's *Alphaville*, the Cybermen and the Daleks of the *Doctor Who* television series, the Cylons of *Battlestar Galactica*, the Borg in *Star Trek: The Next Generation*, the Terminator(s) in the *Terminator* films, and the Agents in *The Matrix* are well-known examples of this tendency, where technological beings take on an uncanny life that at once simulates human life (although not necessarily human form) and threatens to destroy it. In many of these cases, these artificial beings were initially the creation of humans, and part of what makes them threatening is not just that they have assumed a life that is not supposed to belong to them, but also that they have rejected their filiation (their proper place in a "natural" reproductive order or lineage), and rebelled against their creators. This is in fact one of the most common themes of science fiction, dating to its very origins in Mary Shelley's *Frankenstein* (1818).[1] What has become known as a Frankenstein scenario involves any case where a technology created by human beings ceases to be a tool or servant and rebels against its creators, usurping the place supposedly reserved for humans and becoming the master rather than the servant. Variations on this theme continue to the present day, but it is worth noting that even as these representations seem obsessed with distinguishing humans from technology, they also suggest, if only implicitly, that these dangerous, out-of-control technologies are merely projections of humanity's own (worst) traits. In recent manifestations, representations of this Frankenstein scenario have increasingly moved toward a posthumanist questioning of the primacy of the human and its difference from technology. Nonetheless, technology's intimate relationship to humanity – it is after all portrayed as humanity's illegitimate offspring – was there from the very start.

Of course, representations of technologies that come to life have not always been presented as dangerous or threatening. Science fiction is in fact replete with examples of robots and other technological beings who are helpful, loyal, and even endearing, from Astro Boy manga and anime to Robby the Robot in *Forbidden Planet* (1956) to R2-D2 and C-3PO in *Star Wars* to Number Five from *Short Circuit* (1986) to the android Data in the *Star Trek: The Next Generation* series to Doctor Who's robotic dog K-9 or the puppy-like Chappie (2015). A number of subservient fembots or gynoids can also be referenced in this context, from Hadaly in Auguste Villiers de l'Isle-Adam's *L'Ève future* (1886) to Olga in the film *The Perfect Woman* (1949) to the Stepford Wives in Ira Levin's 1972 novel and subsequent film versions to a wide variety of gynoid figures in manga and anime (although these female robots, often designed to replace actual women, introduce an uncanny element not usually present in their anodyne male counterparts). In all of these cases (and many more), however, these beings are presented mainly as servants and companions to humans, incapable – as we are repeatedly told – of harming human beings. These examples owe a strong debt to science-fiction author Isaac Asimov's "Three Laws of Robotics,"[2] which ensured that robots could never harm and must always obey human beings, but Asimov's Laws were already an extension of the older "rule" that technologies exist to serve humanity.

Despite the persistence of these technological themes and stereotypes, there have been a growing number of cases in recent years where the representation of living or autonomous technologies has broken from the opposition that casts good technologies as controllable and subservient, on the one hand, and technologies that are out of human control as dangerous threats, on the other hand. This does not mean, of course, that positive representations of new technologies that enhance human capabilities do not still regularly appear in popular science-fiction media and literature (and in real-life discourses about new technologies), nor does it mean that negative representations of technologies that threaten to manipulate and control humans have faded from the cultural scene. Yet, representations of technology do seem to be changing, no longer adhering to the sharp division between utopian and dystopian depictions. Clearly, this shift in representation suggests that a similar shift has taken place – or is in the process of taking place – in how we see, understand, and relate to technology.

To understand these changes, we must examine more closely the conception of technology at the basis of these utopian/dystopian depictions. That conception – generally seen as taking shape during the Renaissance and closely aligned with western notions of enlightenment, progress, and modernity – rests on the idea that technology, closely linked to a scientific perspective, is an instrument, means, or tool through which human beings are better able to know and understand the world and to achieve the power to control it. It is hardly surprising, then, that when technology has been seen as exceeding human control, it has also been perceived as running amok or as threatening to appropriate humanity's position of control and mastery. Even today, this instrumentalist conception of technology – and its inverse view of technologies that appear out of human control – remains the most common way of thinking about technology. At the same time, however, this conception – with its basis in humanist anthropocentrism – has now begun to seem outmoded.

It is tempting to see this disjunction between technologies and how humans perceive them as itself an effect of rapid technological change: new technologies and the changes associated with them – following the dictates of what French philosopher of technology Bernard Stiegler terms "permanent innovation" – have outpaced the ability of human beings to conceptualize them appropriately. As Stiegler observes, since the advent of industrial society, "Technics evolves *more quickly* than culture."[3] There is indeed a sense in which contemporary technologies have begun to strain the categories and concepts through which we have traditionally defined and represented "technology." At the same time, however, it is important to acknowledge that seeing technology as exceeding cultural understanding – or as "in advance" of human thought – necessarily involves envisioning technology as an autonomous force (and, in Stiegler's conception, an evolutionary force) that affects and often determines human/cultural behaviors. This conception of technology as a force unto itself therefore runs the risk of becoming a kind of *technological determinism*, where technology becomes an *a priori* causal force that not only operates independently of environmental, cultural, economic, political-ideological, or even human determinants but, in fact, serves to mold them.

Although the notion of technology as a determining force may seem to contradict the idea of technology as a tool for human knowledge and use, these two concepts are not necessarily inimical. A number of theorists associated with the Frankfurt School – a group of social and political theorists originally associated with the Institute for Social Research at Goethe University in Frankfurt, formed in the 1920s – have, for example, argued that the rationalizing, instrumentalizing tendency of technology eventually becomes so universally established that it surpasses human control. It becomes, as Herbert Marcuse claimed, a *"technological a priori"* that precedes and informs the development of particular technologies.[4] According to this argument, technological rationality may have begun as a means for humans to gain control over the world, but it eventually comes to operate autonomously, imposing its own logic of calculation, rational planning, and efficiency on humanity. In this sense, the apparent opposition between technological determinism and the instrumental idea of technology is less an opposition than a dialectic: indeed, it is precisely what the principal thinkers of the Frankfurt School, Max Horkheimer and Theodor W. Adorno, referred to as the "dialectic of enlightenment."

In *Dialectic of Enlightenment*, Horkheimer and Adorno outline a historical dialectic – an interplay of opposite but mutually constituting forces – that initially promises to free humanity from enthrallment to natural and supernatural forces via the power of a rational enlightenment that allows human beings to gain an increasing knowledge of and control over the world.[5] Their notion of demythologization clearly draws from German sociologist Max Weber's idea of a "disenchantment of the world," where a mythic, animistic, enchanted view of nature is transformed by the extension of a rationalized, calculative perspective to ever-broader aspects of the world.[6] Through this progressive rationalization, the world comes increasingly to be viewed in quantitative and functionalist terms, becoming a series of objects or resources defined by their ability to be used or exploited by human beings. This instrumental rationality is the very basis of modern technology and techniques – Marcuse will in fact refer to it as "technological rationality."[7] The instrumental conception defines technology as precisely the means by which human beings come to measure, know, and master the world. As Horkheimer and Adorno (and Marcuse) argue, however, as this technological rationality is extended, what had begun as a means to fulfill human ends becomes an end in itself. If rationality and technology had originally "aimed at liberating human beings from fear and installing them as masters,"[8] the extension of these tendencies subjects nature, art, culture, and ultimately human beings themselves to these same processes of quantification, instrumentalization, commodification, and mastery. Humans are, metaphorically at least, technologized by their own zeal to master the world through technology.

From Rationalization to "Informatization"

The classic fictional representation of technological rationality's effect on human beings is Fritz Lang's *Metropolis* (1927). In the film, Joh Fredersen, the Master of Metropolis, builds and rules a supposedly utopian technological city based on the principles of modern design, efficiency, and the assembly-line regimentation of Fordist rationalization. The workers of the city are forced to adapt to – are enslaved by – this "dehumanizing," mechanistic rationalization, as demonstrated by their synchronized, mechanical movements and emotionless expressions. In the workers' rebellion that results – a revolt led by another machine, the "monstrous" robot Maria – the emotions that have been repressed in Fredersen's technological society return with a Frankensteinian vengeance, destroying much of the city. A more recent version of a dystopian technological society may be found in Jean-Luc Godard's *Alphaville* (1965), where the lives of the inhabitants of the city Alphaville are ruled by the computer Alpha 60 according to the dictates of an instrumental, "scientific" logic. Here, too, emotions are repressed, largely through the control of language, with emotionally evocative words – in a gesture reminiscent of George Orwell's Newspeak in

Nineteen Eighty-Four (1949) – removed from dictionaries. The fact that Godard shot the film in contemporary buildings in Paris suggests that the society of the time is already afflicted by a similar technological rationality.

Alphaville suggests that the dehumanizing consequences of technological rationalization extend far beyond an obvious mechanization. It is precisely these broader, cultural-ideological effects that Horkheimer and Adorno emphasize in their discussion of "the culture industry," where the processes of rationalization subsume virtually every aspect of art and popular culture within a commodity-oriented industrial-technological system. Although this system seems to offer consumers the freedom to express their individual tastes by choosing among its many products, these choices are largely illusory variations that never bring the system itself into question. Thus, the processes of rationalization and commodification are internalized, extended into the very consciousness of individuals and society, with the result that human beings (like culture more generally) come to be seen – and often see themselves – in terms of commodified objects and images.

The Frankfurt School's idea of the culture industry bears a close resemblance to what French theorist Guy Debord would later call "the society of the spectacle," where modern society becomes "an immense accumulation of spectacles" that replace what "once was directly lived" with commodified representations, images, and signs.[9] In this society, Debord argues, "the commodity completes its colonization of social life ... commodities are now *all* that there is to see; the world we see is the world of the commodity."[10] The work of another French cultural theorist, Jean Baudrillard, on the commodification of signs, as well as his notions of simulation and the hyperreal, display a similar vision of an increasingly reified world in which every aspect of culture has become subject to commodified simulation.[11] In Debord's and Baudrillard's depictions of a world completely transformed by commodified spectacle or simulation, the dialectic of enlightenment may seem to have reached its logical conclusion. Here, every aspect of life, including human life itself, can be captured and abstracted, manipulated, and disseminated as a commodity via an ongoing process of technological reproduction that seems to operate automatically, without human intervention.

There are a great many fictional as well as theoretical texts that depict versions of a culture or world fallen into simulacra. Among prominent fictional works, one could include Daniel F. Galouye's novel *Simulacron-3* (1964) as well as the films based on it: Rainer Werner Fassbinder's *World on a Wire* (1973) and *The Thirteenth Floor* (1999); Kurt Vonnegut's *Breakfast of Champions* (1973); many of the works of Philip K. Dick, particularly *Ubik* (1969) and *Valis* (1981); almost all of "cyberpunk" fiction, including

William Gibson's Sprawl trilogy, James Tiptree Jr.'s *The Girl Who was Plugged In* (1974), and Neal Stephenson's *Snow Crash* (1991); Don DeLillo's *White Noise* (1985), Viktor Pelevin's *Generation "П"* (1999) and its filmed version *Generation P* (2011); and numerous films, including *Videodrome* (1983), *Ghost in the Shell* (1995) and its sequel *Ghost in the Shell 2: Innocence* (2004), *Dark City* (1998), *The Truman Show* (1998), *eXistenZ* (1999), *The Matrix* trilogy (1999–2003), *Paprika* (2006), *Tron: Legacy* (2010), the documentary *Life 2.0* (2010), and *Inception* (2011). In all of these works, human beings find themselves immersed in a simulated, increasingly digital, "virtual" environment.

Importantly, none of these portrayals depict the obvious rationalization of culture or humans seen in *Metropolis* and *Alphaville*; rather, they present culture as an ever-proliferating circulation of signs, simulacra, and data. Here, humans do not become robotic; they become consumers and users, participating (willingly or unwillingly) in a system that, as most of the protagonists in the above works eventually realize, is deceiving them, and in many cases watching, controlling, and profiting from them. There is a conspiratorial, even paranoid, tone to most of these works, which in some cases even reaches the point where the protagonists discover that their friends and family, and perhaps even they themselves, are technologically reproduced beings controlled by others.

While the paranoid tendency of these works (and many similar works) still sees technology in largely dystopian terms, often as an explicit threat to humanity, it also points to a shift in cultural thinking about technology. Older industrial fears about the technologization of humans are displaced by a more diffuse anxiety about humanity's place in a technocultural system whose operations are so complex that they seem to escape human understanding, much less control. This shift points to a broader, underlying change in the relationship between human beings and this technocultural system. Marxist critic Frederic Jameson has argued that what he dubs "high tech paranoia" literature, as well as the conspiratorial perspective in the work of many cyberpunk authors, involves an attempt to represent "the impossible totality of the contemporary world system."[12] While Jameson sees these cultural representations as indicative of what is largely an economic shift from industrial capitalism to late or consumer capitalism (aka postmodernism), it is impossible to disassociate these cultural and economic changes from technological changes. Political theorists Michael Hardt and Antonio Negri have made this connection explicitly, arguing that the shift from industrial production to a service and knowledge economy involves a process of "postmodernization, or better, informatization."[13]

Beyond the Digital Dialectic

The fact that this increasingly information-based technoculture appears too complex for human comprehension may, from a humanist perspective (including Jameson's Marxist perspective), appear as a diffused but still Frankensteinian threat to human agency. Yet, this also means that it brings into question the humanist subject's presumed position of mastery. It is here that we begin to find an opening for representations of beings who not only go beyond the humanist subject, but who also are not simply a combination of conventional ideas of the human and the technological. Conversely, autonomous technologies and artificial life begin to be seen neither as dystopian threats to humanity nor as friendly but docile servants. It is precisely at the point where these nonhumanist humans and autonomous technologies converge that we can begin to talk about a posthumanist identity.

If the shifting conceptions involved in postmodernism and information technologies open a space to think beyond the old definitions of both technology and the human, it should be clear that neither postmodernism nor information technology can be seen as the cause of a posthumanist perspective or identity. In many ways, they remain thoroughly humanist, still following the dictates of the dialectic of enlightenment. New information technologies routinely promise expanded forms of liberation and self-empowerment to their human users. Indeed, much of the appeal of these technologies is based on their ability to transform their users from passive consumers into active creators and producers. Yet, if the promise of increased individual freedom, expression, and mastery has obviously been central to the appeal of information technologies, this promise is based upon these technologies' ability to translate virtually every aspect of life, nature, and culture into quantitative terms, into data. Whatever is digitalized, transformed into data, becomes an instrumentalized object, liable to control. As human beings, like everything else, become increasingly subject to digitalization, they also become subject to ever-broadening forms of technically-based surveillance and control.

Ironically, users of information technologies have often been willing to participate in their own informatization, supplying information about themselves in exchange for various services that allow them a sense of control, freedom, or self-expression. Information providers frequently encourage users to volunteer information about themselves and to feel empowered by doing so. This situation bears an intriguing similarity to Walter Benjamin's observation that Fascism gave the masses a chance to express themselves, in place of their right to change the property structure of society.[14] In a digital age, this desire for an "empowering" self-expression still seems operative:

however, it is not the masses en bloc, but individual subjects who are offered opportunities for self-expression, which, in many cases, they seem only too glad to accept. Here, as in Benjamin's day, class and property structures, as well as their basis in a possessive individualist subject, remain generally untouched and unthought.

Arguably, then, a new digital dialectic seems to follow from, and amplify, the dialectic of enlightenment. It is not simply users who gain a sense of mastery or self-empowerment through the freedom of choice and expression enabled by information technologies; in many ways, the entire system is based on a presumed mastery. All stakeholders in this information "society" imagine themselves to be empowered by their knowledge of and control over a digitized world. Yet, even as human beings increasingly rely on information technologies to support their own sense of freedom, autonomy, and mastery, they are at the same time subjecting themselves to increasing levels of commodification and control. This leads to a technocentric vicious circle in which individuals, sensing that they are little more than data-points, with little control over the technological networks in which they are immersed, feel the need to employ more technologies to re-buttress their sense of individuality and mastery, thus beginning the cycle anew.

It is precisely the desire to maintain or reestablish a sense of human empowerment that drives this seemingly never-ending cycle of technological addiction. Escaping this cycle therefore demands a reconceptualization of human identity and of technology in nonhumanist and non-instrumental terms. If posthumanism involves an attempt to imagine what a nonhumanist or post-anthropocentric human identity might be, it also necessarily involves a reconceptualization of technology. It is useful, however, to consider first what posthumanism is not.

Imagining a Nonhumanist Posthumanism

Posthumanism does not, as is sometimes assumed, necessarily refer to an evolutionary state *after* the human, an historical stage where human being is transcended by "enhanced" post-humans whose techno-biological capabilities exceed the merely human. This is not to deny that such "enhancements" may be adapted in the future, but simply to question whether they challenge, much less surpass, the traditional definition of the human. Adding technological or even biological enhancements to the human body no more makes one posthuman than wearing eyeglasses, a hearing aid, or a pair of athletic shoes does. As the notion of "enhancement" implies, these visions of post- or transhumans continue to rely on, and in fact reinforce, a humanist conception of the subject, defined by its instrumental mastery over the object world.

Thus, the evolutionary, utopian claims of "transhumanists" mark their project as a perpetuation of the utopian promise of the dialectic of enlightenment; the "post-humans" that they envision are merely enhanced or augmented human subjects, humans with added "superpowers." As I have argued elsewhere, this transhumanist vision actually involves "an all-too-human fantasy: a fantasy of becoming, not posthuman, but superhuman."[15] Similarly, Cary Wolfe has argued that posthumanism should be distinguished from transhumanist ideas, noting, "transhumanism should be seen as an intensification of humanism."[16]

The posthuman does not apply, then, to most of the various superheroes, mutants, and metahumans that populate comic books, young adult literature, manga, anime, and superhero movies. Generally, these figures are simply humans with "special powers" (it is worth noting that these powers, while not technological in the conventional sense, may certainly be seen as prostheses supplementing an *a priori* humanity). Spiderman may have "spider" senses and strength, and the ability to shoot webs from his wrists, but in every other way, he is human. Superman may technically be an alien, the Mighty Thor may be a god, and Harry Potter may be a wizard, but all are recognizably human in their appearance, attitudes, hopes, and desires. Even when these superhuman figures have been physically transformed or mutated, such as Wolverine, The Thing, or even the Teenage Mutant Ninja Turtles (who ostensibly are turtles but who act exactly like US teenagers), they generally still behave like "regular" humans. There are, however, occasional exceptions who might be considered as posthuman, such as Doctor Manhattan in Alan Moore's comic book *Watchmen* (1986)[17] and the later movie version (2009), whose quantum powers change him to the point that he no longer sees or feels as humans do. Moore's descriptions suggest that Doctor Manhattan becomes a nonhuman being, a god who is beyond human understanding, but the suggestion of a being with a different mode of thought and experience may provide more insight into what a posthumanist identity might be than "more human" posthuman characters.

By the same token, the integration of technology into the human body does not necessarily produce a posthumanist identity. In this sense, many of the typical cyborgs of science fiction are – like Iron Man, or Johnny Mnemonic and Molly the Razorgirl from William Gibson's work – for the most part simply humans with technological prostheses. Arguably, it is only to the extent that technology alters the thought processes or experience of the typical human subject that we begin to glimpse the possibilities of posthumanist identity. In this context, Donna Haraway's well-known suggestion of a hybrid, partial, or non-unitary cyborg identity that would undo the "troubling dualisms"[18] of the individual humanist subject – including the divisions of organic and technological, human and animal, self and other, male and female – remains suggestive for any attempt to envision a nonhumanist posthuman identity. Similarly, N. Katherine Hayles has suggested that such an identity might be seen as "a posthuman collectivity, an 'I' transformed into the 'we' of autonomous agents operating together."[19] Here, it becomes obvious that a cyborg or posthumanist identity is not just a matter of adding technology to an already human subject, nor – as Hayles has forcefully argued – of transferring a human mind or self to a computer or robot. Rather, a nonhumanist posthumanism challenges the assumption of an original or essential humanity to which technology necessarily serves as a prosthesis or supplement. As Stiegler has argued – following French philosopher Jacques Derrida's suggestion that supplements inevitably undermine their "origins" – the very idea of the human has, from its origins, always "incorporated" a prosthetic, technological – but not necessarily instrumental – aspect.[20]

Stiegler's argument should remind us that concepts of the posthuman – so frequently linked to visions of advanced technology – involve not only a challenge to traditional notions of the humanist subject but an equally important redefinition of conventional definitions of technology, as suggested by German philosopher Martin Heidegger in his 1954 essay, "The Question Concerning Technology."[21] Heidegger's argument that modernity has overemphasized technology's instrumental aspects, thus eliding an earlier perspective that saw *technē* as a generative or creative process or *poiēsis*, suggests the extent to which any notion of posthuman identity must be tied to a redefining of technology that would emphasize its poietic or autopoietic qualities, rather than its instrumentality.[22]

We might, then, find precedents for such a nonhumanist posthuman identity in some of the technological figures that have been cast as threats to humanity, such as the communally networked yet individual Borg Queen from *Star Trek: First Contact* (1996) or the humanoid Cylons in the reimagined *Battlestar Galactica* (2004–09) who, in the course of the series, come to be regarded more sympathetically. Tom Cohen has suggested that the threatening "liquid metal" T-1000 cyborg from *Terminator 2* offers a model (or metaphor) for seeing identity in fluid and dynamic rather than fixed, unitary terms.[23] The Replicants in *Blade Runner* (Haraway mentions Rachael as a cyborg example) have often been cited as challenging the division between human and technological life, enabling a more sympathetic, less dystopian view of autonomous technology (albeit by stressing the "humanity" of the Replicants). The representation of Motoko Kusanagi in *The Ghost in the Shell* (1995; manga 1989–90) has frequently been cited as an example of a cyborg or posthuman identity, yet it is her merger with the seemingly threatening digital entity, the Puppet Master, that pushes the boundaries of human identity beyond a unitary subject or consciousness, suggesting another option for imagining nonhumanist posthumans.

An even more complex portrayal of merged, collective identities can be seen in the science fiction of Octavia Butler, particularly in the novels of her "Xenogenesis" series, to which Haraway and more recently Bruce Clarke, in his *Posthuman Metamorphosis*, have already drawn attention.[24] There humanity undergoes a genetic merger with an alien species, the Oankali. The Oankali are not technological in a conventional sense, but exist through genetic – or as Clarke argues, "neocybernetic" – engineering, performed by the Oankali's third sex the *ooloi*. As Haraway observes, they "do not build nonliving technologies ... Rather, they are complexly webbed into a universe of living machines, all of which are partners in their apparatus of bodily production."[25] In this context, technology is no longer seen as part of a dialectic that figures it either as *instrumentum*, a means to human ends, or as out-of-control and dangerous. It is instead presented as part of what Chilean biologists Humberto Maturana and Francisco Varela have called an autopoietic system, capable of reproducing and maintaining itself.[26] Butler's novels chart the incorporation of humans into this autopoietic, biotechnological web, from the humans' initial resistance to the Oankali, whom they see as monsters, to a gradual acceptance over several generations as the two species take on one another's traits. The entire series continually questions the very idea of a human essence, while hybrid, biotechnological, interconnected, and genderqueer identities are explored, opening alternative possibilities for posthumanist identities.

Other examples could obviously be added to this short list. I would, however, close by suggesting that – contrary to some views – even representations that depict entities that appear fully technological, alien, or otherwise inhuman (or nonhuman) should be considered as potential models for posthumanist identity. For example, the largely incomprehensible alien presences – and the uncertain effects of their technologies on human beings – that appear in the science fiction of the Strugatsky brothers[27] – as well as films based on their works, such as Tarkovsky's *Stalker* (1979) and Lopushansky's *The Ugly Swans* (2006) – impel us to think beyond the boundaries of the humanist subject and "its" technologies. Rethinking and indeed attempting to reimagine the limits of the human also requires reconceptualizing instrumentalist notions of technology; both are in fact necessary to any conception of posthumanism that hopes to challenge the horizons of the humanist subject.

R. L. RUTSKY

NOTES

1. Mary Shelley, *Frankenstein: Or, the Modern Prometheus* (New York: Penguin Books, 1963).

2. Asimov's laws were first articulated in his short story "Runaround" in 1942. He would modify them in later years. "Runaround" is included in his collection of robot stories, Isaac Asimov, *I, Robot* (New York: Gnome Press, 1950).

3. Bernard Stiegler, *Technics and Time, 1: The Fault of Epimetheus*, trans. Richard Beardsworth and George Collins (Stanford: Stanford University Press, 1998), 15.

4. Herbert Marcuse, *One-Dimensional Man: Studies in the Ideology of Advanced Industrial Society* (Boston: Beacon Press, 1964), 153.

5. Max Horkheimer and Theodor W. Adorno, *Dialectic of Enlightenment*, trans. John Cumming (New York: Continuum, 1989).

6. Max Weber, *The Theory of Social and Economic Organization*, trans. A. M. Henderson and Talcott Parsons (New York: Oxford University Press, 1947), 185.

7. Marcuse, *One-Dimensional Man*, 144–69.

8. Horkheimer and Adorno, *Dialectic of Enlightenment*, 1.

9. Guy Debord, *The Society of the Spectacle*, trans. Donald Nicholson-Smith (New York: Zone Books, 1995), 12 (Thesis 1).

10. Debord, *Society of the Spectacle*, 29 (Thesis 42).

11. See Jean Baudrillard, *For a Critique of the Political Economy of the Sign*, trans. Charles Levin (Saint Louis: Telos Press, 1981); and *Simulacra and Simulation*, trans. Sheila Glaser (Ann Arbor: University of Michigan Press, 1994).

12. Fredric Jameson, *Postmodernism, or, the Cultural Logic of Late Capitalism* (Durham: Duke University Press, 1991), 38.

13. Michael Hardt and Antonio Negri, *Empire* (Cambridge: Harvard University Press, 2000), 280.

14. Walter Benjamin, "The Work of Art in the Age of Its Technological Reproducibility," *Selected Writings*, Vol. 4, 1938–1940, ed. Howard Eiland and Michael W. Jennings, trans. Edmund Jephcott et al. (Cambridge: Harvard University Press, 2003), 269.

15. R. L. Rutsky, "Mutation, History, and Fantasy in the Posthuman," *Subject Matters* 3.2–4.1 (2007): 105.

16. Cary Wolfe, *What is Posthumanism?* (Minneapolis: University of Minnesota Press, 2010), xv.

17. Alan Moore, *Watchmen* (New York: Warner Books, 1987).

18. Donna J. Haraway, "A Cyborg Manifesto: Science, Technology, and Socialist-Feminism in the Late Twentieth Century," *Simians, Cyborgs, and Women: The Reinvention of Nature* (New York: Routledge, 1991), 177.

19. Katherine Hayles, *How We Became Posthuman: Virtual Bodies in Cybernetics, Literature, and Informatics* (Chicago: University of Chicago Press, 1999), 6.

20. Stiegler, *Technics and Time 1*: "The evolution of the 'prosthesis,' not itself living, by which the human is nonetheless defined as a living being, constitutes the reality of the human's evolution, as if, with it, the history of life were to continue by means other than life" (50). Cf. Jacques Derrida, "... That Dangerous

Supplement …," *Of Grammatology*, trans. Gayatri Chakravorty Spivak (Baltimore: Johns Hopkins University Press, 1977).

21. Martin Heidegger, "The Question Concerning Technology," in *The Question Concerning Technology and Other Essays*, trans. William Lovitt (New York: Harper Torchbooks, 1977).

22. A stimulating discussion of posthumanism's relation to technology can be found in Ivan Callus and Stephen Herbrechter's "Critical Posthumanism or, the *Inventio* of a Posthumanism without Technology," *Subject Matters* 3.2–4.1 (2007): 15–29. Callus and Herbrechter suggest the possibility of a critical posthumanism "which would not be overdetermined by technology" (26). Their arguments suggest that in a critical posthumanism, the definition of technology must itself be questioned and broadened to include an "*inventio*" (cf. Heidegger's *poiēsis*) that is not simply a means or instrument for human ends.

23. Tom Cohen, *Anti-Mimesis from Plato to Hitchcock* (Cambridge: Cambridge University Press, 1994), 260.

24. Bruce Clarke, *Posthuman Metamorphosis: Narrative and Systems* (New York: Fordham University Press, 2008), 168–92.

25. Donna J. Haraway, "The Biopolitics of Postmodern Bodies: Constitutions of Self in Immune System Discourse," in *Simians, Cyborgs, and Women: The Reinvention of Nature* (New York: Routledge, 1991), 228.

26. Humberto R. Maturana and Francisco J. Varela, *Autopoiesis and Cognition: The Realization of the Living* (Boston: D. Reidel, 1980).

27. See for example, Arkady and Boris Strugatsky, *Roadside Picnic*, trans. Antonina W. Bouis (New York: MacMillan, 1977); *The Ugly Swans*, trans. Alice Stone Nakhimovsky and Alexander Nakhimovsky (New York: MacMillan, 1987).

15

CLAIRE COLEBROOK

Futures

The future seems to present us with a series of exclusive disjunctions: *either* investment in the future buys into hetero-normative conceptions of reproduction and fruition[1] *or* the future is the horizon for thinking beyond restrictive conceptions of the normalizing present.[2] Either the future holds the promise of technological maturity and of finally reaching the full potential of the intellect,[3] or technology has reached its destructive limit, causing an "epidemic of distraction,"[4] environmental destruction,[5] infantilism,[6] and intensified imperialism.[7] Either the thought of a genuine absolute takes thought away from its anthropocentric enclosure,[8] or humans need to overcome Cartesianism and become attuned to their embodiment[9] and affect.[10] Either humans have finally recognized that the border and threshold they share with animality needs to be problematized to recognize our companionship, kinship, and shared existence,[11] or the human must break with anthropologism and rise to the status of the subject.[12] Either we have entered the Anthropocene and it is game over for humans, who should therefore begin to come to terms with extinction of themselves and others,[13] or the advent of the Anthropocene finally offers humans the chance for revolution, social justice, and an even better planet.[14] Either the future holds the promise of a political universalism that would break free of the history of "man," or that dream of a future is all too European, modern, rational, and all-too-human.

Divided Futures

I will begin by exploring this last apparently exclusive disjunction regarding the future, precisely because the motif of the future – so crucial for twentieth- and twenty-first-century literary theory – harbors both a radically posthuman messianism that is critical of all that has been demanded in the name of humanity and a sustained repetition of theological humanism. This divided sense of the future as both humanist, in its ties to theology and the subject, and posthumanist, in its critique of teleology and eschatology, finds one of its clearest examples in a text given by Jacques Derrida:

> Can one conceive an atheological heritage of the messianic? Is there one, on the contrary, that is more consistent? A heritage is never natural, one may inherit more than once, in different places and at different times, one may choose to wait for the appropriate time, which may [be?] the most untimely – write about it according to different *lineages*, and sign thus more than one *import*. These questions and these hypotheses do not exclude each other. At least for us and for the moment. Ascesis strips the messianic hope of all biblical forms.[15]

"Ascesis" – most commonly, the practice of religious self-discipline – "strips the messianic hope of all biblical forms": the messianic, the hope for a future that is radically other than the present, may emerge from the present but must also gesture infinitely, and absolutely, beyond any of its actualized figures or inherited modes. Derrida recognizes that this future comes from a past and that the past is never one's own, never fully human, never fully past. This deconstructive temporality that acknowledges both the openness *and* inscriptive limits of the future would be posthuman and nonlinear; whatever one thinks, says, intends, experiences, or predicts of the present, the traces through which such experiences occur have an anarchic or untamed quality that will transform the future and the past. (One might think here of the ways Enlightenment liberalism and universalism – with all its apparatuses of technological innovation – both opened and closed its own future, both betraying and generating rights.) Deconstruction is affirmative of both sides of the disjunctions that surround futures; there can be no future without *techne*, but *techne* is also – as the totality of apparatuses that open to the future – what contains and regresses. As early as "The Ends of Man," Derrida had already argued that the figure of "man" has always been defined as the being who has no determined end, and who surpasses any given limit; man is the being who masters and overcomes himself by way of *techne*, which he has always determined as means, extrinsic to his proper end.[16] Yes, one always thinks the future – the true future – from within the relative closure of the present (and so the future "must not be the 'anything whatsoever'"[17]), but precisely because the future is *traced* in the present, its anticipatory marking is open to reiteration and mutation. The very figure of a radical future is bound up with legacies, inheritances, ghosts, and specters of the past; these cannot be erased, but one must also shift terrain: "one must speak several languages and produce several texts at once."[18] Derrida's affirmation of the future's debt to the past asserts history's textual, cultural, and religious finitude, and yet – for all that – it also affirms that this very finite history has never been closed but opens to the infinite.

Whatever the calculations, critical delimitations, dire warnings, hopes, prognoses, promises, and debts of the future, there will always be a future to come. For "us" – living in the present – every potential future is already upon us, but this can have two quite distinct senses. The first sense would be that which has dominated literary and critical theory since deconstruction and which remains within a critical Western liberal heritage of ongoing expansion, universalization, and progressive posthumanism. That is, one would acknowledge that one thinks within a specific lineage but also strives to maintain critical distance from one's own vocabulary. Or, as Richard Rorty argues: "Hope – the ability to believe that the future will be unspecifiably different from, and unspecifiably freer than, the past – is the condition of growth."[19] In this respect, the human would always be looking to a future of the posthuman, where what appears as self-evident, universal, and futural in the present would recognize itself as once more bound with figures, specificities, and logics that are all too human(ist), masculine, heterosexual, Western, Christian, white, imperialist, and ableist. Modernity and the Enlightenment would be ongoing projects[20] for a future envisioned in this first sense, a future that would *both* never arrive *and* be lived as demanding, imminent, and promissory.

If this were so, then one must also recognize that the future of high-technological liberation has been dreamt of at the expense of humans and nonhumans who bear the burden of the world's labour and resource extraction. Yet, rather than nostalgically siding with a world of pre-technological plenitude, one might recognize that there is neither an outside to *techne* nor an innocent posthumanist utopia that would either fulfil or vanquish global neoliberal expansionism. As the French philosopher of technology Bernard Stiegler has argued, technology is a *pharmakon*.[21] It is at once that which both enables a future – for without the capacity to retain, re-inscribe, and re-read a stored past, the future would be impoverished, limited to the range of the simple present – and at the same time precludes a future. This is true both in a highly abstract sense, given that any thought, dream, or hope of a future is composed from the materials, networks, figures, and capacities of the present, and also in a far more limited sense, and it is this second, more limited sense that renders the open and absolutely hospitable future of deconstruction problematic. The promise of the future might not be as nonlinear as the syntheses of thinking and writing can be. That is, while the conditions of experience are nonlinear, with the future always acting to reinscribe the past, the conditions of the planet might not allow for a revivification of what has already been. Or, more accurately, the nonlinearity of experience might be at odds with the nonlinearity (or other line of time) of the planet.

Future Times

Nonetheless, it may well be that as long as one remains within the conditions for *thinking*, or as long as one remains within technologies of thought and cognition, the future is essentially open, while the messianic is necessarily revolutionary. If one can think, speak, predict, calculate, warn, despair, promise, or hope, then one must retain past impressions and anticipate beyond the present; such syntheses of experience require technology in its broadest sense – ranging from the neural networks of the brain and language to books, digital archives, cinema, and television.

The textuality or technology of time and futurity is at once what makes experience possible *and* what generates lines of time and futurity beyond present experience. As Derrida established in his ongoing debate with John Searle, if one can speak and think with a present context, then this is because whatever is conceptualized relies upon a network of traces that has a mobility that exceeds any context.[22] If there is a crucial difference between the nonlinearity of time conceived as *real* (in the manner of T. S. Eliot's open whole of time) and the nonlinearity of time that is generated from inscriptive systems, then we seem to be back at another disjunction. Should we think about the future as that which unfolds from the complexity of technical traces and textual conditions, *or* as that which has a reality quite independent of human experience? One of the main criticisms of late twentieth-century's theory of futurity concerns the extent or range of what we mean by temporality. Is the radical openness of the future possible only if we rely on what may be thought, rather than on what is physically, materially, or environmentally possible? Climate change and the advent of the Anthropocene have forced theorists to think beyond cognitive and technical conditions, sometimes by extending the insights of deconstruction and sometimes by demanding a different theoretical plane altogether.

According to David Wood, grasping this complexity of deconstruction's future is crucial for any environmentalism precisely because ecological destruction has resulted from a simple linear temporality that extracts the earth's resources for its own immediate consumption, without a sense of the debt we owe to the past or future. Wood's focus on time and futurity in Derrida expands the conditions of temporality (debt, mourning, anticipation) to what lies well beyond the human:

> [E]nvironmentalism finds itself in an often problematic and aporetic space of posthumanistic displacement with which deconstruction is particularly well equipped to offer guidance. But ... equally ... environmental concerns can embolden deconstruction to embrace at least what I have called a "strategic materialism," or the essential interruptibility of any and every idealization ...
> [A] deconstructive embrace of materialism, would be this: we tend to think of

matter and spirit, or matter and mind as somehow opposed, and hence as unable to be thought of in the same space. But we can, I believe, get beyond this reductive understanding of opposition without falling into the arms of dialectical synthesis.[23]

For Wood, the way beyond the idealism of dialectical opposition is to recognize a materiality that is beyond human agency and cognition, while also accepting the imbrication of humanity with a nature that is never reducible to the experience we have of it. However, one might want to ask (as Timothy Clark has done) whether a focus on the conditions of thinking and experience does not generate an openness of futurity that is possible only by precluding thought of ecological conditions and depletions:

> A geographical and geological contingency, the finitude of the earth, now compels us to trace the anthropocentric enclosure of inherited modes of thinking and practice. ... The epoch whose intellectual closure is now visible, the "flat earth" epoch so to speak, inaugurates the need to think a bounded space in which the consequences of actions may mutate to come back unexpectedly from the other side of the planet.[24]

However, there might be yet another way to approach the exclusive disjunctions that mark the future. Whereas deconstruction – in its Derridean form – focused on the ways in which thinking and experience harbored traces and ghosts that would generate multiple futures, Clark speaks of mutations from the other side of the planet. What is this other side? And how many "sides" does the planet have, and how many times or futures do all these sides open?

Whatever else might seem uncertain, climate change is closing off and unifying the future: the future of this earth is now threatened for "all" of us. This englobing of the future, or limitation to the future from the other side of the planet, generates yet another exclusive disjunction where climate change has *either* forced a "tragedy of the commons" upon us (because we all share one globe and all face resource depletion and the accusation of destroying the planet as one species)[25] *or* climate change has intensified racial, colonial, and class divisions to the point of producing different futures and even a bifurcation of *homo sapiens*.[26] The theory of the Anthropocene claims that we are once again united at species level, while the politics of climate change divides "us" more than ever. In this respect, the exclusive disjunctions that mark futures today are of a different intensity from previous centuries and decades, and for several reasons (mass media, technological acceleration, speed and distance of communications, the volatilities of climate change, the new existential threats of AI, nano, and viral technologies and the violent subsuming by globalism of all spaces and times).

Inclusive Disjunctions

Precisely because of this intensity, what imposes itself upon us is a breakdown of exclusive disjunction in favor of inclusive disjunction. The future is *both* rigidly linear (bound to a contracting planet and materiality that is increasingly less open) *and* nonlinear (*not* because past and future fold back and forth but because any seeming "now" or present is accompanied by multiple points of view and potential futures, both human and nonhuman). Here, I draw upon Deleuze and Guattari, who theorized inclusive disjunction against the Oedipal logic of exclusive disjunction (I am *either* male *or* female, *either* subjected to the law *or* abandoned to psychosis, *either* inside language and structure *or* cast outside into indifference).[27] Inclusive disjunction is also quite distinct from the "bourgeois" logic that Deleuze describes in *Difference and Repetition* where one operates with "on the one hand ... on the other hand."[28]

Deleuze and Guattari's criticism of exclusive disjunction is radically posthumanist and post-subjective. As the history of logic going back to Aristotle maintained, one cannot consistently affirm both "a" and "not-a." However, if one were to adopt a sense of a divergent and open whole – such as all the possible perspectives that life unfolds (the point of view of life, of organisms, of rocks, of humans, of silicon) – then one might say that there *is* and *is not* a future. This would contrast directly with the compromises of liberal critique and irony. The liberal subject acknowledges the insistence of ideals, but nevertheless mourns their impossibility. On the one hand, we acknowledge that speaking about *the* future, *the* human, or *the* posthuman perpetuates centuries of Eurocentric hegemonic universalism; on the other hand, without any gesture to the universal, "we" would abandon "others" to particularity, while "we" are blessed with the grand perspective of cultural, historical, and ethical relativism.[29] Exclusive disjunction operates with an "either/or," while "on the one hand ... on the other hand" keeps the distribution and distinction of the "either/or" but allows the subject the somewhat good conscience of compromise. In both cases – exclusive disjunction and the logic of "on the one hand ... on the other hand" – compromised thinking precludes any future that is not ultimately subjective (even, or especially, if it declares itself to be posthumanist). As long as there is a *subject*, a being for whom the world exists as a historical entity with decisive outcomes, a subject who deems himself to be the outcome and agent of history, then there will always be "a" future that will emerge from a negotiated and interpreted line of time.

There has been much talk of nonlinear history, especially in a posthumanist mode. Manuel de Landa's *A Thousand Years of Nonlinear*

History[30] anticipates much that now might be included in the "nonhuman" turn.[31] Rather than a history of individuals or social agents, de Landa's book charts dispersed, multiple, overdetermined, and primarily nonintentional processes of emergence. Well before claims regarding the Anthropocene (and the non-temporal and technical complexity of "nature"), de Landa destroyed the opposition between humans as historical agents and nature as timeless, *and* refused the reliance on equilibrium that allowed natural and human history to stabilize. Language, for example, does not emerge, transform human history, and then persist as "a" structure; rather, all emergences are part of an ongoing and volatile dynamism that has multiple vectors and thresholds: "the move away from energetic equilibrium and linear causality has reinjected the natural sciences with historical concerns."[32]

For de Landa, the consequences of nonlinearity and far-from-equilibrium dynamism are political. One neither submits to nature as though it were fateful and determining (as in the manner of Social Darwinism) nor does nature's historicity preclude the striving for a better future. The future cannot be utopian in the sense of an achieved, planned, and stable beatitude. On the contrary, if one aims for greater degrees of freedom among the components of the political whole (which would include multiple times and spaces), then one loses "man" as single agent in a grand unfolding historical trajectory, but gains "humanity" (which would be multiple, exposed, precarious, dynamic, and no longer contained by the illusion of temporal stability). According to de Landa,

> we will need to destratify reality itself, and we must do so without the guarantee of a Golden Age ahead, knowing full well the dangers and possible restratifications we may face . . . [D]espite all the cautionary tales about simplistic calls for anarchic liberation, there is in these new theories a positive, even joyful conception of reality. And while these views do indeed invoke the "death of man," it is only the death of the "man" of the old "manifest destinies," not the death of humanity and its potential for destratification.[33]

If de Landa's past is the outcome of unforeseen events and connections (where potentials emerge that could not have been calculated given the multiplicity of factors and intensities), then one might conclude that any future from such a vantage point would not be poised *between* two possibilities (where *either* the geo-engineering capitalists win the climate wars *or* climate change becomes the harbinger of a new socialism and justice for all). Once a history of dynamism and multiple forces is written, or once one begins to note the ways in which technology, climate, "nature," geopolitics, ecosystems, and markets enabled the present to emerge, de Landa suggests, one might have a sense of the future's range of potentiality (but not its enumerated possibilities). One might, if one recognizes the multiple composition and emergence of the past, open the future beyond what appears to be self-evident. Despite the non-intentionality of nonlinear history, the past's contingency and composition enable the thought of an intentional future. This intentionality, though, is not the achievement of the proper, not the choice between or among outcomes based on humanity arriving at technological maturity (Bostrom) or final justice (Klein). On the contrary, the emphasis – if there is to be a future in any real sense – is on *unmaking* or *destratification*. De Landa's "humanity," then, is not the "man" who frees himself from nature to achieve self-determination and critical distance from the world, but a potential for intensified volatility and multiplicity, a counter-destiny or counter-future, at odds with what appears to be fateful.

As I have already suggested, De Landa's work is an anticipation of a mode of nonhuman thinking that will abandon a history of teleology while affirming, rather than lamenting, contingency. Bruno Latour, champion of the agency of nonhumans, clarifies this point:

> What has been made so quickly can be unmade just as quickly. What has been designed may be redesigned. There is not fate in the vast landscape of inequalities we associate with the economy and their unequal distribution of "goods" and "bads," only a slowly built set of irreversibilities. Now that historicity has shifted from the *stage* to the *backstage* of human action – namely, from second nature to first nature – activists should ally themselves with the globe against the global.[34]

Latour's position is also posthumanist and nonlinear: agency is attributed to the globe, and the globe, in turn, presents itself as the ethical choice for our allegiance (against the global*ism* of certain "human" self-interests). Like de Landa, Latour is critical of fateful and teleological conceptions of history, but whereas de Landa insists on the historicity and nonlinearity of "nature" such that "man" as agent of history becomes one force among others in a dynamic system, Latour notes an alarming tendency to re-inject *non-history* into a specific aspect of human life – namely the economic – creating a "second nature" that now bears all the transcendence and determinism that once characterized "first nature" in its seeming timelessness. The affect of capitalism, for Latour, is a certain resignation or fatalism with regard to what had once been dynamic, contested, political, and volatile. Economic processes appear more and more like implacable and transcendent laws, operating with the regularity and timelessness that once marked "nature."

The political and human future that de Landa opened by destratifying nature and rendering it dynamic has been displaced by the seeming exemption of the economic order. What Latour's diagnosis suggests is a certain return of the linear, a sense of destiny now attributed to economic "reality." Latour describes a "slowbuilt set of irreversibilities": we cannot simply move back along a line of time, for the world is composed and emerges from multiple and intensive forces. Adding and subtracting days does not give you the same thing earlier or later, for each moment in time alters just *what* is being mapped by time and history. There is not "a" world that goes through the line of time, nor is there a humanity that goes through history; what calls itself human, and what the human deems to be inhuman or "outside" is formed and de-formed along multiple strata. There is neither "a" line of time nor multiple *lines*, but there are bifurcations, intersections, potentialities, redundancies, and archaisms. Latour's "slowly built" set may be *unmade*, even though its unmaking cannot return us to what was before the making (if what is slowly built is nevertheless *irreversible*).

In this sense, one might want to rethink the residual linearity and humanism that resides in reading the contingency and inhumanity of the past in order to open a future that would not simply happen *to us*. Is there not one way in which a certain nonlinearity (or history as made and built rather than destined) allows for a domesticating rehumanization of the future? We may no longer be *homo faber*, masters of time, but we regain even more by becoming masters of unmaking, negating, and annihilating. By contrast, the thought of *linearity* might be radically inhuman, if one were to accept multiple lines. That is, rather than regaining the future by insisting on our capacity to unmake, deform, and destratify, perhaps we could be open to lines of making or becoming not our own. No matter how we read the contingency, dynamism, and nonfatal nature of the past, the future is not one we choose; the future seems to be choosing us. The depletion of resources, ocean acidification, and viral volatility brought about by the complexities of global travel and markets, the melting of the polar ice-caps, rising sea-levels, ever-more intertwined and *seemingly* inscrutable financial systems, the threats to cognition by new technologies and overconsumption: yes, these present such a complexity that it is impossible to predict *what* will happen. But should that preclude us or discourage us from acknowledging *that no matter what* (like a steady and unstoppable march) "it" will happen? There will be a time of the nonhuman, or the no-longer human.

Eternal Recurrences

Perhaps all that has presented itself as posthuman in terms of historical contingency and nonlinearity refuses irreversibilities that are not "slowly built" and not capable of being unmade. Rather than exclusive disjunction – either this *or* this – de Landa and Latour, in different ways, open and destratify the future, unlocking more futures that present themselves as possible. But what if, instead, one were to think of an inclusive disjunction where there is and is not a future; this is not a greater range of potentialities, but the coexistence of potentialities that are "incompossible."[35] Humanity faces its destined end, *and* humanity has a future. How might we live the present in this truly posthuman mode?

Consider Nietzsche's multivalent challenge of eternal return (especially as re-read through Deleuze): if everything that ever was and will be, will recur over and over again, then nothing has ever truly passed once and for all, and nothing is ever *merely possible*, but will indeed come into being, and has come into being, and will continue to come into being. One way to think about the eternal return – one of many – is as a radically de-subjectifying procedure that also destroys the disjunction between linear and nonlinear temporalities. The eternal return destroys any single temporal point of view; all our potential futures are already fully real (if virtual) as are all the non-actualized pasts, and yet the actualization of any event transforms the whole, always and eternally. Such a temporality is at once nonlinear, demanding that any event be considered in relation to every other potentiality, without any sense of privileged cause or ground. And yet the eternal return is also multiply linear; there is the world of capitalist over-production that eliminates the human species and all organic life *once and for all, and* there is the human world where the thought of such annihilation generated a love of other fates, *and* there is the world where – amid all the threats of climate change – something absolutely untoward opened other lines (felicitous for humans, or absolutely destructive).

Such a conception of multiple worlds, multiple futures, and multiple lines of time is especially important if one wishes to accommodate literary culture into time and futurity. Twentieth- and twenty-first-century literature and cinema have already played out multiple pasts and futures. Lars von Trier's *Melancholia* (2011) ended the world; Danny Boyle's *Sunshine* (2007) joyously extinguished those who tried to save the world; Maggie Gee's *Ice People* witnessed the planet freezing over, while the same author's *The Flood* depicts a city submerged (and class-riven) by water.[36] J. G. Ballard also wrote of future worlds that were both drowned *and* drought-stricken.[37] All these texts are not simply presentations of non-existent entities; on the contrary, these futures *are real*. We live in a present in which futures of flooding, drought, ice ages, resource depletion, and – as in Alexis Wright's *Swan Book* – of intensified racial violence are intrinsic to the lived "now."[38] Rather than the eternal return being a static whole, it allows every event to have multiple lines of potentiality as part of its reality. Nothing justifies or invalidates anything else *prima facie*. There is no reason other than one's own parochialism to favor or sustain the human point of view. The only sufficient reason is the affirmation of all that becomes – human and inhuman.[39]

If "one" adopts the point of view of eternal return, one does not have a life defined and delimited by one's chosen and finite path; one will pass through all potentialities, becoming male and female and animal and inorganic. This "one" cannot be a bounded body folded around its own point of view, but might be something like a monad, and this monad – unlike Leibniz's monads that all perceive the same world but from different perspectives – opens to all the other perspectives from which other worlds unfold.

In more concrete terms, and quite specifically in relation to posthuman futures, one might say that there is a future of hope and human survival that is utterly joyous, and a future where humans cease to be, and that this too should elicit joy; there is a future in which humanity transforms itself to save life and the planet, and a future in which this is intended but fails to be actualized. Living the present with these multiple futures is not only post-humanist in its acceptance of times and worlds beyond our own; it is also hyper-political, for rather than assume the value and existence of "our" future and survival, the question of just "who" we are remains open. If humanity affirms itself, it does so – eternally – not as that which exists for all time, but as that which comes into being and passes away, and does so with the joyous sense that "all time" is composed of nothing more than becomings. One affirms survival *and* extinction, technology *and* its annihilation, humanity *and* its non-being.

NOTES

1. Lee Edelmann, *No Future: Queer Theory and the Death Drive* (Durham: Duke University Press, 2004).
2. José Esteban Muñoz, *Cruising Utopia: The Then and There of Queer Futurity* (New York: New York University Press, 2009).
3. Ray Kurzweil, *The Singularity is Near: When Humans Transcend Biology* (New York: Viking, 2005); Nick Bostrom, *Superintelligence: Paths, Dangers, Strategies* (Oxford: Oxford University Press, 2014).
4. Marc E. Weksler and Babette B. Weksler, "The Epidemic of Distraction," *Gerontology* 58.5 (2012): 385–90.
5. Jo Confino, "How Technology has Stopped Evolution and Is Destroying the World." www.theguardian.com/sustainable-business/technology-stopped-evolution-destroying-world.
6. Bernard Stiegler, *Taking Care of Youth and the Generations*, trans. Stephen Barker (Stanford: Stanford University Press, 2010).
7. Michael Adas, *Machines as the Measure of Men: Science, Technology, and Ideologies of Western Dominance* (Ithaca: Cornell University Press, 1989); Daniel Headrick, "The Tools of Imperialism: Technology and the Expansion of

European Colonial Empires in the Nineteenth Century," *Journal of Modern History* 51.2 (1979): 231–63.

8. Quentin Meillassoux, *After Finitude*, trans. Ray Brassier (London: Continuum, 2008).

9. Susan Bordo, *Unbearable Weight: Feminism, Western Culture, and the Body* (Berkeley: University of California Press, 1993); Elizabeth Grosz, *Volatile Bodies: Toward a Corporeal Feminism* (Bloomington: Indiana University Press, 1994).

10. Melissa Gregg and Gregory J. Seigworth, eds., *The Affect Theory Reader* (Durham: Duke University Press, 2010).

11. Donna Haraway, *The Companion Species Manifesto: Dogs, People, and Significant Otherness* (Chicago: Prickly Paradigm Press, 2003); Cary Wolfe, *What is Posthumanism?* (Minneapolis: University of Minnesota Press, 2010).

12. Alain Badiou, *Theory of the Subject*, trans. Bruno Bosteels (London: Continuum, 2009).

13. Roy Scranton, "Learning How to Die in the Anthropocene," accessed July 12, 2015, http://opinionator.blogs.nytimes.com/2013/11/10/learning-how-to-die-in -the-anthropocene/.

14. Naomi Klein, *This Changes Everything: Capitalism vs. the Climate.* (New York: Simon and Schuster, 2014).

15. Jacques Derrida, *Specters of Marx: The State of the Debt, the Work of Mourning, and the New International*, trans. Peggy Kamuf (New York: Routledge, 1994), 168.

16. Jacques Derrida, "The Ends of Man," in *Margins of Philosophy*, trans. Alan Bass (Chicago: Chicago University Press, 1972).

17. Derrida, *Specters of Marx*, 211.

18. *Ibid.*

19. Richard Rorty, *Philosophy and Social Hope* (London: Penguin, 1999), 120.

20. Jürgen Habermas, "Modernity – An Incomplete Project," trans. Seyla Ben-Habib, in *The Anti-Aesthetic: Essays on Postmodern Culture*, ed. Hal Foster (New York: New Press, 2002), 3–15.

21. Bernard Stiegler, *Technics and Time 1: The Fault of Epimetheus*, trans. Richard Beardsworth and George Collins (Minneapolis: University of Minnesota Press, 1998).

22. Jacques Derrida, *Limited Inc.* (Baltimore: Johns Hopkins University Press, 1977).

23. David Wood, "Specters of Derrida: On the Way to Econstruction," in *Ecospirit: Religions and Philosophies for the Earth*, ed. Laurel Kearns and Catherine Keller (New York: Fordham University Press 2007), 286–87.

24. Timothy Clark, "Some Climate Change Ironies: Deconstruction, Environmental Politics and the Closure of Ecocriticism," *The Oxford Literary Review* 32.1 (2010): 134.

25. Stephen Mark Gardiner, *A Perfect Moral Storm: The Ethical Tragedy of Climate Change* (New York: Oxford University Press, 2011).

26. Accessed July 12, 2015, http://news.bbc.co.uk/2/hi/uk/6057734.stm.

27. Gilles Deleuze and Felix Guattari, *Anti-Oedipus*, trans. Robert Hurley, Mark Seem, and Helen R. Lane (London: Continuum, 2004).

28. Gilles Deleuze, *Difference and Repetition*, trans. Paul Patton (New York: Columbia, 1994), 225.

29. Denise Ferreira da Silva, *Toward a Global Idea of Race* (Minneapolis: University of Minnesota Press, 2007).

30. Manuel De Landa, *A Thousand Years of Nonlinear History* (New York: Zone Books, 1997).

31. Richard Grusin, ed., *The Nonhuman Turn* (Minneapolis: University of Minnesota Press, 2015).

32. De Landa, *Nonlinear History*, 14.

33. *Ibid.*, 274.

34. Bruno Latour, "On Some of the Affects of Capitalism," accessed July 12, 2015, www.bruno-latour.fr/sites/default/files/136-AFFECTS-OF-K-COPENHAGUE .pdf.

35. Gilles Deleuze, *The Fold: Leibniz and the Baroque*, trans. Tom Conley (London: Athlone, 1993), 63.

36. Maggie Gee, *The Ice People* (London: Richard Cohen Books, 1998); Maggie Gee, *The Flood* (London: Saqi, 2005).

37. J. G. Ballard, *The Drowned World* (New York: Doubleday, 1965); J. G. Ballard, *The Drought* (St. Albans: Triad, 1978).

38. Alexis Wright, *The Swan Book* (Artarmon: Giramondo, 2013).

39. Gilles Deleuze, *Nietzsche and Philosophy*, trans. Hugh Tomlinson (New York: Columbia University Press, 1983), 48–49.

FURTHER READING

Aarseth, Espen J. *Cybertext: Perspectives on Ergodic Literature.* Baltimore: The Johns Hopkins University Press, 1996.

Abel, Jessica and Matt Madden. *Drawing Words and Writing Pictures: Making Comics from Manga to Graphic Novels.* New York: First Second, 2008.

Agamben, Giorgio. *The Man without Content.* Stanford: Stanford University Press, 1999.

The Open: Man and Animal. Stanford: Stanford University Press, 2003.

Alexander, Marguerite. *Flights from Realism: Themes and Strategies in Postmodernist British and American Fiction.* London: Edward Arnold, 1990.

Allen, Valerie. *On Farting: Language and Laughter in the Middle Ages.* New York: Palgrave Macmillan, 2007.

Aretoulakis, Emmanouil. "Towards a Posthumanist Ecology: Nature without Humanity in Wordsworth and Shelley." *European Journal of English Studies* 18:2 (2014): 172–90.

Askin, Ridvan, Andreas Hägler, and Philipp Schweighauser. "Introduction: Aesthetics after the Speculative Turn." *Speculations: A Journal of Speculative Realism* 5 (2014): 6–38.

Avanessian, Armen and Suhail Malik, eds. *Genealogies of Speculation: Materialism and Subjectivity since Structuralism.* London: Bloomsbury, 2016.

Badmington, Neil. *Alien Chic: Posthumanism and the Other Within.* New York: Routledge, 2004.

ed. *Posthumanism.* New York: Palgrave, 2000.

Balsamo, Anne. *Technologies of the Gendered Body: Reading Cyborg Women.* Durham: Duke University Press, 1996.

Barad, Karen. *Meeting the Universe Halfway: Quantum Physics and the Entanglement of Matter and Meaning.* Durham: Duke University Press, 2007.

Bedini, Silvio A. "The Role of Automata in the History of Technology." *Technology and Culture* 5:1 (1964): 24–42.

Bell, David and Barbara Kennedy, eds. *The Cybercultures Reader.* London: Routledge, 2000.

Benesch, Klaus. *Romantic Cyborgs: Authorship and Technology in the American Renaissance.* Amherst: University of Massachusetts Press, 2002.

Bennett, Jane. *Vibrant Matter: A Political Ecology of Things.* Durham and London: Duke University Press, 2010.

Bertens, Hans. *The Idea of the Postmodern: A History*. London: Routledge, 1995.

Best, Steven and Douglas Kellner. *Postmodern Theory: Critical Interrogations*. London: Macmillan, 1991.

Blackford, Russell. "Symposium on Posthuman Science Fiction, with Gregory Benford, Maureen Kincaid Speller, Andrew M. Butler, Helen Merrick and Joe Haldeman." *Foundation* 78 (Spring 2000): 83–103.

Boluk, Stephanie, Leonardo Flores, Jacob Garbe, and Anastasia Salter, eds. *Electronic Literature Collection 3* (Electronic Literature Organization, 2016), http://collection.eliterature.org/3/.

Borras, Laura, Talan Memmot, Rita Rayley, and Brian Kim Stefans, eds. *Electronic Literature Collection 2* (Electronic Literature Organization, 2011), http://collection.eliterature.org/2/.

Bostrom, Nick. "Why I Want to Be a Posthuman When I Grow Up." In *Medical Enhancement and Posthumanity*. Eds. Bert Gordijn and Ruth Chadwick, 1007–137. Dordrecht: Springer, 2008.

Bradley, Arthur. *Originary Technicity: The Theory of Technology from Marx to Derrida*. New York: Palgrave Macmillan, 2011.

Brooker, Peter, ed. *Modernism/Postmodernism*. London: Longman, 1992.

Bruce, Douglas J. "Human Automata in Classical Tradition and Medieval Romance." *Modern Philology* 10 (1913): 511–26.

Bryant, Levi, Nick Srnicek, and Graham Harman, eds. *The Speculative Turn: Continental Materialism and Realism*. Melbourne: Re. Press, 2011.

Bryden, Mary, ed. *Beckett and Animals*. Cambridge: Cambridge University Press, 2013.

Bukatman, Scott. *Terminal Identity: The Virtual Subject in Postmodern Science Fiction*. Durham: Duke University Press, 1993.

Burdet, Michael. S. *Eschatology and the Technological Future*. London: Routledge, 2014.

Caughie, Pamela, ed. *Virginia Woolf in the Age of Mechanical Reproduction*. New York: Garland, 2000.

Chaney, Michael A., ed. *Graphic Subjects: Critical Essays on Autobiography and Graphic Novels*. Madison: University of Wisconsin Press, 2011.

Chapuis, Alfred and Edmond Droz. *Automata: A Historical and Technological Study*. Trans. Alec Reid. Neuchatel: Éditions du Griffon, 1958.

Chute, Hillary. *Graphic Women: Life Narrative and Contemporary Comics*. New York: Columbia University Press, 2010.

Outside the Box: Interviews with Contemporary Cartoonists. Chicago: University of Chicago Press, 2014.

Cixous, Hélène. "Animalmessie." (Choix des textes et introductions par Marta Segarra). *Animal Traces/Tierspuren/Traces Animals*, ed. Manuela Rossini. *figurationen* 1 (2014): 15–40.

Clark, Andy and David J. Chalmers. "The Extended Mind." *Analysis* 58 (1998): 10–23.

Clarke, Bruce. "Evolutionary Equality: Neocybernetic Posthumanism and Margulis and Sagan's Writing Practice." In *Writing Posthumanism, Posthuman Writing*. Ed. Sidney I. Dobrin, 275–97. Anderson, SC: Parlor Press, 2015.

Clarke, Bruce and Mark B. N. Hansen. "Neocybernetic Emergence: Retuning the Posthuman." *Cybernetics and Human Knowing* 16:1–2 (2009): 83–99.

Cohen, Jeffrey Jerome, ed. *Animal, Vegetable, Mineral: Ethics and Objects.* Washington, DC: Oliphaunt Books, 2012.

Cohen, Jeffrey Jerome. *Medieval Identity Machines.* Minneapolis: University of Minnesota Press, 2003.

    Stone: An Ecology of the Inhuman. Minneapolis: University of Minnesota Press, 2015.

Colebrook, Claire. *Death of the Posthuman: Essays on Extinction.* Ann Arbor: Open Humanities Press, 2014.

    Gilles Deleuze. London: Routledge, 2002.

Connor, Steven. *Postmodern Culture: An Introduction to Theories of the Contemporary.* Oxford: Blackwell, 1989.

Crane, Susan. *Animal Encounters: Contacts and Concepts in Medieval Britain.* Philadelphia: University of Pennsylvania Press, 2013.

Crawford, T. Hugh. "Networking the (Non) Human: *Moby-Dick*, Matthew Fontaine Maury, and Bruno Latour." *Configurations* 5:1 (Winter 1997): 1–21.

Cultural Critique 53 (Winter 2003), special issue on Posthumanism. Eds. Bart Simon, Jill Didur, and Teresa Heffernan.

Danius, Sara. *The Senses of Modernism: Technology, Perception, and Aesthetics.* Ithaca: Cornell University Press, 2002.

Davis-Floyd, Robbie and Joseph Dumit, eds. *Cyborg Babies: From Techno-Sex to Techno-Toys.* London: Routledge, 1998.

De Landa, Manuel. *A Thousand Years of Nonlinear History.* New York: Zone Books, 1997.

de Mello, Margo, ed. *Speaking for Animals: Animal Autobiographical Writing.* New York: Routledge, 2013.

Deleuze, Gilles. *Francis Bacon: The Logic of Sensation.* Trans. Daniel W. Smith. Minneapolis: University of Minnesota Press, 2003.

Dery, Mark, *Escape Velocity: Cyberculture at the End of the Century.* New York: Grove Press, 1996.

Dinello, Daniel. *Technophobia!: Science Fiction Visions of Posthuman Technology.* Austin: University of Texas Press, 2006.

Diski, Jenny. *What I Don't Know About Animals.* New Haven: Yale University Press, 2011.

Docherty, Thomas, ed. *Postmodernism: A Reader.* London: Harvester Wheatsheaf, 1993.

Dowd, Garin. *Abstract Machines: Samuel Beckett and Philosophy after Deleuze and Guattari.* Amsterdam: Rodopi, 2007.

Dozois, Gardner R., ed. *Supermen: Tales of the Posthuman Future.* New York: St. Martin's Griffin, 2002.

Dunham, Jeremy, Iain Hamilton Grant, and Sean Watson. *Idealism: The History of a Philosophy.* Durham: Acumen, 2011.

Edelman, Lee. *No Future: Queer Theory and the Death Drive.* Durham: Duke University Press, 2004.

Eisner, Will. *Comics and Sequential Art.* New York: W. W. Norton, 2008.

Esposito, Roberto. *Immunitas: The Protection and Negation of Life.* Trans. Zakiya Hanafi. Malden, MA: Polity Press, 2011.

Ferguson, Frances. *Solitude and the Sublime: Romanticism and the Aesthetics of Individuation.* New York: Routledge, 1992.

Foster, Thomas. *The Souls of Cyberfolk: Posthumanism as Vernacular Theory.* Minneapolis: University of Minnesota Press, 2005.

Fuery, Kelli. *New Media: Culture and Image.* Basingstoke: Palgrave Macmillan, 2009.

Fukuyama, Francis. *Our Posthuman Future: Consequences of the Biotechnology Revolution.* London: Profile Books, 2002.

Garcia, Tristan. *Form and Object: A Treatise on Things.* Trans. Mark Allan Ohm and Jon Cogburn. Edinburgh: Edinburgh University Press, 2014.

Gatens, Moira. *Imaginary Bodies: Ethics, Power and Corporeality.* London: Routledge, 1996.

Gilbert, Scott F., Jan Sapp, and Alfred I. Tauber. "A Symbiotic View of Life: We Have Never Been Individuals." *The Quarterly Review of Biology* 87:4 (December 2012): 325–41.

Gitelman, Lisa. *"Raw Data" Is an Oxymoron.* Cambridge: MIT Press, 2013.

Gomel, Elana. *Science Fiction, Alien Encounters, and the Ethics of Posthumanism: Beyond the Golden Rule.* New York: Palgrave Macmillan, 2014.

Goody, Alex. *Technology, Literature and Culture.* Cambridge: Polity Press, 2013.

Graham, Elaine L. *Representations of the Post/Human: Monsters, Aliens, and Others in Popular Culture.* Manchester: Manchester University Press, 2002.

Green, Jeremy. *Late Postmodernism: American Fiction at the Millennium.* Houndmills: Palgrave, 2005.

Gross, Aaron and Anne Vallely, eds. *Animals and the Human Imagination: A Companion to Animal Studies.* New York: Columbia University Press, 2012.

Grosz, Elizabeth, ed. *Becomings: Explorations in Time, Memory, and Futures.* Ithaca: Cornell University Press, 1999.

Grosz, Elizabeth. *The Nick of Time: Politics, Evolution, and the Untimely.* Durham: Duke University Press, 2004.

Volatile Bodies: Toward a Corporeal Feminism. Bloomington and Indianapolis: Indiana University Press, 1994.

Hacking, Ian. "Autistic Autobiography." *Philosophical Transactions of the Royal Society B, Biological Sciences* 364:1522 (May 2009): 1467–73.

Haney, II, William S. *Cyberculture, Cyborgs and Science Fiction: Consciousness and the Posthuman.* New York: Rodopi, 2006.

Haraway, Donna J. *When Species Meet.* Minneapolis: University of Minnesota Press, 2008.

Hassan, Ihab. *The Postmodern Turn: Essays in Postmodern Theory and Culture.* Columbus: Ohio State University Press, 1987.

Hauskeller, Michael, Thomas D. Philbeck, and Curtis D. Carbonell. *Electronic Literature: New Horizons for the Literary.* Notre Dame: University of Notre Dame Press, 2008.

eds. *The Palgrave Handbook of Posthumanism in Film and Television.* London: Palgrave MacMillan, 2015.

Hayles, N. Katherine, *Writing Machines.* Cambridge, MA: MIT Press, 2002.

Hayles, N. Katherine, Nick Montfort, Scott Rettberg, and Stephanie Strickland, eds. *Electronic Literature Collection 1* (Electronic Literature Organization, 2008), http://collection.eliterature.org/1/.

Herbrechter, Stefan. *Posthumanism: A Critical Analysis.* London: Bloomsbury, 2013.

Herbrechter, Stefan and Ivan Callus, eds. *Posthumanist Shakespeares.* London: Palgrave MacMillan, 2012.

Hillis, Ken. *Digital Sensations, Space, Identity, and Embodiment in Virtual Reality.* Minneapolis: University of Minnesota Press, 1999.

Hillmann, David and Ulrika Maude, eds. *The Cambridge Companion to the Body in Literature.* New York: Cambridge University Press, 2015.

Hird, Myra J. "Animal, All Too Animal: *Blood Music* and an Ethic of Vulnerability." In *Animals and the Human Imagination: A Companion to Animal Studies.* Eds. Aaron Gross and Anne Vallely, 331–48. New York: Columbia University Press, 2012.

Hoesterey, Ingeborg, ed. *Zeitgeist in Babel: The Postmodernist Controversy.* Bloomington: Indiana University Press, 1991.

Hunt, Alastair and Matthias Rudolf, eds. *Romanticism and Biopolitics: Praxis* (Romantic Circles, 2012). www.rc.umd.edu/praxis/biopolitics.

Hutcheon, Linda. *The Politics of Postmodernism.* New York: Routledge, 1989.

Idel, Moshe. *Golem: Jewish Magical and Mystical Traditions on the Artificial Anthropoid.* Albany: SUNY, 1990.

Jacobs, Naomi. "Posthuman Bodies and Agency in Octavia Butler's Xenogenesis." In *Dark Horizons: Science Fiction and the Dystopian Imagination.* Eds. Raffaella Baccolini and Tom Moylan, 91–112. New York: Routledge, 2003.

Joy, Eileen A. and Craig Dionne, eds. "When Did We Become Post/Human?" *Postmedieval* 1:1–2 (2010).

Kakalios, James. *The Physics of Superheroes.* New York: Gotham Books, 2005.

Kedem, Nir, ed. *Deleuzian Futures. Deleuze Studies* 5, supplement (December 2011).

Kelley, Theresa M. "Romantic Interiority and Cultural Objects." In *Romanticism and Philosophy in an Historical Age: Praxis* (Romantic Circles). www.rc.umd .edu/praxis/philosophy/kelley1/tk1.html.

Kelly, James Patrick and John Kessel, eds. *Digital Rapture: The Singularity Anthology.* San Francisco: Tachyon Publications, 2012.

Khalip, Jacques, "The Ruin of Things." In *Romantic Frictions: Praxis* (Romantic Circles). www.rc.umd.edu/praxis/frictions/HTML/praxis.2011 .khalip.html.

Kirby, Vicki. *Quantum Anthropologies: Life at Large.* Durham: Duke University Press, 2011.

Kuusisto, Stephen. *Planet of the Blind.* New York: Dial, 1998.

Lake, Christina Bieber. *Prophets of the Posthuman: American Fiction, Biotechnology, and the Ethics of Personhood.* Notre Dame: University of Notre Dame Press, 2013.

Latour, Bruno. *Reassembling the Social: An Introduction to Actor-Network-Theory.* Oxford: Oxford University Press, 2005.

Lejeune, Philippe. "Autobiography and New Communication Tools." In *Identity Technologies: Constructing a Self Online.* Eds. Anna Poletti and Julie Rak, 247–58. Madison: University of Wisconsin Press, 2014.

Lévy, Pierre. *Cyberculture.* Minneapolis: University of Minnesota Press, 2001.

Lilly, John Cunningham. *The Mind of the Dolphin: A Nonhuman Intelligence.* Garden City, NY: Doubleday, 1967.

Further Reading

Luhmann, Niklas. "The Autopoiesis of Social Systems." In *Essays on Self-Reference*, 1–20. New York: Columbia University Press, 1991.

Lussier, Mark and Kaitlin Gowan. "The Romantic Roots of *Blade Runner*." *Wordsworth Circle* 43:3 (2012): 165–72.

Lyotard, Jean-François. "Can Thought Go On Without a Body?" In *The Inhuman*. Trans. Geoffrey Bennington and Rachel Bowlby, 8–23. Stanford: Stanford University Press, 1991.

Mao, Douglas. *Solid Objects: Modernism and the Test of Production*. Princeton: Princeton University Press, 1998.

Margulis, Lynn. *Symbiotic Planet: A New Look at Evolution*. New York: Basic Books, 1998.

Margulis, Lynn and Dorion Sagan. *Microcosmos: Four Billion Years of Microbial Evolution*. Berkeley: University of California Press, 1997.

Maturana, Humberto and Francisco J. Varela. *Autopoiesis and Cognition: The Realization of the Living*. Boston: Riedel, 1980.

Maude, Ulrika. *Beckett, Technology and the Body*. Cambridge: Cambridge University Press, 2009.

McCloud, Scott. *Understanding Comics: The Invisible Art*. New York: Harper Perennial, 1994.

McHale, Brian. *Constructing Postmodernism*. London: Routledge, 1992. *Postmodernist Fiction*. London: Methuen, 1987.

Meillassoux, Quentin. *The Number and the Siren: A Decipherment of Mallarmé's Coup de Dés*. Falmouth: Urbanomic, 2012.

Meyer, Steven. *Irresistible Dictation: Gertrude Stein and the Correlations of Writing and Science*. Stanford: Stanford University Press, 2001.

Milburn, Colin. *Nanovisions. Engineering the Future*. Durham: Duke University Press, 2008.

Mitchell, J. Allan. *Becoming Human: The Matter of the Medieval Child*. Minneapolis: University of Minnesota Press, 2014.

Mitchell, Robert and Ron Broglio, eds. *Romanticism and the New Deleuze, Praxis* (Romantic Circles, 2008). www.rc.umd.edu/praxis/deleuze/.

Moore, Adrian William. *The Evolution of Modern Metaphysics: Making Sense of Things*. Cambridge: Cambridge University Press, 2012.

Morrison, Susan Signe. *The Literature of Waste: Material Ecopoetics and Ethical Matter*. New York: Palgrave Macmillan, 2015.

Morton, Timothy. *Hyperobjects: Philosophy and Ecology after the End of the World*. Minnesota: University of Minnesota Press, 2013.

Nelson, Ted. *Literary Machines: The Report on, and of, Project Xanadu Concerning Word Processing, Electronic Publishing, Hypertext, Thinkertoys, Tomorrow's Intellectual Revolution, and Certain Other Topics Including Knowledge, Education and Freedom*. Sausalito, CA: Mindful Press, 1980.

Nicol, Bran, ed. *Postmodernism and the Contemporary Novel: A Reader*. Edinburgh: Edinburgh University Press, 2002.

Nusselder, André. *Interface Fantasy: A Lacanian Cyborg Ontology*. Cambridge, MA: MIT Press, 2009.

Olney, J., ed. *Autobiography: Essays Theoretical and Critical*. Princeton: Princeton University Press, 1983.

Further Reading

Oser, Lee. *The Ethics of Modernism: Moral Ideas in Yeats, Eliot, Joyce, Woolf and Beckett.* Cambridge: Cambridge University Press, 2007.

Palmeri, Frank. *Humans and Other Animals in Eighteenth-Century British Culture: Representation, Hybridity, Ethics.* Aldershot: Ashgate, 2006.

Parikka, Jussi. *The Anthrobscene.* Minneapolis: University of Minnesota Press, 2014.

Pekar, Harvey and Joyce Brabner, with drawings by Frank Stack. *Our Cancer Year.* Philadelphia: Running Press, 1994.

Plumwood, Valerie. "Being Prey." In *The Ultimate Journey: Inspiring Stories of Living and Dying.* Eds. James O'Reilly, Sean O'Reilly, and Richard Sterling, 128–46. San Francisco: Travelers Tales, 2000.

(Post) Human Lives. Eds. Gillian Whitlock and G. Thomas Couser. *Biography* 35:1 (2012).

Pressman, Jessica, Mark C. Marino, Jeremy Douglass. *Reading Project: A Collaborative Analysis of William Poundstone's Project for Tachitoscope {Bottomless Pit}.* Iowa City: University of Iowa Press, 2015.

Punday, Daniel. *Narrative Bodies: Towards a Corporeal Narratology.* New York: Palgrave Macmillan, 2003.

Rand, Richard, ed. *Futures: Of Jacques Derrida.* Stanford: Stanford University Press, 2002.

Robertson, George. *FutureNatural: Nature, Science, Culture.* London: Routledge, 1996.

Robertson, Kellie. "Medieval Materialism: A Manifesto." *Exemplaria* 22 (2010): 99–118.

Rohman, Carrie. *Stalking the Subject: Modernism and the Animal.* New York: Columbia University Press, 2008.

Ross, Stephen, ed. *Modernism and Theory: A Critical Debate.* New York: Routledge, 2009.

Schultz, Mark, Zander Cannon, and Kevin Cannon. *The Stuff of Life: A Graphic Guide to Genetics and DNA.* New York: Hill and Wang, 2009.

Sebastian, John T., ed. *Croxton Play of the Sacrament.* Kalamazoo: Medieval Institute Publications, 2012.

Segarra, Marta. "Hélène Cixous's Other Animal: The Half Sunken Dog." *New Literary History* 37:1 (Winter 2006): 119–34.

Senior, Mathew, David L. Clark, and Carla Freccero, eds. "Animots: Postanimality in French Thought." *Yale French Studies* 127 (2015).

Shaviro, Steven. *The Universe of Things: On Speculative Realism.* Minneapolis: University of Minnesota Press, 2014.

Without Criteria: Kant, Whitehead, Deleuze, and Aesthetics. Cambridge: MIT Press, 2009.

Short, Sue. *Cyborg Cinema and Contemporary Subjectivity.* Basingstoke: Palgrave Macmillan, 2004.

Simondon, Gilbert. *On the Mode of Existence of Technical Objects.* Trans. Ninian Mellamphy. Ontario: University of Western Ontario, 1980.

Sloterdijk, Peter. "Rules for the Human Zoo: A Response to the *Letter on Humanism.*" *Environment and Planning D* 27 (2009): 12–28.

Smith, Daniel W. *Essays on Deleuze.* Edinburgh: Edinburgh University Press, 2012.

Further Reading

Smith, Marquard and Joanna Morra, eds. *The Prosthetic Impulse: From a Posthuman Present to a Biocultural Future*. Cambridge, MA: MIT Press, 2006.

Smith, Sidonie A. and Julia Watson, eds. *Reading Autobiography: A Guide for Interpreting Life Narratives*. Minneapolis: University of Minnesota Press, 2001.

Springer, Claudia. *Electronic Eros. Bodies and Desire in the Postindustrial Age*. Austin: University of Texas Press, 1996.

Stark, Hannah and Jonathan Roffe, eds. *Deleuze and the Non/Human*. London: Palgrave, 2015.

Steel, Karl and Peggy McCracken. "The Animal Turn: Into the Sea with the Fish-Knights of Perceforest." *Postmedieval* 2:1 (2011): 88–100.

Stiegler, Bernard, *Technics and Time, 2: Disorientation*. Trans. Stephen Barker. Stanford: Stanford University Press, 2009.

Technics and Time, 3: Cinematic Time and the Question of Malaise. Trans. Stephen Barker. Stanford: Stanford University Press, 2010.

Tabbi, Joseph. *Postmodern Sublime: Technology and American Writing from Mailer to Cyberpunk*. Ithaca: Cornell University Press, 1996.

Thompson, E. P. "Time, Work-Discipline, and Industrial Capitalism." In *Customs in Common*, 352–403. New York: Norton, 1993.

Truitt, E. R. *Medieval Robots: Mechanism, Magic, Nature, and Art*. Philadelphia: University of Pennsylvania Press, 2015.

Vaccari, Andrés and Belinda Barnet. "Prolegomena to a Future Robot History: Stiegler, Epiphylogenesis and Technical Evolution." *Transformations* 17 (2009). Accessed October 25, 2015. www.transformationsjournal.org/journal/issue_17/article_09.shtml.

Vint, Sherryl. *Bodies of Tomorrow: Technology, Subjectivity, Science Fiction*. Toronto: University of Toronto Press, 2007.

Waldby, Catherine. *The Visible Human Project. Informatic Bodies and Posthuman Medicine*. London: Routledge, 2000.

Walters, Gregory J. "Transhumanism, Post-Humanism, and Human Technological Enhancement." *Existenz: An International Journal in Philosophy, Religion, Politics and the Arts* 8:2 (Fall 2013): 1–13.

Waugh, Patricia. *Practicing Postmodernism: Reading Modernism*. London: Edward Arnold, 1992.

Weber, Samuel. *Mass Mediauras: Form, Technics, Media*. Stanford: Stanford University Press, 1996.

Whitehead, A. N. *Science and the Modern World*. Cambridge: Cambridge University Press, 1926.

Williams, Ian. *The Bad Doctor: The Troubled Life and Times of Dr. Iwan James*. Brighton: Myriad Editions, 2015.

Wilson, Elizabeth. *Neural Geographies: Feminism and the Microstructure of Cognition*. London: Routledge, 1998.

Wolfe, Cary. *What is Posthumanism?* Minneapolis: University of Minnesota Press, 2010.

Wurth, Kiene Brillenburg, ed. *Between Page and Screen. Remaking Literature through Cinema and Cyberspace*. New York: Fordham University Press, 2012.

Yaszek, Lisa. "Science Fiction." In *The Routledge Companion to Literature and Science*. Eds. Bruce Clarke with Manuela Rossini, 385–95. New York: Routledge, 2011.

Further Reading

Yi, Dongshin. *A Genealogy of Cyborgothic: Aesthetics and Ethics in the Age of Posthumanism.* Farnham: Ashgate, 2010.
Zylinska, Joanna, ed. *The Cyborg Experiments: The Extensions of the Body in the Media Age.* London: Continuum, 2002.

Special Journal Issues

Cultural Critique 53 (Winter 2003): Posthumanism. Edited by Bart Simon, Jill Didur, and Teresa Heffernan.
Social & Cultural Geography 7:4 (2006): Posthuman Geographies. Edited by Noel Castree and Catherine Nash.
Subject Matters 3:2/4:1 (2007): Posthuman Conditions. Edited by Neil Badmington.
Postmedieval 1:1/2 (2010): *When* Did We Become Post/human? Edited by Eileen A. Joy and Craig Dionne.
Technical Communication Quarterly 19:1 (2010): Posthuman Rhetorics and Technical Communication. Edited by Andrew Mara and Bryon Hawk.
NORA – *Nordic Journal of Feminist and Gender Research* 19:4 (2011): Post-Humanities. Edited by Cecilia Åsberg, Redi Koobak, and Ericka Johnson.
Biography 35:1 (2012): (Post) Human Lives. Edited by Gillian Whitlock and G. Thomas Couser.
Subjectivity 5:3 (2012): Posthumanist Subjectivities. Edited by Ivan Callus and Stefan Herbrechter.
The European Journal of English Studies 18:2 (2014): European Posthumanism. Edited by Stefan Herbrechter, Ivan Callus, and Manuela Rossini.
Word & Text 6:1/2 (2016): Proto-Posthumanisms. Edited by Marija Grech.

INDEX

Index

Index

Index

Index

Index

Index

Index

Index

Index

Cambridge Companions to ...

AUTHORS

TOPICS